THE SOVIET UNION AND TERRORISM

THE
SOVIET UNION
AND TERRORISM

Roberta Goren
edited by Jillian Becker
with an introduction by Robert Conquest

GEORGE ALLEN & UNWIN
London   Boston   Sydney

THE SOVIET UNION AND TERRORISM

Roberta Goren
edited by Jillian Becker
with an introduction by Robert Conquest

GEORGE ALLEN & UNWIN

London   Boston   Sydney

George Allen & Unwin (Publishers) Ltd,
40 Musuem Street, London WC1A 1LU, UK

George Allen & Unwin (Publishers) Ltd,
Park Lane, Hemel Hempstead, Herts HP2 4TE, UK

Allen & Unwin, Inc.,
9 Winchester Terrace, Winchester, Mass. 01890, USA

George Allen & Unwin Australia Pty Ltd,
8 Napier Street, North Sydney, NSW 2060, Australia

First published in 1984.

British Library Cataloguing in Publication Data

Goren, Roberta
The Soviet Union and terrorism.
1. Terrorism - Government policy - Soviet Union
2. Soviet Union - Foreign relations - 1975-
I. Title II. Becker, Jillian
322.4'2 HV6433.S65
ISBN 0-04-327073-5
ISBN 0-04-327074-3 Pbk

Library of Congress Cataloging in Publication Data

Goren, Roberta.
The Soviet Union and terrorism.
Bibliography: p.
Includes index.
1. Terrorism - Government policy - Soviet Union.
2. Soviet Union - Foreign relations - 1917-
I. Becker, Jillian,1932 II. Title.
HV6431.G64 1984 327.1'2 84-12366
ISBN 0-04-327073-5 (alk. paper)
ISBN 0-04-327074-3 (pbk. : alk. paper)

Set in 10 on 11 point Melior by Art Associates (Manchester) Ltd.
and printed in Great Britain by Mackays of Chatham.

Contents

Preface

What This Book Is About

The Soviet Union has always had one supreme aim: to establish Communism everywhere on earth, as an unchallengeable orthodoxy, the only Truth and the only Way, and itself as the universal absolute power which enforces and guards and perpetuates it. To realize this awful ambition, it has used without compunction whatever means and methods, however immoral, however dishonourable, however unjust or cruel or bloody or devastating, which have seemed most likely to bring success according to time, place and circumstance. One method it has always used, with varying degrees of intensity, is terrorism.

After the Second World War, when the Soviet Union found itself at a very considerable disadvantage because the United States had developed weapons of vast, unprecedented, destructive capability, which would ensure Soviet defeat if the two powers went to war against each other, the policy-makers of the Kremlin concentrated on other ways to gain their ends. They gave increased attention to the use of non-violent methods — intensified proselytizing by means of propaganda and indoctrination; infiltration of Western institutions by their agents; a campaign for 'peace', to stir up public opinion in the open societies against maintaining nuclear weapons, and in general to hobble Western defences. But they did not give up the use of violence. On the contrary, they promoted it clandestinely, more widely, and with more determination and ruthlessness than ever before, in every possible form - active subversion and sabotage, civil strife and riot, full-scale insurrection and armed revolution, and the employment of large surrogate armies, led by officers well trained in the communist countries, and well equipped with Russian and Czech weaponry.

In the late 1960s an era of terrorism began. Organized terrorist groups struck within the liberal democracies of Western Europe and North America, and in the less secure countries of South America and Africa. Groups of different nationalities acted with and for each other. One of them, the Palestine Liberation Organization, became the chief and central agency for dispensing terror and death, for supplying fighters, arms, money, training, orders and advice to customers of every shade of political and ideological coloration who were eager or willing to destroy, terrify and kill. And the power for which it acted as agent in its mission of global partisan warfare was the Soviet Union.

That supremely important theme is what this scholarly, thoroughly-researched book deals with, and those are the inescapable conclusions to which it leads. Quietly, authoritatively, analytically, without the least intention to startle, or petrify, or excite its readers, it brings us to the realization that World War Three IS BEING WAGED, and has been waged for decades now, against the West - while most of us in the West, our governments, our press and news analysts remain blind to the nature of the aggression, and to the intention behind it, while it threatens to destroy our world piecemeal, surreptitiously, by ambush, by attack from behind the camouflage of causes with other names, by the guerrilla stealth of some who live treacherously and often unrecognizably among us. Even now that the USSR has its own nuclear weapons, the reduction of the West by direct attack remains impossible to it, and will remain impossible as long as the West keeps itself effectively armed. So the little bombs, the hand guns, the grenades go off instead, killing innocent people by tens rather than millions, but at the same time weakening the foundations of our world to bring about our downfall.

The author died a few weeks after finishing her difficult task. The message she left behind her is frightening, but if it brings us to a new understanding of the danger which threatens us both from outside and within our gates, teaches us its nature, its source, and its mechanism, she will have done a very great service. If we believe her, her work will have the reward it deserves. Far more vitally, if we act on the information she has brought to light, we can save ourselves.

A note on the Editing

This book was written as an academic thesis. I have made no attempt to re-write it for the general reader, so it retains the quality of a doctoral dissertation. This means that repetition has not been eliminated. Editing has been limited to making the meaning clearer where I thought this necessary. The style and content are the author's and have not been altered except in small particulars. Some points have been qualified or enlarged by editorial notes which appear at the foot of the relevant page. A very few, and very minor, errors of statement have been cut out. None of the points corrected or omitted make any difference to the author's general thesis.

Appendix C, *How the ANC became a Communist Front* has been added by me.

Jillian Becker
London
April, 1984

Introduction

This book is the result of research under the direction of my friend the late Leonard Schapiro, one of the West's handful of truly profound students of Soviet matters. His death, and that of the author of this work, in the meantime, together deprive us of too much irreplaceable seriousness and understanding of the Soviet mind and Soviet intentions and actions.

In Professor Schapiro's place, I have been asked to introduce this work. I cannot do so as he would have done. Not merely had he the closest scholarly relationship with the author, but he was also personally concerned with, and knowledgeable about, the Soviet connection with the terrorist organizations of today, as I am not.

As a learner rather than a teacher, then, it is appropriate for me to say that I have learnt much about this important and inadequately studied subject from these pages. In the best traditions of scholarship Mrs Goren has pursued the inevitably scanty, yet in the end cumulative and decisive, evidence of the long established but (especially in late years) increasingly important involvement of the Soviet regime in sponsoring, arming and training groups which have sought to influence the world by the bomb and the hijack.

We must indeed distinguish, as does the author herself. Terrorism is a vague word. Support for and arming of guerrillas is one thing; of small groups of indiscriminate urban bombers and aeroplane hijackers another. She well develops the inconsistent and inconstant way in which Leninists, from their earliest history, abjured 'individual' terrorism, if only from tactical motives, yet saw a range of actions from scattered incidents to general insurrections as part of the legitimate spectrum of the struggle against hostile regimes.

The original Leninist 'tactical' objection to 'individual terror' was based on the idea that it did not produce useful political results, and if anything caused revulsion among potential supporters. In recent years, it might be thought, such things as random bombings have become so widespread that the Kremlin may feel that these disadvantages have to some degree disappeared. At any rate, support for terrorist organization, with occasional rebukes to their most revolting killings of innocents, now seems to be Moscow's accepted tactic. But the author also makes it clear that from early Soviet times such support has been given in circumstances or areas where the advantages seemed to outbalance the admitted negatives. It is thus to be seen as a tactical weapon in the process of unlimited expansion as and when possible to which Leninism, and their political mind-set in general, commits Soviet leaders.

This book does not deal in detail with 'terrorism' in the sense understood by the original Russian terrorists of the last century – the assassination of specific individuals. It was this, rather than other aspects of 'terrorism', which Lenin held unadvisable. There were various exceptions, but it does not seem to have been until about the end of 1936 that the NKVD formed its 'Adminstration of Special Tasks' under Major of State Security Yakov Serebryanski, with the original purpose of killing defectors from the NKVD itself as with the cases of Agabekov and Reiss. Soon Trotsky and his entourage became targets - several being killed before the final operation assassinated Trotsky himself in 1940. In the 1950s the same section organized the killings of the Ukrainian emigré leader Stepan Bandeka, and others, with the assassins being awarded orders by the Soviet Government. And later this principle was extended to other 'disloyal' subjects of the Soviet empire - including, or so it now appears, the Polish Pope.

This subject is a study in itself which may yet deserve referring to as a minor supplement to this striking and most useful book. Far more important on the world scale is the scholarly establishment of the evidence of the nature of the relationship between the USSR and autonomous or partly autonomous terrorist organizations abroad at the present, which the author has done so effectively in these pages, and which makes her work an indispensable handbook for all who wish to understand crucially important aspects of the world as it is today.

Robert Conquest

Acknowledgements

The author gratefully acknowledges the invaluable advice and support extended by Professor Leonard Schapiro, Professor Emeritus of Political Science with Special Reference to Soviet Studies at the London School of Economics and Political Science, while supervising this work.

The author is also much indebted to all those who granted her interviews and contributed information which was used in this study. In particular, the author wishes to thank, in alphabetical order: Jillian Becker, author and researcher; Mr John Bushnell, US Department of State, Washington DC; US Ambassador Kingman Brewster; Mr J. Churba, Washington DC; Dr Ray S. Cline, Center for Strategic and International Studies, Georgetown University, Washington DC; Mr Michael Elkins, BBC correspondent in Israel; General Shlomo Gazit, Israel; Mr Isar Harel, Israel; Mr Edward S. Heyman, Washington DC; Dr Hans Joseph Horchem, Head of the Office for the Protection of the Constitution, West German Government; Mr Robert Hubert, House Committee on International Relations, Washington DC; Mr Ephraim Ilin, Israel; Dr Brian Jenkins, Rand Corporation, California; Dr Robert Kupperman, Washington DC; Professor Walter Laqueur, Center for Strategic and International Studies, Georgetown University, Washington DC; Sir David McNee, QPM, New Scotland yard; Dr Ariel Merari, Institute for Strategic Studies, Tel Aviv University; Mr Edward Mickolus, McLean, Virginia; Mr Joseph V. Montville, US Department of State, Washington DC; Mr Robert B. Morley, US Department of State, Washington DC; Dr Dick Mulder, The Hague, Holland; Ambassador Anthony Quainton, US Department of State, Washington DC; Dr Yaacov Roi, Chairman of the Russian and East European Center, Tel Aviv University; Mr Evo Spalatin, House Committee on International Relations, Washington DC; Mr Robert Whalley, Private Secretary to Sir Robert Armstrong, London. Those not mentioned are omitted by their own request but are nevertheless thanked.

Special thanks are given to Dr Galia Golan, Hebrew University of Jerusalem, who not only was generous with her time but made available to me the facilities of the Russian Research Institute's library of Soviet press information which proved an invaluable asset to the research; to Dr Leon Gouré, Washington DC, for always being supportive and helpful in his criticism; and Mr Zvi Hartman and Mr Rafael Vago at the Tel Aviv University Russian and East European Research Centre for their generous help in the use of their excellent library of Soviet material.

The author is deeply indebted to many personal friends who faithfully assisted in various ways. In alphabetical order these are: Mr George E. Agree, Mr Charles C. Cushing, Mr Louis B. Eaton, Mr Dan Eshel, Mr Richard W. Richardson, General Dan Tolkowsky, Dr J. E. Warren, and Mr Brian Wolfson.

Finally, my husband and daughters who have exhibited extended patience, support and love.

Abbreviations

A. General

AJIL	American Journal of International Law
ASIL	American Society of International Law
BBC/SU	Summary of World Broadcasts/Soviet Union
BYIL	British Yearbook of International Law
CHEKA	Chrezvychainaia Kommissia
	All-Russian Extraordinary Commission for
	Combating Counter-Revolution
CIA	United States Central Intelligence Agency
CO	Colonial Office Documents, British Government
Comintern	The Third Communist International
CP	Communist Party
CPSU	Communist Party of the Soviet Union
CPUSA	Communist Party of the United States
DGI	Direcion General de Inteligencia (Cuba)
DST	Direction de Securité Territoriale
ECCI	Executive Committee of the Communist
	International
FGCI	Italian Communist Party Youth Organization
FO	Foreign Office Documents, British Government
GAOR	United Nations, General Assembly, Official
	Records
GPRA	Provisional Government of the Republic of Algeria
GRU	Glavnoe Razvedyvatelnoe Upravlenie
	Chief Intelligence Directorate - Red Army
HCIS	House Committee on Internal Security, US
	Congress
ICAO	International Civil Aviation Organization
ICLQ	International and Comparative Law Quarterly
IDF	Israel Defence Forces
IISS	Institute for International and Strategic Studies,
	London
FBIS	Foreign Broadcast Service, Washington DC
KGB	Komitet Gosudarstvertnoi Bezopasnosti
	Committee for State Security
KPD	Communist Party of Germany (West Germany)
LNTS	League of Nations Treaty Series
MER	Middle East Record, Shiloah Institute, Tel Aviv
	University
MEW	Marx and Engels Werke

MOR	Monarchist Confederation of Russia
NKVD	Narodny Kommissariat Vnutrennikh Del
	People's Commissariat of Internal Affairs
OAU	Organization of African Unity
OGPU	Obedinnoe Gosudarstvennoe Politicheskoe
	Upravlenie
	The Unified State Political Administration
PCA	Parti Communiste Algérien
PCE	Parti Communiste Egypitien
PCF	Parti Communiste Français
PCI	Partito Comunista Italiano
QB	Queen's Bench
RUSI	Royal United Services Institute for Defence
	Studies, London
SACP	South African Communist Party
SCOR	United Nations, Security Council, Official Records
SIAIS	Subcommittee to Investigate the Administration of
	the Internal Security Laws of the Committee of the
	Judiciary, U.S. Senate.
SID	
SWB	Summary of World Broadcasts, same as BBC/SU
UAR	United Arab Republic
UN Doc.	United Nations Document
UNGA	United Nations General Assembly
UNTS	United Nations Treaty Series
USIS	United States Information Service
USPD	German Independent Democratic Party
PNA	Palestine National Assembly
PNC	Palestine National Council

B   Terrorist and Paramilitary Groups

ANC	African National Congress
BR	Brigate Rosse
DRH	Dutch Red Help
ELN	Ejercito de Liberaciòn Nacional (Bolivia)
EOKA	National Organization for Cyprus Fighters
ERP	Ejercito Revolucionaria del Pueblo (Argentina)
ETA	Euzkadi ta Azkatasuna (Basque)
FALN	Fuerzas Armadas de Liberaciòn Nacional (Puerto
	Rico)
FAR	Fuerzas Armadas Rebeldes (Guatemala and
	Argentina)
FLN	Front de Libération Nationale (Algeria)

FLQ	Front de Libération du Quebec
GAP	Gruppi di Azione Partigiana
GARI	Gruppos de Acciòn Revolucionaria Internacionalistas (Spain)
GRAPO	Grupo Revolucionario Antifascista Primero Octubre (Spain)
INLA	Irish National Liberation Army
IRA	Irish Republican Army
JCR	Junta de Coordinaciòn Revolucionaria
JDL	Jewish Defense League
JRA	Japanese Red Army (Rengo Sekigun)
M2J	Movement of the Second of June
MAR	Movimiento de Acciòn Revolucionaria (Mexico)
MIR	Movimiento de Izquierda Revolucionaria (Chile)
MLN	Movimiento de Liberaciòn Nacional (Tupamoras - Uruguay)
MPLA	Movimento Popular para a Libertaciao de Angola
PDFLP	Popular Democratic Front for the Liberation of Palestine (PLO)
PFLP	Popular Front for the Liberation of Palestine (PLO)
PLO	Palestine Liberation Organization
RAF	Rote Armee Fraktion
TLA	Turkish Liberation Army
TPLA	Turkish People's Liberation Army

1

Introduction

This book is about war: the war which the Soviet Union is waging on the West - indirectly. In practical terms, international terrorism is power projection. It is the physical manifestation of a bid for power.

That remains true whether one wishes to analyse the problem of political terrorism from the psychological or sociological underlying causes which propel an individual to kill as a means of satisfying his or her own need for self-assertion - for an expression of power and invincibility - often legitimized by a political rationale, or from the strictly political context of a group perpetrating murderous deeds as a means of drawing attention to its cause. In the latter case, the group achieves power in the terrorist act itself and in the harnessing of concentrated publicity through the media exposure which a terrorist act inevitably receives; that attention, it could be argued, has proved to be the greatest expression of the power of the terrorist group.

This is not to say that the group is at all times aiming at a total takeover of the established political order. Hence it is not the classical notion of a power takeover at the top which is contemplated. The terrorist groups operating in European liberal democracies, for example, have until now shown no such inclination. Even though each organization has espoused its own individual reasons for carrying out terrorist acts, ranging from the anarchist mentality of the Movement of the Second of June (M2J) of West Germany, to the 'national liberation' claims of the Irish Republican Army (IRA), to the 'class struggle' of the Brigate Rosse (BR) of Italy, each has achieved power by the perpetration of the acts themselves and has been either unwilling to go further or incapable of doing so.

An international terrorist event is equally a manifestation of power when it is state-initiated. For example, Colonel Qaddafi of Libya extended his power all the way to London when he had several leading dissident civilians assassinated there. The same extension of power was achieved by the Bulgarian government with the murder of the Bulgarian émigré who worked for the BBC in

London, for example. In these cases, the extension of state power is demonstrated not only to other dissidents but also to the states in whose territory the crimes are perpetrated.

However, perhaps most importantly, international terrorism is power from the point of view of the sponsor state. In the context of global power politics with the existing potential for nuclear devastation, international terrorism can be a greater source of power than was previously suspected. The importance which must be given to the problem of international terrorism cannot, in fact, be overstated, particularly when evaluating the necessary Western response. The sponsor state runs little risk of confrontation with the adversary and thus avoids a nuclear engagement. The use of terrorism therefore becomes a tactic in a larger objective.

There has been until now a reluctance in the West to acknowledge the immense importance of terrorism in the overall strategic context, and only recently Ambassador C. E. Quainton, while director of the United States Department of State's Office for Combating Terrorism, stated his opposite view as follows: 'Terrorism, brutal and savage though it may be, is still a relatively minor problem in comparison with the many other pressing economic, social and political priorities of the planet and of our country.'[1] However, this view, which has frequently been echoed by numerous political analysts, lacks the global perspective which is so necessary for the proper evaluation of the worldwide pattern of aggression that international terrorism has acquired in the last fifteen years. Terrorism is both a political and a strategic problem and must qualify as a collective political priority for the Western liberal democracies.

Perceptions and Conceptualization of International Terrorism

International terrorist incidents have, on average, increased since 1968 and there were more casualties of international terrorism in 1980 than any preceding year in that period, as Figures 1.1 and 1.2 demonstrate.

Although terrorism is certainly not the invention of the political world of the twentieth century, its dramatic growth since 1968 has been greatly enhanced by specific conditions belonging to this century. The invention of television with instant satellite relay has suddenly given small unknown groups the possibility of a worldwide publicity campaign. The fact that most terrorist incidents have taken place in the more liberal states may in part be due to the availability of this instant publicity. Under an

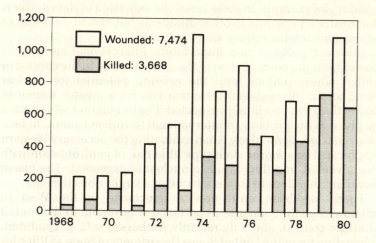

Figure 1.1 *Deaths and injuries due to international terrorist attacks.*
Source: CIA Study, *Patterns of International Terrorism 1980* (National Foreign Assessment Center, 1981).

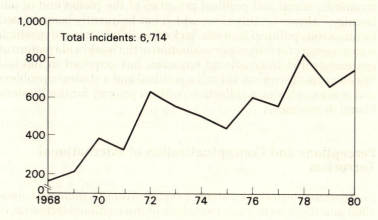

Figure 1.2 *International terrorist incidents.*
Source: CIA Study, *Patterns of International Terrorism 1980* (National Foreign Assessment Center, 1981).

authoritarian regime terrorists can be cut off from their media audience in the target country, thereby losing all the expected impact of their actions.

With the freely available media, small groups of terrorists can achieve heavy leverage against powerful opponents by focusing large publicity on politically small events. The impact is mostly psychological and meant for media coverage.

Moreover, the proliferation and incredible sophistication of modern weapons have enabled small numbers to do great harm. In 1973, for example, the Italian police burst in on five Arab terrorists who were setting up SA-7 missiles in a rented apartment four miles from Rome's Leonardo da Vinci Airport. These missiles were intended for use against an Israeli civilian airliner. The SA-7 is a Soviet heat-seeking, precision-guided missile. It can be carried comfortably on a man's back and can destroy a plane at altitudes of up to 6,500 feet. United States intelligence sources have reported that SA-7 missiles have surfaced in almost all Arab countries and some African nations, including Mozambique.[2] Libya has obtained from the USSR large quantities of RPG-7 rockets which weigh under ten pounds, can be hand carried and can destroy a tank, a speaker's platform, or a limousine. In this connection, the IRA is known to have used RPG-7 rockets against armoured British military vehicles and police installations.

There is, in addition, increasing evidence of active co-operation between various terrorist groups.[3] The pilgrims at Lod Airport in Israel were massacred by Japanese Red Army (JRA) members acting for the Palestine Liberation Organization (PLO). The terrorists who raided the Vienna OPEC meeting were made up of elements from the Popular Front for the Liberation of Palestine (PFLP), a PLO group, and the Baader-Meinhof gang (Rote Armee Fraktion, RAF), the West German anarchist group. Also, the promotion of armed struggle by means of a so-called 'guerrilla international' was carried out by the Junta for Revolutionary Co-ordination (JCR), initiated during 1974 by the Argentine ERP (Trotskyist People's Revolutionary Army). It included the Bolivian ELN, the Chilean MIR and the Uruguyan MLN-Tupamaros, with offices and a press agency (APAL) in Paris.[4] A special unit of the Irish Republican Army Provisionals was known to be training Black nationalist guerrillas for action in Rhodesia to be sent to operate in Mozambique.[5] IRA members have been trained in PLO camps in the Middle East, and the PLO was the overall co-ordinator of international terrorism.

The twentieth century will have to be described by later historians as the century of wars and revolutions. The growth of nationalism, which led naturally to emancipatory moves by various nations at the end of the First World War, resulted in the final dismantling of the Western colonial empire. However, to attribute all the events of this century to a natural pattern of evolvement would be to discount state behaviour as a factor influencing political events. In 1917 Soviet communism turned the tables on the West's overwhelming ascendancy and as a consequence the Western democracies have found themselves in an ideological defensive posture ever since. This Western position has been of the greatest importance as a contributory factor to the general weakening of the West's political power worldwide. Clearly, the successes enjoyed by the Soviet Union over the years cannot all be attributed to its foresight.

It is, however, the debate of recent years, revolving as it has around war and the justifiable use of violence, which most determines the importance that international terrorism has acquired. Since 1945 and the first atomic weapon, the very nature of war has undergone a radical change with the introduction of the deterrent 'as the guiding principle in the armament race'.[6] This deterrent factor 'aims in effect at avoiding rather than winning the war it pretends to be preparing. It tends to achieve its goals by a menace which is never put into execution, rather than by the act itself'.[7] The technological developments which have reached unprecedented levels have, in fact, made war in the classical sense an impossibility, if not an absurdity, and this new perception of war forms the basis of the policy of confrontation of the two superpowers. Whereas wars used to be fought to achieve peace, there has recently been an increased substitution of 'cold' wars and proxy wars for 'hot', direct wars. Since the Second World War and particularly since the middle 1960s, the growing shift of emphasis from wars to revolutions and so-called urban warfare has been of paramount importance. In the early 1960s Hannah Arendt predicted that 'revolution, in distinction to war, will stay with us into the foreseeable future' and she went on to say that 'those will probably win who understand revolution, while those who still put their faith in power politics in the traditional sense of the term and, therefore, in war as the last resort of all foreign policy, may well discover in a not too distant future that they have become masters in a rather useless and obsolete trade'.[8]

It is unfortunately true that most sincerely idealistic revolutions in this century have not been able to produce a limited government guaranteeing civil rights and liberties. In fact more often than not one sort of repressive regime has taken the place of another repressive regime. Often what has been represented as a left-wing 'liberating' regime overthrowing a right-wing repressive regime is no less reactionary than its predecessor, as was the Bolshevik Party replacing the Czarist *ancien régime*, for example, although in this case the liberator surpassed the oppressor by a staggering margin. As compared with the 14,000 recorded executions which were carried out during the last fifty years of Czarism, there are various estimates of up to 12 million individuals executed in the first twenty years of Bolshevik rule.[9]

It is important, in the present context, to say a few words about the stigmatizing terminology which appears to constrict Western liberal democratic policy evaluations. The natural revulsion to Hitler's horrors has created a situation where 'left', which was presumed to be the opposite of nazism, has been regarded as 'good' and 'liberating'. This distinction has handicapped proper evaluation of particular situations. Nazism, which is generally regarded as 'right-wing', differed little from Leninist-Marxist communism, both in expressed ideologies and in foreign policy goals.[10] Moreover, the parallels which can be drawn between the factual implementation of the two policies only add to this view. Perhaps what is not widely known is that Communist Party members in Germany (KPD) made up the very early membership of the Nazi Party, and there was a consistent attraction between the two camps. The opposition which was perceived by the Western allies as existing between the Nazi and Marxist ideologies and as *de facto* polarizing them was due, on the contrary, to their similarity of goals rather than the opposite. In the context of this study, therefore, it is essential to understand that what are labelled as 'right-wing' terror and 'left-wing' terror are often co-operative ventures which aim at the identical goal of disruption and are not always fighting each other. The growing evidence of co-operation between such groups should therefore not be regarded as anything unusual. There is a definite blurring of distinctions when extreme 'right' and extreme 'left' meet in the nethermost regions of political fanaticism. What must be clear is that there cannot be any 'good' terrorism carried out against Western liberal democracies.[11]

No matter what real grievance a terrorist may have, it is the fact that he is sponsored to any extent from abroad which is of interest for foreign policy evaluations. Although one often hears the argument that the terrorist will accept help from wherever he can get it - and that is, of course, true - the fact that a given state would want to sponsor him at all gives rise to the question, why? For example, if Italian terrorism is aided and abetted from abroad, then the sponsor state must have certain political or strategic goals in mind which may or may not be identical to those of the terrorist group.[12] In either case it can be said that the group is being used as a proxy. In this way, the group is satisfied because it receives the necessary logistical support for its activities, and the sponsor state is satisfied because it must perceive the terrorist activities carried out by the group as beneficial to its own goals.

Whereas there can always be found endemic reasons for people turning to terror, a greater understanding of the importance of the logistical and material support necessary for this activity would benefit the quality of the West's response to this threat. The reality of the suicidal nature of a nuclear confrontation is reflected in a greater effort at self-restraint in terms of avoiding dangerous confrontational issues in the conduct of international relations by the superpowers. It is also reflected in the assiduous attempts at nuclear arms limitation. This re-emphasizes the proportionately greater increase in value as a tactical weapon which international terrorism has acquired.

There are at least two qualitative comments to be made regarding the international terrorism which has flourished since 1968. First, what can and must be noted is the conspicuous absence of terrorism in the Eastern bloc countries, at least of the type which has plagued Western liberal democracies in particular. None of the groups which have been active in and against the West has operated against the Eastern bloc countries since the early 1960s. Even though Central Intelligence Agency (CIA) statistics[13] on yearly incidents of international terrorism include, for example, the Soviet Union as a geographical area where a small number of terrorist incidents have taken place, the base structure of the groups and the targets of these terrorists differ greatly from those which operate in the West, such as the PLO. The hijackers in the Soviet Union were mostly Jewish 'refuseniks' who desperately wanted to leave the country. They had no organization in the classical conspiratorial cell structural sense and they lacked political objective. Between 1968 and 1980 the CIA lists a total of sixty-two terrorist incidents as having occurred in the USSR/ Eastern Europe geographical area. Of these, twenty-nine attacks were directed against United States targets. Neither the hijackings nor the attacks against United States targets could be viewed as politically aimed at the government of the Soviet Union (see Figures 1.3 and 1.4).

Secondly, the traditionally accepted view that terrorism was the only weapon available to the weak and desperate fighting against foreign oppression, and therefore to be condoned, was based on the philosophical liberalism of the nineteenth century which saw this oppressive foreign rule as a justifiable target; but the proliferation of terrorism in Western liberal democracies cannot be condoned in the same manner, so this view requires a re-evaluation. The actions of the Red Brigades or the Rote Armee Fraktion can be called acts neither of desperation nor of weakness for they are perpetrated in countries which exemplify the parliamentary alternatives that allow for political change to be effected by non-violent means, and they are largely carried out by wealthy middle-class individuals.

In the last fifteen years international terrorism has often contributed to the escalation which leads to civil wars, factional strife, revolutions, or *coups d'état*. In fact, with the benefit of

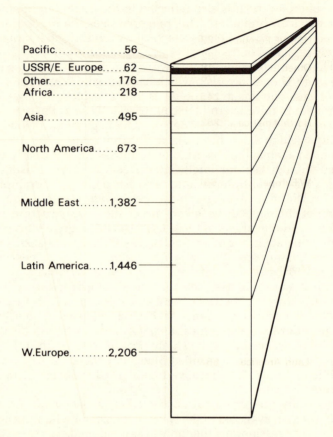

Figure 1.3 *Geographic distribution of international terrorist attacks, 1968-80.*

Source: CIA Study, *Patterns of International Terrorism 1980* (National Foreign Assessment Center, 1981).

hindsight, it now appears to be the case that two main types of international terrorism have developed, distinctly bisected into near-perfect geographic sections, both of which have mainly been erosive to the West's overall position in the balance of power. For the purposes of this study these two categories are defined as (1) revolutionary terrorism and (2) sub-revolutionary terrorism.

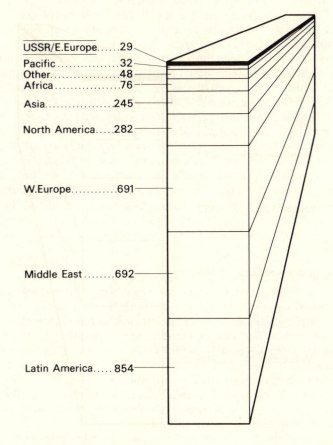

USSR/E.Europe......29
Pacific................32
Other..................48
Africa................76
Asia..................245
North America.....282
W.Europe............691
Middle East........692
Latin America.....854

Figure 1.4 *Geographic distribution of international terrorist attacks directed against US targets, 1968-80.*
  Source: CIA Study, *Patterns of International Terrorism 1980* (National Foreign Assessment Center, 1981).

(1) Revolutionary Terrorism
This type of terrorism involves the systematic use of terrorist tactics against civilian targets, both living and material, with the objective of bringing about political revolution - the overthrow of the existing political order. It has been legitimized ever since the French Revolution which provided the sanctification of violence in the name of the people. In the twentieth century it has affected mainly

Third World countries which were still shedding European colonialism or which had strong links with the Western powers after their decolonization. This terrorism has usually preceded what is normally defined as the revolution itself, or the civil war, having been used as a tactic to create a sense of tension and fear in the country. It is interesting to note that the targets of revolutionary terrorism have often been foreign to the expressed conflict. Thus in El Salvador, where a military right-wing dictatorship is being fought by left-wing groups, the primary targets of attacks have included civilians, embassies and private facilities belonging to the United States, Israel and other Central American countries. On 11 January 1980, for example, the Panamanian embassy in San Salvador was stormed by the 28 February Popular League (LP-28). They held hostages, including two ambassadors (Costa Rica and Panama), and demanded the release of other LP-28 members held in prison in San Salvador.[14] On 16 September 1980 the American embassy was badly damaged by a rocket attack launched by the ERP. In Guatemala the pattern has been similar with, for example, the Spanish embassy being taken over by leftists on 31 January 1980.[15]

(2)   Sub-Revolutionary Terrorism

This type of terrorism can best be described as acts of terrorism perpetrated against civilian targets, both living and material, by groups having political motives or ideologies but whose aims fall short of revolution. The terrorist groups operating in Western liberal democracies mostly fall into this category. This definition would apply to the PLO as well as to indigenous groups operating within any given country in Western Europe, such as the BR or the RAF. The PLO has mainly operated on the European continent without ever intending to create a revolution there. This type of terrorism is agitational by definition.

In both of these categories there are two necessary common denominators:

(a)   an organized group using terrorism must exist or be created;
(b)   the groups must receive massive logistical and material support in order to sustain their activities for any length of time.

In both categories, where this logistical support comes from a sponsor state there ensues an automatic internationalization of the conflict. This applies to both indigenous and foreign groups.

Definitional Problems

Any definition of international terrorism is certain to arouse dispute and the ultimate judgement of the right to use terrorism as a political factor is bound to be subjective. So far the definitional problems of terrorism have evaded a universally accepted consensus.

The difficulties stem, on the one hand, from the varying interpretations given to a particular 'terrorist' act by the world at large, by the terrorists who perpetrate it, and by the country or countries which might reap some benefit from such an act. Human nature tends to protect its own, and where violence comes into the picture this tendency is perhaps most visible in the immediate distinction made between just and unjust terror. The validity of some causes, such as resistance to an oppressive totalitarian regime or the right of self-determination, are justified in the eyes of the perpetrators of the violence as excusable and an acceptable alternative to accession through legitimate routes. Where these legitimate routes are absent, the use of violence has normally been acceptable and has not led to long philosophical discussions on its merits. However, even in cases where there are no alternatives to violence to overthrow an oppressive regime, terrorist attacks on civilian targets and even on family members of the oppressive ruler must be deemed unacceptable and terroristic if liberal democracies are to deal effectively with the problem.

A large part of the difficulties in reaching a clear understanding of terrorism stem from semantical and terminological differences which have been perpetrated by writers, politicians and the public information media, to a point of total confusion. The terms 'terrorist', 'freedom fighter', 'partisan', 'commando', 'guerrilla fighter', are very often used interchangeably although they all mean something different and each carries with it a value judgement. Some of these terms are discussed next in order to clarify this confusion.

Terrorism

By this is meant violence usually associated with the authority in any given area, such as government terror, used to coerce, repress, or destroy human life and property by force and intimidation. This type of terrorism has most often been identified with the Jacobins during the period of the French Revolution (the Reign of Terror, 1793-4) when several thousand people were guillotined and mass arrests took place in order to liquidate all internal counter-revolutionary elements.[16] This same sort of terror - terrorism to retain power - has been applied by many governments; for example, Stalin (the Great Purge), and Khomeini in Iran. As discussed earlier, this so-called 'official terrorism' or state terror can also be exported to assassinate enemies of the state or to sponsor insurgents in another country.

International Terrorism

This describes violent acts and/or campaigns of violence and threats against civilian targets used across the national borders of a given state for political purposes and falling outside the normally accepted rules of international diplomacy and war.[17] These acts are committed by individuals or organized groups operating as allegedly independent entities under no official state umbrella and wearing no uniform. These terrorists resort to hijackings, bombings of civilian populations at random, kidnapping and killing businessmen and diplomats often connected to a foreign state and usually not connected to the 'cause'. The 'revolutionary terrorism' and 'sub-revolutionary terrorism' categories defined earlier both form part of international terrorism.

Guerrilla Warfare

The word 'guerrilla' was coined during the Peninsular War (1808-14), when the Spanish partisans, under such leaders as Francisco Mina, proved unconquerable even by the armies of Napoleon 1. The *Columbia Encyclopedia* describes guerrilla warfare as 'fighting by other than regularly organized military forces in areas occupied by the enemy'. This form of military struggle was greatly developed during the American Civil War and during this century has become a major weapon used by communist powers in their conflict with the West.[18] Guerrilla warfare is therefore a form of war (Spanish for 'little war') aiming at the overthrow of the established power and normally only attacking military and strategic targets. If guerrillas obey the laws of 'civilized warfare' they are entitled to be treated as prisoners of war when captured.[19] The term 'guerrilla' has all too often been used as a catch-all term by the public information media to describe violent acts by international terrorists, thereby automatically bestowing on the latter an aura of legitimacy.

'National Liberation'

This is a phrase coined by the Third World nations to describe the process of decolonization, as expressed in the Declaration for Granting of Independence to Colonial Countries and Peoples in 1960.[20] It legitimizes the use of force to destroy colonialism (meaning past Western colonialism only) and often this force is represented by the use of terrorist tactics. The term is now used to describe an attack on the established order even when colonialism no longer exists.

The attempts at defining international terrorism are naturally made complex by political realities, as the peregrinations of the United Nations Ad Hoc Committee on International Terrorism have indicated. As an example, in 1973 France proposed a narrow definition of the problem as follows:[21]

> heinous act of barbarism committed in the territory of a third state by a foreigner against a person possessing a nationality other than that of the offender for the purpose of exerting pressure in a conflict not strictly internal in nature.

Another attempt came from a group of non-aligned nations which offered the following definition:[22]

> acts of violence and other repressive acts by colonial, racist, and alien regimes against peoples struggling for their libera- tion . . . tolerating or assisting by a state or organization of the remnants of fascists or mercenary groups whose terrorist activity is directed against other sovereign countries; acts of violence committed by individuals or groups of individuals which endanger or take innocent human lives or jeopardize fundamental freedoms or affect the inalienable right to self- determination and independence of all peoples under colonial and racist regimes and other forms of alien domination . . . acts of violence committed by individuals or groups of individuals for private gain, the effects of which are not confined to one State.

Carlton and Schaerf have pointed out[23] that the above definition for international terrorism jeopardizes fundamental freedoms and defines only acts committed by 'others' as international terrorism. Needless to say, the Ad Hoc Committee failed to reach agreement on what international terrorism is.

Since the nineteenth century political crimes have had to pass the test of extraditability to fall under the 'justifiable' violence and therefore non-extraditable crime category. In 1890 murder committed during a political disturbance was held to be non- extraditable by an English court if it could be proven to be part of an organized attempt to seize power.[24] A few years later this point was expanded with the decision that acts of violence, even though politically motivated, would not be protected from extradition, and therefore not considered political crimes, if they were not part of that organized attempt to seize power.[25] The rationale used in the rule against the extradition of purely political offenders was that they did not, like 'common criminals', generally represent a threat to the life or property of citizens of other states.[26] The political terrorist today, however, does represent a threat to the life and property of citizens of his or other states and his crimes should therefore be treated as criminal and extraditable if there is to be any hope of outlawing the perpetration of this crime. Under international law, when the stability of other states or innocent human life and consequently international order are threatened, then the person who commits such an act ceases to be a political offender and becomes a criminal.[27]

International terrorists can be paralleled to offenders under the Genocide Convention and the Geneva Conventions of 1949. Offenders are deprived of the benefit of non-extradition under those Conventions because 'crimes against humanity or the rules of war are of international concern and should not be protected because they happen to have a national political objective'.[28] In spite of this rationale, and reflecting the recent evolvement of the concepts of war as discussed above, on 22 April 1977 a committee of the International Red Cross Conference of the Geneva Convention countries met in an attempt to update the 1949 texts on prisoners of war. The vote was 65 to 2 with 19 abstentions to extend prisoner-of-war status, protection and privileges to terrorists. (Britain abstained, Israel and Brazil voted against, and the United States surprisingly joined the other sixty-four countries voting in favour of the resolution - among which were the USSR, East Germany and Libya.) It cannot be overemphasized that this type of blurring of the distinction between a soldier whose unfortunate business it is to kill - preferably other soldiers - and civilians or alleged 'liberationists' who murder other civilians is a dangerous development in the West's fight against international terrorism. This proposal, in fact, exemplified a new 'collective legitimization' of violence and must serve to re-emphasize the necessity of a re-evaluation of the whole problem which would lead to a greater acceptance of the view that terrorism is now being exploited as a tactic in a larger conflict.

Within the sub-revolutionary category of international terrorism where the ultimate aim of the group and/or the sponsor falls short of revolution, the agitational goal of this type of terrorism can be defined as *indirect aggression*,[29] which in turn brings us to the close relationship which exists between international terrorism and subversion. Usually defined as the systematic attempt to undermine a society with the ultimate goal of causing the collapse of law and order and loss of confidence in the state, subversion can also be said to occur often during a period of time immediately preceding a revolutionary war or a so-called 'national liberation' war. The classic example of this type of activity was the terrorism which immediately preceded what was to develop into the Vietnam War and took place as part of the general conflict as well. That war followed the pattern developed by Mao Tse-tung and Vo Nguyen Giap. [30] As Brian Crozier has pointed out, revolutionary wars do not just happen. They necessitate a structural progression which begins with the creation of a subversive apparatus that will lead to terrorist activity on a random and sporadic scale, eventually escalating into guerrilla war. Ultimately, when there has been sufficient disruption, a 'revolutionary final offensive' will occur. This pattern is repeated in all revolutions or civil wars.

It is consequently of the utmost importance not to omit from any definition of international terrorism the subversive elements of its making. Subversion and clandestine support for murder on an organized scale add a dangerous dimension to an activity which would otherwise be limited to small groups of lunatics acting on their own and with no outside support.

Perceptions and Conceptualization of the Soviet Union

The USSR has had a continuity of leadership and internal structure since 1917 which permits trend analysis and attempts to establish whether the Kremlin has pursued a consistent policy towards international terrorism, if any policy is present, and so forth.

The Soviet Union has used an ideological scaffolding which has itself remained a constant feature and has both supported and legitimized the Kremlin's foreign policy behaviour. This ideology is perpetually aggressive by definition, forecasting as it does the inevitable demise of the 'capitalist enemy' and the triumph of communism. Does this necessarily imply that the USSR would actively, if covertly, support any activity which would hasten this inevitability - even terrorism - though it objects to its use in principle, or is all this mere rhetoric to be considered irrelevant? And, furthermore, does the USSR really object to the use of terrorism in principle?

Officially, the Soviet Union professes an abhorrence on principle to terrorism. Publicly, particularly in the forum of the United Nations, but also in the official press and radio statements, the Soviet Union actively supports Marxist-Leninist 'partisans' fighting for 'national liberation'.

There are, of course, many problems related to any analysis of Soviet behaviour. These problems are mostly those of interpretation and conceptualization rather than lack of information. And foremost is the tendency to perceive Soviet foreign policy in terms of Western value judgements. Often when Soviet behaviour is, in the opinion of the Western observer, 'unrealistic', there is a tendency to dismiss it as not possible. Particularly without allowing for Soviet flexibility in their decision-making process, Soviet objectives are often evaluated in terms of an 'either-or' approach. However, the Kremlin views the international sphere as a dynamic changing milieu necessitating equally dynamic and flexible policies and responses. So where in this text I speak of Soviet policy as being 'opportunistic', the definition to be applied to that term is 'the exploitation of favourable conditions within the context of their overall objectives', and *not* an unplanned, *ad hoc* type of behaviour. One can often see sharp and sudden changes in Soviet direction depending on their assessment of the balance of forces; however, these shifts take place within the scope of policy objectives which remain the same.

In fact it can be said that Soviet foreign policy has always been based on the achievement of long-term goals, and in contrast to Western liberal democracies whose electoral systems preclude such continuity of purpose, the Communist Party of the Soviet Union (CPSU) has proved over the years that it can be pragmatic, flexible and, therefore, opportunistic, in order to keep its ultimate objective within reachable reality.

Paramount to any analysis of the Soviet Union's position on the question of international terrorism is the setting down of certain perceptions about its general global outlook which inevitably form part of a decision-making process. The fact that it views itself as the champion and leader of the global 'anti-imperialist struggle' is perhaps the most important ideological base. What it calls 'proletarian internationalism' makes it, *ipso facto* and by its own definition, the backer and sponsor of global revolutionary and national liberation movements. It is also, however, supremely aware of its critical need of United States and West European economic aid and investments and must therefore avoid behaviour which would jeopardize the satisfying of this need. As a consequence, the Kremlin sees itself as an opportunistic, flexible negotiator. It sees the struggle for predominance between capitalism and socialism as inevitable and to achieve its own predominance it utilizes a vast number of concurrent or alternate strategies. The strongest determining influence on its decision-making is real fear of a nuclear confrontation with the United States. And, finally, the Soviet Union has had since 1917 strong desires to make political gains in Western Europe and the Middle East. A loss of influence by the United States is perceived by the Kremlin as a political gain for itself even though it may not have replaced the United States in that particular area.

Method of Approach

These concepts will be further developed as this study progresses. The analysis of the Soviet Union's attitude and policy on international terrorism has been placed in a historical setting in the belief that Soviet behaviour in relation to the West can best be analysed and understood in the perspective of time. Declassified documents from the British Foreign Office form the greater part of the factual information presented for the historical period. In addition, the legal perceptions by the USSR on aggression and indirect aggression are set down in the belief that they form the framework within which the Kremlin sees itself functioning and are useful indicators of its decision-making process. Marxist-Leninist ideology on terrorism is discussed in an attempt to establish whether the USSR is opposed to the use of terrorism for political gains as a matter of principle. Since the Soviet Union uses this ideology, whether out of true belief or out of necessity, and justifies its behaviour by falling back on Leninist statements in particular, it is deemed important to clarify the question. The contemporary section is based on an analysis of Soviet official pronouncements at the United Nations, or in the press and in radio broadcasts, to present the Soviet position in their own words. The Western press, academic studies on terrorism, and interviews with high-level government personnel in various countries in the Western liberal democracies form the background of the factual information necessary for this study. Where specific permission was granted to this author to quote the interview, this has been done.

It is hoped that this study of Soviet behaviour in relation to international terrorism will prove useful in furthering understanding in the West of the problem in general and will help in developing the appropriate response to it.

Notes

1. Excerpt from a speech (Quainton, 1979).
2. Jonathan Kwitny, 'The Terrorists', *Wall Street Journal*, 1 Jan. 1977.
3. Brian Crozier distinguishes between 'transnational terrorism' and 'international terrorism', preferring to use the former, in the belief that the second term might imply the existence of a 'terrorist international' in the sense of an international body coordinating the activities of terrorists in different countries. U.S. Congress. Senate. Committee of the Judiciary. Subcommittee to Investigate the Administration of the Internal Security Act and other Internal Security laws (hereinafter referred to as SIAIS), *Terroristic Activity: International Terrorism*. Part 4, Hearings, 94th Congress, 1st session, 14 May 1975.

4. Staar (ed.) (1976), p. xxvii.
5. *Daily Telegraph* (London), 21 Dec. 1976. Information reported as coming from Washington's daily newspaper on defence and foreign affairs.
6. Arendt (1979) p.15.
7. See Aron, 'Political Action in the Shadow of Atomic Apocalypse', in Lasswell and Cleveland (1962).
8. Arendt (1979) p. 18.
9. Tolstoy (1981) p. 15; (see also Conquest (1970) and Ulam (1965). Various estimates of deaths attributable to the Chekas are to be found in Appendix C of Leggett (1981).
10. See Shirer (1960).
11. For further examples of early Nazi-Communist cooperation see Daycock (1980), particularly Chapter II and Appendix II.
12. Although there is a technical difference between providing aid to a terrorist group and totally sponsoring one, there is no substantive difference when evaluating this aid as a policy decision by the sponsor State. The degree of sponsorship might indicate a decision of a strategic nature to promote more or less activity at any given time. Obviously, the more comprehensive the sponsorship the greater the implication of control over the group's activities by the sponsor State. In either case, it indicates a policy decision by the sponsor State to support that group.
13. See the yearly CIA Reports on International Terrorism since 1967. Their statistics include, for example, hijackings in the US committed by unstable individuals lacking political motives but exclude cross-border terrorist attacks by the PLO into Israel.
14. This incident ended with the capitulation by the El Salvador government to the terrorist demands and to the release of the prisoners. Negotiations took three days and all hostages were released.
15. Of the more than 30 terrorists and hostages involved, the only survivors were the Spanish Ambassador and one of the attackers.
16. *The Columbia Encyclopedia*, 3rd Edn, 1963, p. 1784.
17. Carlton and Schaerf, (eds) (1975) p.21.
18. Cf. Malaya against the British, Indo-China against the French and later the Americans, and Cuba against Batista.
19. Cf. Mao-Tse-tung (1978), (1969); Otto Heilbrunn (1962), (1963).
20. UNGA, Resolution 1514 (XV).
21. Report of the *Ad Hoc Committee on International Terrorism*, GAOR, 28th Session, Suppl. no. 28, A/9028, 1973, p. 21.
22. Algeria, Congo, Guinea, India, Mauritania, Nigeria, South Yemen, Syria, Tanzania, Yemen, Yugoslavia, Zaire and Zambia. *Ibid.*
23. Carlton and Schaerf (eds) (1975) p. 21.
24. *Re Castioni* (1980), 1 QB, 149, 156, 159.
25. *Re Meuniers* (1894), 2 QBD, 415 and 419.
26. Green (1962) p. 329; Harvard Research in International Law (1935).
27. *Re Meuniers* as in note 25.
28. J.E.S. Fawcett, in BYIL, v. 34, 1956, p. 391. See also Pella (1938).
29. See Chapter 3 of this study.
30. Brian Crozier, Testimony to the U.S. Senate, SIAIS, Committee of the Judiciary, 14 May, 1975, p. 180.

2

Marxist-Leninist Ideology on Terrorism

Western leaders and their analysts have often tended to discount Soviet ideology as 'mere rhetoric' and as having little or no bearing on Soviet official behaviour in the decision-making process governing their internal and external policies. This tendency has often been increased when the strong assertions made by the Politburo have contradicted preconceived sets of assumptions by Western leaders, as for example United States assumptions of détente.[1] The argumentation discounting the importance of ideological pronouncements would state either that this ideology was directed only to foreign communists or that it was strictly inconsequential.

The communist doctrine is, however, a rigid, theoretical system which demands sacrosanct obedience to its laws if it is to succeed. The oracular nature of its assertions, declaring as they do that communism is the only 'truth' and therefore not to be questioned, can be favourably equated with a theology requiring uncompromising, literal obedience.

If the leaders of the Soviet state are true 'believers', then the doctrinal nature of Soviet assertions cannot be discounted as mere rhetoric, for fanaticism has usually tried to fulfil its own oracles. On the other hand, if the assumption is made that the leaders are pragmatists and do not really believe in the doctrine, it can be argued that the repetitive presence of ideological communism must be deemed to fulfil another need - that of justification of behaviour. In this case, the ideological rhetoric equally cannot be discounted as mere rhetoric. It is clear that in order to keep the masses happy and, in particular, to keep them subdued, the theoretical objective of world communism must remain a tangible goal and confidence in the leadership must be perpetually reinforced by righteous doctrinal statements. This ideological scaffolding needs to be supported in its turn by behavioural actions which would justify continued belief in the system. Therefore, it can be said that the ideology is self-reinforcing and requires to be taken quite literally.[2]

Perhaps owing to these Western assumptions which have refused to evaluate Soviet ideology at literal value, Western analytical thinking has revolved around the theme that in the matter of terrorism, Marxist-Leninist ideology was opposed to its use in achieving political goals.

For example, it is often stated that Marx and Engels were not enthusiastic about the use of terrorism[3] and that 'terrorism as such had little or no support from official Soviet ideology . . .

Both Marx and Lenin made explicitly clear statements regarding the question of the applicability of terrorism to achieve political ends. Bearing in mind the context within which both of them wrote, with world revolution being the theoretical tangible goal, terrorism was discussed by both as part of that overall programme, and the question then revolved around whether terrorism was a useful tool to hasten and facilitate the communist cause at any given time, or whether it should be discarded 'on principle'.

It was Karl Marx who wrote in *Das Kaptial* (first translated into Russian in 1872) that 'force is the midwife of every old society pregnant with a new one'. It was also Karl Marx who vehemently blamed the French *communards* of 1871 for not having imitated the Jacobins in their use of terrorist methods. He added that 'violence is itself an economic power'.[5]

He presented a clear argumentation of the same theme in an article where he explained that '. . . the cannibalism of the counter-revolution will itself convince the people that there is only one means to shorten, simplify and concentrate the death agony of the old society and the bloody birth pangs of the new, one means only - revolutionary terrorism'.[6] This was not an unusual statement for Marx to introduce and was, in fact, a recurring theme which appeared in one way or another throughout his voluminous writings. In the last issue of the *Neue Rheinische Zeitung* of 18 May, 1849, he wrote an article in which he classified the future use of terrorism according to who the perpetrators were: 'When our turn comes we will not excuse our terrorism. But royal terrorists, terrorists by the grace of God and the law, are brutal, contemptible and vulgar in their practice, cowardly, secretive and double-faced in their theory, and in both respects entirely without honour'.[7] So his condemnation of terrorism, if it is to be so perceived, is one-sided and similar to the arguments extended today by the Soviet government but using different terminology. What Marx called 'our terrorism', which he justified since the other side's terrorism is 'contemptible', has today become the term 'freedom fighter' or 'national liberation'. This notion of the cause justifying the use of violence was certainly not Marx's invention. St Thomas Aquinas was followed by Machiavelli in expounding the necessity of violence for the founding of new political bodies and the reforming of corrupt ones.[8] Robespierre justified terror as 'the despotism of liberty against tyranny'. And what Marx set down was then enthusiastically taken up and expanded by Lenin.

Even though Lenin was most likely a 'believer' in Marx's dialectical materialism doctrinal themes, his own writings are imbued with pragmatic interpretations of his own.

The ideas which are identified as Leninism on the subject of terrorism basically revolve around his notion of an organized political *élite* as being the necessary ingredient to achieve successful Marxist communism, and are extensions of this same emphasis. In the same way that he had objected in 1902 to the idea of the proletariat attempting to bring about a revolution without a group of leaders who would dictate the manner and the timing of such a revolution, he also objected to what he called the 'individual terrorist' attempting on his own to bring about revolution. In what has come to be known as the chief Leninist political strategy treatise, *What Is To Be Done?*, the main distinction he made on this matter was in fact between what he called the 'amateur terrorist' and the 'professional revolutionary'.[9] This distinction was tantamount to saying that the necessary ingredient for success was premeditation and a base structure to support the action, as opposed to *ad hoc* individual behaviour. Answering his critics, he stated that what he objected to was the idea of a few terrorists 'engaged in single combat with the government'.[10] He offered instead a '*revolutionary organization* with *professional revolutionaries*'.[11] 'Such an organization', he explained, 'must of necessity be not too extensive and as secret as possible'.[12] The cellular structure and clandestine nature of this type of revolutionary group would ensure his control.

Lenin repeatedly pointed out that to reject terrorism was philistine. His only qualifications for its use were the when and the where, and his insistence on the organizational structure which had to be present to support that use as part of an overall concerted plan of action. During the 1905 abortive revolution he had assiduously preached revolutionary tactics, instructing in great detail on the assassination of policemen, 'and on the use of every conceivable weapon, from rifles and bombs to knuckle-dusters and boiling water . . .'.[13]

Lenin's obsession with maintaining personal control over happenings and the Party structure, and his own profound distrust of spontaneity (*stikhiinost*), greatly influenced his outlook on revolutionary tasks in general. Centralization was his main theme for success, and terrorism was no exception to this organizational view. His terminology emphasized phrases such as 'armed struggle', 'partisan warfare', and 'professional revolutionaries' - euphemistic expressions for agitational activity of one sort or another, including the use of terror tactics - within the overall revolutionary aim.

Lenin was in effect a pragmatic, ruthless leader and organizer. Although not espousing the view that terror tactics were the *only* way to achieve revolution, as Bakunin had done, he maintained that terrorism was a useful tactic if employed in conjunction with 'other methods of combat'.[14]

Thus when Lenin was against what he called 'individual' terrorism perpetrated by a lone actor, possibly insane, but mostly not organized and controlled, he was saying that he would like a controlled situation. Anything to the left of his party and remotely out of his control was to be considered an 'infantile disorder' and therefore to be condemned. In his *'Left-Wing Communism, An Infantile Disorder*, he explained the Bolshevik position as follows:[15]

Of course we rejected individual terror only on grounds of expediency, whereas people who were capable of condemning 'on principle' the terror of the Great French Revolution, or in general, the terror employed by a victorious revolutionary party which is besieged by the bourgeoisie of the whole world, had already been ridiculed and laughed to scorn by Plekhanov, in 1900-1903, when he was a Marxist and a revolutionary.

In 1916, regarding the attempted assassination of the Austrian Prime Minister, Count Sturg, he wrote '*We do not at all oppose political killing*' (original emphasis), and he went on again to qualify the use of terrorism as needing to be part of a concerted plan for an uprising, or some other revolutionary undertaking. He condemned that particular attempted assassination only on the basis of its being a 'single, isolated and unco-ordinated act'.[16]

In this treatise *Partisan Warfare* he argued that Marxism 'never will reject any particular combat method, let alone reject it forever . . . At present European Socialists regard parliamentarism and trade unionism as their main method of struggle. Previously they favoured the armed uprising . . . [they] are perfectly willing to favour the uprising again should the situation change in the future.'[17]

This theme recurred often in Lenin's writings.[18] Again in *Partisan Warfare*: 'Marxism does not tie the movement to any particular combat method. It recognizes the possibility that struggle may assume the most variegated forms . . .'[19] He explained the development of what he called 'armed struggle' as a phenomenon which emerged as a consequence of the Russian Revolution. He defined it thus: 'Armed struggle is waged by small groups of individuals, some of whom are members of revolutionary parties.'[20] As part of this 'armed struggle', he included the killing of individuals and the 'expropriations' of government and private funds - the latter activity having been enthusiastically accepted by Lenin with the help of Stalin even after the 1906 Congress had outlawed it - both of which are terroristic tactics by any definition.

Lenin differentiated between what he called 'traditional Russian terrorism, which he regarded as the work of plotting intellectuals, and 'armed struggle', which was now to be taken on by 'workers or unemployed persons who are members of combat groups'.[21] This again is the distinction between the 'individual terrorist' and the centralized revolutionary organization. In fact, he clearly countered criticism from some quarters that the use of terrorism had weakened the movement, by explaining that it was not the use of terrorism but 'the weakness of the party, which does not know how to *take those actions into its own hands.*' (original emphasis). Explaining further that Marxists favoured class struggle as opposed to social peace, he encouraged Marxists to regard 'partisan struggles' as just one of the forms of civil war and therefore a matter of course in revolutionary progress. 'Terrorist partisan acts against representatives of the violent regime . . . are *recommended*' (original emphasis).[22]

Lenin's conceptualization of the revolutinary process was tantamount to a 'package deal', a pragmatic strategy to satisfy an ideological theory which was to include preparation for every method of struggle to cover any and every eventuality. As he saw it, 'the revolution itself must not by any means be regarded as a single act (as the Nadezhdins apparently imagine) but as a series of more or less powerful outbreaks rapidly alternating with periods of more or less intense calm'.[23]

If one had to use only one word to describe Lenin's philosophy of revolution, flexibility would be the one which would describe it best. He often argued that compromise was a necessity for success. Insisting on a centralized organization, which was to form the basis of the monolithic apparatus which we are familiar with today, he said:[24]

Only such organization would ensure the *flexibility* [original emphasis] required by a militant Social-Democratic organization, i.e. the ability to adapt itself immediately to the most diverse and rapidly changing conditions of struggle, the ability, 'on the one hand, to avoid open battle with an enemy of overwhelming strength when he has concentrated all his forces at one spot and, on the other hand, to be able to take advantage of the awkwardness of his enemy and attack him whenever and wherever he least expects'.

And again:

The strictest loyalty to Communist ideas must be combined with the ability to make necessary compromises, to scheme, to sign agreements, to zigzag, to retreat . . . anything to hasten the coming to power of Communism.

In *'Left'-Wing Communism, An Infantile Disorder*, mentioned earlier and written in 1920 well after the October 1917 revolution, Lenin extended his revolutionary aims to the 'world working-class movement' and saw 'the historical mission of the Soviets as the grave-digger, heir and successor to bourgeois parliamentarism, and of bourgeois democracy in general'.[25] Equating politics with war, he reiterated the need for mastering 'all means of warfare'.[26]

In his chapter dealing with 'A "conspiratorial" organization and "democracy" in *What Is To Be Done?*, he had implied that he was flattered to be compared to the Narodnaya Volya which he called 'that magnificent organization' . . . ,[27] just as Marx had done earlier in a letter to his daughter Jenny Longuet.[28]

The Narodnaya Volya (The People's Will) was the outgrowth in 1879 of a split in the ranks of the Zemlya i Volya (Land and Liberty). This original revolutionary party had been formed out of the Populist movement in the early 1870s in St Petersburg and had quickly been joined by men such as M. A. Natanson, A. D. Mikhailov and G. V. Plekhanov. The Zemlya i Volya set up for the first time a specialist terror group which engaged in various terror attacks. Inspired by these was the attempted assassination of General Trepov, Governor of St Petersburg, by Vera Zasulich. Although Zasulich did not manage to kill Trepov and did not technically belong to any group, the publicy of the case did much for the morale of the Zemlya i Volya.

The split of 1897 had largely been due to dissension within the group on the utility of terrorist tactics. Plekhanov broke with Zemlya i Volya and formed Chernyi Peredel (Black Partition), a group which advocated economic and social actions and which eventually grew into the Social Democratic Party (SDs). The other group, the Narodnaya Volya advocated the use of terrorist methods as an effective means of promoting the revolution. The belief was based on the notion that the publicity and the agitational qualities of political assassinations were necessary and that terrorism would show 'the light' to the masses. IN 1881 Czar Alexander II was killed by a team of bomb-throwers belonging to that group. A child who happened to be near the coach died as a result of the same incident.[29]

The Narodnaya Volya did not survive the reactionary regime of Alexander III (1881-94) and eventually some of its original members regrouped to form the Social Revolutionary Party (SRs) in the 1890s in direct competition with Plekhanov's Social Democratic Party. The journal published by the SRs. *Revolutionary Russia*, explained the revolutionary tactics endorsed by that party: 'Terrorist acts must be carefully organized. They must be supported by the party which directs their action and will assume moral responsibility for them'.[30] This mode of conflict was the same one which Lenin repeatedly emphasized throughout his writings, and his favourable reaction to being compared with the Narodnaya Volya was therefore consistent with his expressed belief that terrorism had to be used as part of an overall revolutionary plan with centralized control.

The events of 1905 (Bloody Sunday) had, in fact, seen an increased co-operation between Lenin and the terrorist SRs. Lenin controlled overall operations while technical expertise was provided by Krasin, a member of the Central Committee of the Fourth Congress. In 1906, with the help of Stalin, Lenin had enthusiastically continued to carry out 'expropriations' of government and private funds to enrich the coffers of his group. This he did even though the Menshevik majority had outlawed these activities at the Congress which took place earlier in the same year.[31] He even had gone as far as to take over a small 'Military-Technical Bureau' set up purportedly for 'defensive' action against right-wing terror.

Lenin's ideology was to be given structural realism by Leon Trotsky, the organizer of the armed forces of the new state. After the revolution, in 1920, Leon Trotsky wrote his influential tract on terrorism. It was a response to Karl Kautsky's severe attack on bolshevism and its use of terrorism. The Red Terror - an expression largely used with pride by both Lenin and Trotsky - had been in fully swing for over two years when the book appeared, variously published in translation as *Terrorism and Communism, The Defense of Terrorism* and *Dictatorship vs Democracy*.[32] Although it was written primarily as a justification for the repressive terror engaged in by Lenin and the Bolsheviks to maintain control of the leadership, in it one can also find the Bolshevik philosophy on the use of terrorism as a tool for achieving the political goal of socialism in general. Trotsky wrote in essence the same views which both Marx and Lenin had expressed before him: 'the revolution', he said, 'does require of the revolutionary class that it should attain its end by all methods at its disposal - if necessary, by an armed uprising, if required, by terrorism'.[33] He explained again that the kind of force, or the degree of force, to be used is 'not one of principle' but a 'question of expediency'.[34] He found terrorism to be an all-important aspect of the 'struggle' for the success of communism. 'Terror can be very efficient against a reactionary class which does not want to leave the scene of operations. *Intimidation* [original emphasis] is a powerful weapon of policy, both internationally and internally'.[35] He also echoed Marx's idea of justified terror when he wrote:

> The terror of Tsarism was directed against the proletariat . . . Our Extraordinary Commissions shoot landlords, capitalists, and generals who are striving to restore the capitalist order. Do you grasp this . . . distinction? Yes? For us Communists it is quite sufficient.

Both Lenin and Trotsky repeatedly equated revolution with war, and given the terrorist tactics fell within the scope of both, it is an all-important point to keep in mind when evaluating present-day power politics.[36] In the 1936 preface to the French edition of his book *Terrorism and Communism*, Trotsky argued that 'the main objective of revolution, as of war, was to break the will of the foe . . . if required by terrorism'.[37]

Engels had regarded all wars as 'organized violence'. Lenin followed suit and placed his emphasis on the selection of tactical weapons necessary at any given time, including the use of terrorism, in order to attain the ultimate goal: the destruction of the capitalist society and its replacement with communism. In *State and Revolution* he had clearly stated that 'the supersession of the bourgeois state by the proletarian state is impossible without a violent revolution'.[38]

In discussing the controversy which took place in 1873, where Marx and Engels were seen to be refuting the Anarchists, Lenin explicitly rationalized his ideas on methodology and ultimate aims in his interpretation of what Marx meant by that refutation, and he did it in a few paragraphs which exemplify the two salient features that characterize Leninism: flexibility and monolithic elitism. In *State and Revolution* he argued that Marx 'opposed the proposition that the workers should renounce the use of arms, of organized violence, *that is, the state*, which is to serve to 'crush the resistance of the bourgeoisie'. 'The state', he said, 'is a special organization of force: it is an organization of violence for the suppression of some class', the class being the bourgeoisie.

He agreed with the ultimate aims of the Anarchists on the

question of the abolition of the state. But he emphasized that to attain that aim, temporary use of the very instruments of power which were selected for destruction was essential to achieve that destruction.

The Hegelian dialectic which Marxism - Leninism adopted as its main theme, the historical determinism which exculpates the perpetrator of any aggressive action by its very inevitability, was to allow Lenin and his followers to shed the burden of responsibility for their actions. Within that context, the expectancy of revolutionary violence was built in.

For any student of Soviet behaviour, what must be the most salient point when reviewing printed material issued by the Soviet government is the constant repetition of Marxist-Leninist dogma as explanatory affirmations of Party policy. Lenin remains to date the authoritative back-up most quoted by Soviet policy-makers.

Given this self-stated importance, it would be totally inaccurate to attempt any analyis of Soviet attitude and policy in regard to international terrorism without giving the same emphasis to Leninist writings as the USSR does itself.

What stands out from studying the voluminous tracts which deal with this question is that in Marxist-Leninist ideology, terrorism had always been viewed as a useful tactical weapon in the overall world revolutionary war process, to be used when deemed expedient, and as a part of the multi-faceted strategies necessary for the ultimate success of socialism. At not time did either Marx or Lenin object to its use 'on principle'. The position which Lenin established against what he called 'individual' terrorism is not in contradiction to this, but only a reaffirmation of his obsession with the centralization concept - the idea of a professional revolutionary *élite* controlling events. Marxist-Leninist philosophy in general is not an 'individualist' philosophy at any event, deploring as it does individual intiative of any sort which does not conform to the Central Party authority.

Lenin espoused terrorism in the same way as he did the use of legality, diplomacy and compromise: as an instrument of revolution and one more weapon in the arsenal of class struggle. In this respect, it is to be regarded as part of the Soviet concept of strategies of war.

Notes

1. See Kohler *et al.* (1974) for a discussion on these assumptions. (Also, see Labedz (1979) part I.
2. It is interesting, in the context of international terrorism in Western

democracies, that a very high percentage of terrorists were once ardent Catholics. In fact, even Lenin was apparently religious until the aga of 18. See Giorgio Bocca (1978) p. 7 where he discusses this point with regard to left-wing terrorism in Italy which he claims was fathered by *cattocommunismo*.

3. Laqueur (1977a) p.152, (1978) p.199
4. Galia Golan (1980) p.210
5. Karl Marx, (1962) p. 779 (v.1 Ch.24) for an informative view of Marx, see Carr (1934); for an historical perspective of Russia leading up to 1917, see Pipes, (1979).
6. Karl Marx, 'Victory of the Counter-Revolution in Vienna' in *Neue Rheinische Zeitung*, Nov. 7, 1848. This journal was edited by Marx himself. See *Marx Engeles Werke* (MEW) (1956-68) v. V, p. 457.
7. See *MEW*. v. VI, p. 505
8. See Machiavelli (1982) pp 65-6, 92, 95
9. 'What is to be done?' in Lenin (1958-66) v 6, pp 1-192 Esp. pp. 105, 110, for example
10. *Ibid.* p. 77
11. *Ibid.* pp. 111-127, emphasis in original.
12. *Ibid.* p.114.
13. Lenin (1958-66) v.11, p. 342
14. V. I. Lenin (1946-50) v. 14, p.5 (*Partisan Warfare*).
15. This jibe at Plekhanov was a criticism of the latter's positions on the way the revolution should be conducted, outstanding among which was his pleading to forego terrorist methods altogether. Plekhanov based his plea on effectiveness values rather than moral values as he considered terror a waste of time. See Asprey (1975) p. 288.
16. Lenin (1958-66) v. 49, pp 311-14 (Letter to Koritschoner 25 Oct. 1916) "Blanquism" is discussed by Lenin in "The Congress summed up", Lenin (1946-50) v. 10, p. 360.
17. Lenin (1946-50) v. 14, pp. 1-12
18. See *'Left'-Wing Communism, An Infantile Disorder, Letters on Tactics* and *State and Revolution*, written in 1917, first published in 1918, Lenin (1958-66) v.41, p. 38, v.21 p. 138 and v.33, p. 26 respectively.
19. Lenin (1946-50) v.14, p.1 (*Partisan Warfare*)
20. *Ibid.* p.4.
21. *Ibid.* p.6. Lenin had earlier (1901) criticized the SRs for their individual uncoordinated acts of terrorism which were not part of an overall military strategy, see Lenin (1935 -7) v.4. pp. 108-109.
22. *Ibid.* p. 10.
23. Lenin, (*What is to be done?*.
24. *Ibid.* p. 176
25. Lenin (1958-66) v. 41, p 75 ('*Left'-Wing Communism*); see also *Imperialism, The Highest Stage of Capitalism*, Lenin (1946-50) v.22, pp. 175-290.
26. Lenin (1958-66) v. 41, p. 81 ('*Left'- Wing Communism*)
27. Lenin (1958-66) v.6, pp. 134-7. ('What is to be done?')
28. See *MEW*, v. XXXV, p. 179.
29. Laqueur mentions that even Marx and Engels believed that Russia was on the verge of revolution as a result of *Narodnaya Volya* actions. Plekhanov wrote that he could no longer speak out against terrorism as the intelligentsia believed in terror 'like in God' Laqueur (1977c) p. 34
30. No. 7 of the Journal, as cited in Spiridovich (1930)
31. See Schapiro (1970) p. 90.
32. Trotsky (1961)
33. *Ibid.* p. 58.
34. *Ibid.*

35. *Ibid.*
36. See Chapter 3 of this study for the Soviet views on war and aggression.
37. Trotsky (1961) p. 58.
38. Lenin (19 -) v. 33, p. 28. He added that the 'proletariat needed ... an organisation of violence for the purpose of crushing the resistance of the exploiters', p. 26.

3

Legal Aspects

Problems of Defining Aggression

The existence today of weapons of total destruction has brought about an upheaval of ideas on war and of the notions of 'aggression' and the right to 'self-defence'. The League of Nations and the United Nations have both dedicated endless efforts to reaching a definition of aggression, and the Soviet Union has played a leading role in these attempts.

Arguments for and against an established definition of aggression have flourished over the years. The era of the League of Nations saw the term 'aggression' being used more meaningfully as a legal concept, as an attempt to limit the legality of engaging in war itself. The United Nations adopted without a vote the report of the Special Committee on the Question of Defining Aggression in 1974[1], thus pursuing the attempts at reaching a definition.

As has been pointed out by Bassiouni,[2] problems of aggression arise from the endeavours to define it. It has been argued that no workable definition can be reached and the attempts should therefore be dropped. It has also been argued that any definition should only mark a starting point, because an enumerative definition can never be all-inclusive. In other words, the problems of reaching a definition of aggression at the United Nations are a direct reflection of the realities of global power politics.

For the purposes of this study, the Soviet Union's position on aggression and indirect aggression and an examination of its official statements on international terrorism at the United Nations will be analysed in order to clarify the official legal position of the Soviet government on these questions. International terrorism, falling as it does within the scope of revolutionary and sub-revolutionary goals, as defined earlier, is directly influenced by legal perceptions of the permissibility of the use of force.

Before doing so, however, it is necessary to put down the conceptualization and perceptions of general Soviet behavioural norms vis-à-vis international law.

(1) After its initial repudiation of international law in 1917, the

USSR set about reversing its position by participating in the Brest-Litovsk Treaty, a pragmatic compromise necessary for its survival at the time, and it has since attempted to remould international law to fit Soviet needs.[3]

(2)   The Soviet Union claims the existence of two types of international law: general international law and 'socialist international law', the latter being applicable only between socialist states. This 'socialist international law' in effect claims that the USSR is the arrogated leader of the entire socialist bloc, and that where the essence of the Communist Party's power in any given member of the bloc is affected by an internal situation it ceases to be a matter of domestic jurisdiction and becomes the concern of the entire bloc led by the USSR.[4] The rationale is that since Soviet socialism is inevitable and, where established, irreversible, a deviationist state can legally be invaded by a neighbour to restore the model.

(3)   Soviet attitudes towards the principle of prohibition of intervention and the sovereignty of states are therefore governed by the duty to render 'brotherly' assistance and help. In a recent Soviet international law textbook the authors elucidate this point:[5]

> The mutual assistance of socialist states in the struggle for peace and in resistance to the aggressive plotting of imperialism, as well as in suppressing its effort to export counter-revolution, has important meaning. Clear examples of this are the international actions of the USSR and of other socialist countries during the events in Hungary (1956), in Czechoslovakia (1968), in the assistance given to the heroic Vietnam people in repulsing imperialist aggression and in unifying its fatherland.

(4)   The dialectical ideology is the governing basis of Soviet formulations in the legal world and should form the background of any interpretation of Soviet diplomatic positions and official argumentation.

The Russian word for aggression is *aggressiya*,[6] a word whose first usage the 1950 edition of the *Slovar' sovremennogo russkogo literaturnogo yazyka*[7] attributes to Stalin. In fact, the word became accepted as a Russian word not earlier than 1911 and became commonly used in Soviet speech and writing in 1933. That year also marked the Soviet Union's initial contribution to attempts at legally defining aggression. This coincidence can be explained.

For the USSR there were three powers in the 1930s which were expansionist in outlook as well as militarily formidable: Germany, Italy and Japan. Of those three countries, at least Germany and Japan could well be expected to indulge their expansionist appetites at the expense of the USSR, and one must remember that in 1933 the Soviet perception of this threat was governed in great part by the inadequate state of its army which had only just begun its reconstruction and modernization programme. The Soviet Union, therefore, vigorously attempted to prevent this expansionism, first by postulating the policy of 'collective security' throughout the 1930s,[8] and secondly by attempting to persuade world opinion that a definition of aggression was a necessity.

The legal adviser of the Permanent Soviet Mission to the United States, Evgeny N. Nasinovsky,[9] characterized the draft resolution submitted by the Soviet Union to the League of Nations in 1933 as a major 'contribution towards confirming and developing the principle of banning wars of aggression'. That resolution read as follows:

(1)   The aggressor in an international conflict shall be considered that state which is the first to take any of the following actions:
  (a)   Declaration of war against another state.
  (b)   The invasion by its armed forces of the territory of another state without declaration of war.
  (c)   Bombarding the territory of another state by its land, naval, or air forces or knowingly attacking the naval or air forces of another state.
  (d)   The landing in, or introduction within the frontiers of, another state of land, naval, or air forces without the permission of the government of such state, or the infringement of the condition of such permission, particularly as regards the duration of sojourn or extension of area.
  (e)   The establishment of a naval blockade of the coast or ports of another state.
(2)   No considerations whatsoever of a political, strategic, or economic nature, including the desire to exploit natural riches or to obtain any sort of advantages or privileges on the territory of another state, no references to considerable capital investments or other special interest in a given state, or to the alleged absence of certain attributes of state organization in the case of a given country, shall be accepted as justification of aggression as defined in Clause 1.
  In particular, justification for attack cannot be based upon:
  A.   The internal situation in a given state, as for instance:
    (a)   Political, economic, or cultural backwardness of a given country.
    (b)   Alleged maladministration.

      (c) Possible danger to life or property of foreign residents.

      (d) Revolutionary or counter-revolutionary movements, civil war, disorders, or strikes.

      (e) The establishment or maintenance in any state of any political economic or social order.

B. Any acts, laws, or violations of a given state, as for instance:

      (a) The infringement of international agreements.

      (b) The infringement of the commercial, concessional, or other economic rights or interests of a given state or its citizens.

      (c) The rupture of diplomatic or economic relations.

      (d) Economic or financial boycott.

      (e) Repudiation of debts.

      (f) Non-admission or limitation of immigration, or restriction of rights or privileges of foreign students.

      (g) The infringement of the privileges of official representatives of other states.

      (h) The refusal to allow armed forces transit to the territory of a third state.

      (i) Religious or anti-religious measures.

      (j) Frontier incidents.

(3) In the case of the mobilization or concentration of armed forces to a considerable extent in the vicinity of its frontiers, the state which such activities threaten may have recourse to diplomatic or other means for the peaceful solution of international controversies. It may at the same time take steps of a military nature, analogous to those described above, without, however, crossing the frontier.

This 1933 proposed definition by the Soviet Union clearly indicated a reflexive view of the world situation at the time and of Soviet low-level capacity to fight a war. There was no provision for outlawing any forms of indirect aggression, for example. It also provided a list of conditions, all or some of which could be found to exist within the Eastern bloc of countries. By their exclusion from the proposed definition, any justification for the possible invasion of Soviet territory would thus be removed.

One year earlier the USSR had attempted to make further progress towards a more precise definition of aggression in four bilateral non-aggression treaties signed in 1932 with Finland, Latvia, Estonia and Poland. This legal process did not, however, deter the annexation by the USSR of some of the signatories shortly thereafter, which it claimed took place at the request of these states.[10]

However, it was the 1950 Korean War which spurred the Kremlin into greater activity in attempting to reach a definition of aggression. The USSR found itself in a position to embarrass the United States government which could hardly deny that its troops were 'bombarding the territory of another state, whether by land, sea, or air'. Consequently, the Soviet Union revived its 1933 draft definition at the First Committee of the General Assembly of the United Nations on 6 November 1950 and presented it as a new endeavour. There was only one real change in this definition: the substitution of the word 'attacker' for 'aggressor'. This Soviet proposal was referred to the International Law Commission by a resolution on 17 November 1950 but the Commission could not reach agreement on a definition. When the Security Council became paralysed by the veto prerogative exercised by the Soviet representative against peacekeeping matters, the International Law Commission renewed its efforts and reported in favour of 'a general and abstract definition' because an enumerative definition could not be exhaustive and might therefore limit the freedom of judgement of competent organs.[11]

It was not until 1967, however, that the Soviet Union again proposed that further meetings be held to establish the'much-needed' definition.[12] Three drafts were submitted to the Special Committee on the Question of Defining Aggression which was established by the General Assembly in Resolution 2330 (XXII) of 19 December 1967. The Soviet Union's draft proposal requested that the General Assembly declare that 'armed aggression (direct or indirect) is the use by a state, first, of armed force against another state contrary to the purposes, principles and provisions of the Charter of the United Nations.'[13]

The timing of this new intensive interest on the part of the USSR to reach an agreed definition of aggression was spurred on by the scale of United States involvement in Vietnam and by the Arab-Israeli War. The Soviet Association of International Law held its eleventh meeting from 31 January to 2 February 1968, and dedicated much time to these two events and to the concept of aggression. L. I. Savinki delivered a report entitled 'US Aggression in Vietnam - an International Crime'; V. I. Lisovskii spoke about 'Israeli Aggression against the Arab States - an International Crime'; and V. I. Lazarev discussed 'On Defining the Concept of Aggression'; while the interrelationship of the concepts of aggression and intervention was expounded by M. K. Korostarenko.[14] Lazarev argued that the 1953 Soviet draft definition was obsolete and was in favour of a definition of aggression which would separate armed aggression from less tangible forms of aggression or intervention. This seemed to reflect the official view when the 35-member Special Committee met in June-July 1968 and the USSR favoured giving priority to defining armed aggression, requiring in addition a distinction between aggression and legitimate self-defence. According to the Kremlin, the final and exclusive power of determining the existence of an act of aggression was to be given to the Security Council where the veto power was in effect.[15]

Immediately following the invasion of Czechoslovakia in 1968, the Soviet representative on the Special Committee introduced a new draft definition of aggression which is a perfect example of the attempts the Soviet Union has made to mould international law to its own needs.[16] In essence, it was once again very much the same text as the 1933 version which has already been briefly discussed. The only change was the omission of the last half of subclause *d* of Paragraph 1 on the infringement of conditions of permission to introduce forces within another's territory. The Soviet Union, of course, had forces stationed in Czechoslovakia prior to the invasion and this omission reflected that situation as well as the Czechoslovakian objection to the presence of those troops.[17]

An analysis of this 1968 draft, however, indicates that it would not prevent the use of force in accordance with the United Nations Charter, 'including its use by dependent peoples in order to exercise their inherent right of self-determination in accordance with General Assembly Resolution 1514 (XV)'. This provision is much more alarming than the elimination of subclause *d*, for, where all attempts at finite demarcations are made on the one hand to give the definition an air of legality, this one statement lays no restrictions on what kinds of force can be used by dependent peoples, nor is there an agreed definition of 'self-determination', 'dependent', or 'peoples'.[18] For example, Professor M. I. Lazarev, in his commentary on the renewed attempt to define aggression, clearly argues that 'the armed struggle of a colonial nation against armed forces of a parent state does not come under the definition of aggression'.[19]

For the first time the notion of defining indirect aggression with an inclusion of terrorism was introduced by the Soviet Union in its 1968 draft proposal and Paragraph 2 read as follows:

> The use by a state of armed force by sending armed bands, mercenaries, terrorists, or saboteurs to the territory of another state and engagement in other forms of subversive activity involving the use of armed force with the aim of promoting an internal upheaval in another state or a reversal of policy in favour of the aggressor shall be considered an act of indirect aggression.

This clause should be contrasted with the allowances made by the 'dependent peoples' clause and would indicate that the Soviet application of this indirect aggression clause would be strictly limited to what it calls 'counter-revolution'.

The Soviet government has in fact followed the dicta of Marx and Lenin and declared that aggression is peculiar to 'class' societies and that it therefore follows that, by definition, the Soviet Union is incapable of such guilt.[20] In another definition 'aggression' is possible only between *states*[21] and it therefore cannot include the 'brotherly help' extended by the CPSU to other communist parties or proletariats during a war of 'liberation'. It is then further asserted in this argument that the rules concerning aggression do not apply to 'civil wars' or to wars of 'national liberation'.[22]

In the most recent consensus on defining aggression - the 1974 Definition of Aggression adopted by the United Nations General Assembly - one can find many loopholes which leave 'aggression' in an undefined state. The explicit mention in Article 5 of that Definition[23] of a people's right to use force in the struggle for self-determination extended this right to 'peoples under military occupation' and it was implied that these peoples had the right to receive assistance from third states. This argument was strongly opposed by Western states. However, the Soviet Union and its satellites, even though supporting self-determination, were simultaneously anxiously denying that anything in the definition could affect a state's right to 'police action' against dissident movements, thus demonstrating an ambivalent position which indicated an increased concern in the USSR about the growing dissident movements within its borders - a problem which is surely bound to become a major issue for that country in the not too distant future. This position also reflects the Soviet conception of the existence of two international legal systems. Although the USSR does endorse the use of force for self-determination to gain sympathy and votes from the Third World nations, and to provide itself with the necessary legal flexibility for fulfilling its own expansionist goals around the world, the Kremlin leaders may ultimately prove to have been shortsighted when self-determination becomes a major contention among the annexed countries and peoples which now form part of the USSR.[24]

Defining Indirect Aggression

The Soviet position on aggression notwithstanding, the abstract concept of aggression itself transgresses the legal parameters set by the term 'aggressive war'. The thermonuclear devastation potential which might occur from the escalation of a traditional confrontational war between the superpowers has brought about a proportional increase in the importance which must be given to the concept of indirect aggression, of which international terrorism is a part.

It is a hard truth that it is often the direct armed action of third states which conditions the 'self' in 'self-determination', not to mention the 'self' which is successful in its use of force.

However, it has become increasingly evident that the borderline between internal affairs and international affairs is very blurred indeed in the area of armed conflict.[25] More recently attention has been focused on the thin margin between civil war fought entirely within a single state and so-called international civil wars, in which the actions of third parties affect the conflict.

Examples such as the bloody struggle in Lebanon in 1975-6 (involving the PLO forces opposed by Christian rightists) followed by the invasion of Lebanon by Syrian forces in the guise of a 'peacekeeping' force authorized by the Arab league, the Ethiopian-Somalian war and the civil wars in Central America are all indicative of the close connections and overlaps which exist between civil wars, wars of 'national liberation' or 'self-determination', and international indirect aggression using surrogate forces - terrorist acts or guerrilla incursions, or both, from neighbouring states, or with the aid of sponsor states.

One of the processes of indirect aggression is the exercise of coercion through the medium of rebel groups in the target state. The idea that this process could exist at all was acknowledged by the Soviet Union in 1933. The aggression treaties signed by its government recognized that aggression could be committed by: 'Provision of support for armed bands formed in the territory of another state, or refusal, notwithstanding the request of the invaded state, to take in its own territory all the measures in its power to deprive those bands of all assistance and protection.'[26]

As a direct response to criticism by many Latin American states that the original Soviet 1933 draft omitted any mention of 'indirect aggression', the USSR altered that draft in 1950 with the following addition:[27]

(1) (. . .)
(2) (. . .)
(3) An act of indirect aggression *[aggressiya]* committed by a state includes:
    (a) Encouraging subversive activity against another state (terroristic acts, sabotage, etc.).
    (b) Promoting the stirring up of civil war in another state.

(c)   Promoting an internal coup in another state or a change of policy to please the aggressor.
(4)   An act of economic aggression . . .
(5)   An act of ideological aggression by a state is:

(a)   Encouraging war propaganda.
(b)   Encouraging propaganda for the use of atomic, bacteriological, chemical, or other types of weapons of mass destruction.
(c)   Promoting the propaganda of fascist-nazi views, racial or national exclusiveness, or hatred or disparagement towards other peoples.

However, during the preparations leading up to the 1974 Consensus Definition of Aggression the Soviet Union found it unacceptable to add the words 'however exerted', which were requested by the Western Six (USA, UK, Australia, Canada, Italy and Japan), after the reference to armed force in the definition which stated that: 'Aggression is the use of armed force by a state against the territorial integrity or political independence of another state, or in any other manner inconsistent with the Charter of the United Nations.'[28]

Within this context and the better to understand the USSR's paradoxical position in the debate on aggression, it is useful and informative briefly to examine the Soviet Union's ideological foundations with regard to wars and aggression, as they form the background of the decision-making process which the Kremlin has to implement when dealing with the subject.

Marxist-Leninist philosophy states that war is the result of the existence of classes in society: war is a feudal, capitalist phenomenon and not a communist one. With the establishment of communism throughout the world, war will necessarily disappear. In the interim, the process of revolution by the proletariat will 'liberate' and prepare the world for this communism.

It must be pointed out, however, that the Marxist utopia of communism is not yet a reality in the Soviet Union itself. There exists in the USSR a ruling class which, just like any non-Marxist ruling class, can utilize war or aggression to further its own class interests. The conflict which exists between the two communist states of the USSR and China indicates clearly that the Kremlin interpretation of Marx's theory on the disappearance of war in a communist world implies that this world must be and can only be Soviet-communist.

Marxist-Leninist philosophy permits the ruling class to initiate a war given two sets of conditions:

(1) war should be the most expedient instrument in furthering that interest at that particular time and in those particular circumstances;

(2) victory must be assured.

In Marxist eyes the height of political irresponsibility is to initiate a war when other methods might attain the same goal at considerably less cost. Until the invasion of Afghanistan by the Soviet army in December 1979 the USSR had never before engaged in aggressive war unless victory was certain. It is most probable that Afghanistan was a gross error of underestimation and not a departure from that policy.

The French Revolutionaries, whom Marx and Lenin admired as the first 'revolutionaries', and the French Revolution, which was regarded by them as the only 'just war', were much in favour of wars to liberate peoples from oppressive monarchs and therefore favoured initiating a war to reach this objective.[29]

Civil wars were regarded as taking place between 'exploiters' and 'exploited' in a given country and were, therefore, looked upon as beneficial to the cause. These civil wars were considered inevitable in a capitalist society. In his *A Caricature of Marxism* and *On the Disarmament Slogan*[30] Lenin stated that it is almost always only as a result of such a civil war that capitalism can be ended in favour of the revolution. He stated the same notion in many of his writings with greater subtlety: the triumph of communism is inevitable; to achieve this inevitable triumph, a revolution must take place. However, the 'bourgeoisie' would naturally oppose such a revolution with ferocity and therefore a civil war would of necessity result. In *Partisan Warfare* Lenin explained his position thus:

No Marxist can consider civil war (or partisan war, as one of its forms), to be *in principle* abnormal or demoralizing. A Marxist bases himself on the class struggle, and not on social peace. At certain periods of sharp political and economic crises, the class struggle develops into open civil war (i.e. into armed struggle between two sections of the people). At such time, a Marxist is *obliged* to support this civil war. (Original emphasis)

Lenin's attitude to the Irish Revolt in 1916 indicates clearly this view of civil wars. Castigating those who he said would villify the Irish Rebellion by calling it a 'putsch', he wrote: 'The term "putsch", in its scientific sense, may be employed only when the attempt at insurrection has revealed nothing but a circle of conspirators or stupid maniacs, and has aroused no sympathy among the masses.'[31]

As Vigor[32] argues correctly, to approve of civil wars from the point of view of the 'oppressed', or of 'wars of national liberation' from the point of view of the colony, indicates approval of the initiation of such wars. For otherwise there would be no revolution.

In *The Civil War in France*[33] Marx had reproached the Commune for *not* starting a civil war, and largely attributed its subsequent downfall to this failure. When the Revolutionary French Government of 1792 embarked on war - an invasion of Europe - after the battles of Valmy and Jemappes it was, again according to Marx, spreading its revolutionary principles by force of arms. This type of act of aggression was approved by Marx as long as it was committed by revolutionaries for revolutionary purposes.

Since the Second World War there have been many bloody upheavals in the world, but a formal declaration of war seems to have become a thing of the past. The utilization of more subtle breaches of the peace, such as the support of subversive activities, including the financing and training of terrorists, and the fomenting of civil strife, has become the norm rather than the exception. The utility of these tactics is self-evident: they evade the legal difficulties of defining who is the aggressor and thus avoid direct confrontations in the context of superpower relationships.

The greater incidence of surrogate warfare has equally increasingly become an alternative mode of conflict. The presence of Cuban and East German soldiers fighting on African territory for the USSR is but one of the most recent examples of this trend.

Both these techniques of indirect aggression - the subversive activities and the use of surrogate forces - are devices of concealment, avoiding direct confrontation between the major powers. This concealment technique is even being used by terrorist groups themselves which disclaim responsibility for acts purportedly carried out by 'renegades' or 'extremists' of their group, thereby systematically creating a mythical image which does not reflect the reality. This, in particular, has consistently been the technique used by the PLO when acts such as the Munich Olympics massacre have shocked the world to such an extent that any identification with the deed would prove negative to the group and its search for political legitimation. This increase in concealment techniques indicates the growing utility which indirect aggression methods have acquired.

In problems of defining aggression and indirect aggression, the USSR has played a leading role which directly reflects its perception of its own position in the world balance of power. However, the Marxist ideological foundations have predetermined its legal conceptualization of these problems. Aggression, as defined by the Soviet Union, whether direct or indirect, only exists if such an action is taken by a non-revolutionary Western state, the emphasis being on both 'non-revolutionary' and 'state'. So it follows that from the Soviet perception, aggression is never committed by the USSR or any socialist bloc state. For example, Cuba, being a 'progressive socialist state', never commits an act of aggression as defined by international law.

Although this position does not in any way alter the legality or illegality of any particular violent act, it is clearly indicative of a Soviet opportunistic behavioural pattern on these questions. The emphasis on both an undefined aggression and the support of 'national liberation' allows the Soviet Union to appear as a legal member of the Society of Nations while at the same time supporting the use of force against a large number of these nations by championing those subnational groups needing 'liberation' from the Soviet point of view.

The Soviet Union has found itself increasingly opposing any accuracy in legal definitional discussions of aggression, including indirect aggression. In fact, the 1971 edition of the *Diplomaticheckii slovar'* (Diplomatic Dictionary) has removed the qualification that 'no political, strategic, or economic considerations' could justify aggression.

The Law of Nations by which Western civilization is bound places states under an obligation not to participate in terrorist activities within the territory of another state.[34] It places them under the further obligation not to conduct hostile propaganda against another state.[35] When direct application of violence is not called for, manipulating the opinions and attitudes of a target state's population can be very effective, and can often lead to insurgency.

The doctrine of non-intervention prohibits a state from assisting the rebels of another state during an ongoing civil war, and even as recently as 1965 the General Assembly again condemned indirect aggression by declaring that 'no state shall organize, assist, foment, finance, incite, or tolerate subversive, terrorist, or armed activities directed toward the violent overthrow of the regime of another state, or interfere in civil strife in another state'.[36]

At an earlier date, in 1948, highly effective political infiltration and threats of the use of force by the USSR resulted in a successful *coup d'état* by the Czech Communist Party in Czechoslovakia. Although the Soviet Union's veto in the Security Council prevented any action on the matter, the debates on the question clearly revealed a consensus that the activities of the USSR would have constituted serious violations of the Charter, if proved.[37] The Soviet delegates argued that no tangible evidence for those charges was produced, and there was implicit in that argument a recognition that such conduct would in fact have been illegal,[38] even if viewed from a Marxist perspective.

UN Resolutions on International Terrorism: the Soviet Position

The specific issue of international terrorism has been discussed off and on in the public forum since the 1960s. However, the response of the United Nations and other multilateral organizations which are concerned with curbing international terrorism has been far from spectacular. And the political polarization in the world certainly makes it very unlikely that the United Nations, or any other organization, will deliver a co-ordinated and effective policy on the subject.

These shortcomings notwithstanding, the Soviet argumentation presented during the preparatory meetings leading up to the various Conventions on Terrorism are interesting in themselves, and are indicative of the public posture which the Kremlin has taken on this problem.

The most common type of international terrorism which proliferated in the late 1960s was aerial hijacking of civilian aircraft. Although between 1960 and 1967 there was a very high incidence of aerial hijackings, most of the incidents were committed for private or personal reasons by persons seeking political asylum, escaping criminal process, evading family responsibilities, or suffering from psychological disturbances.

The year 1968, however, marked the initiation of aerial hijacking and the taking of hostages in its new role: the political one. The Popular Front for the Liberation of Palestine (PFLP), a part of the PLO, was the main perpetrator of this type of violence, and hijacking for political blackmail was initiated by it in April 1968 with the seizure of an El Al Israel airliner which was commandeered to Algiers.

The Soviet Union has based its position on terrorism issues at the United Nations on the same quality of argumentation and the same ideological foundations which form the basis of its position on the concept of aggression in general. The interest, or lack of interest, it has shown to the various conventions on the subject has largely reflected the way the Kremlin viewed its needs at any particular time. Thus, whereas the USSR, SSR Ukraine and SSR Byelorussia had not participated at all in the 1963 Tokyo Convention on Aerial Hijacking,[39] in 1970 these three members of the United Nations showed a flurry of interest and activity on the subject and participated in the conference proceedings at The Hague from the outset.[40] This sudden reversal of attitude and shift towards demanding a strong convention against hijackings was a direct result of the fact that the Soviet Union itself had suffered two successful hijackings just before the Conference convened, thus underscoring the Soviet Union's own perception of its vulnerability to such acts.[41]

In the debate which followed the voting on Resolution 2645[42] Mr Dmitry Kolesnik, representing the USSR, strongly emphasized the urgent need to suppress hijacking, and to regard such acts as serious criminal offences. Thus in this very narrow context of terrorism the Soviet Union was willing to withold political recognition from individuals involved in such hijackings. In the case of the two particular hijackings it had suffered in 1970, however, both perpetrated by Lithuanian citizens who hijacked an Aeroflot airliner, killing a stewardess and wounding a pilot and a co-pilot, the perpetrators were granted political asylum in Turkey.[43] The political element - the political extortion - which characterizes hijackings taking place in the Western liberal democracies was non-existent in these cases.

On 8 September 1972 the following item was included, as being urgent of particular importance, on the agenda of the United Nations General Assembly: 'Measures to Prevent Terrorism and other forms of violence which endanger or take innocent lives or jeopardize fundamental freedoms . . .'[44] During the discussions of the Sixth Committee of the United Nations on this question, the Soviet representative stated that Marxism-Leninism rejected international terrorism as a method of revolutionary action because it weakened the revolutionary movement and deflected the workers from the mass revolutionary struggle. We have already seen, however, that Lenin specifically addressed himself to this question and concluded that terrorism was a useful method of revolutionary upheaval when deemed expedient and controlled by the Party. So this public position which bases itself on Leninist dogma can only be viewed as an attempt at cosmetic legitimacy. The Soviet spokesman, in fact, went on to say that the entire experience of revolutionary and national liberation movements showed that the recognition of terrorism as the *principal method* of combat led to a division of forces and diverted active militants from their real task[45] (emphasis added). This formulation does not disallow it as one of the usable methods.

The USSR further reiterated during the discussions that it supported the legitimate struggle of the Arab people of Palestine for the restoration of their inalienable rights. It went on to qualify that statement by criticizing certain acts of terrorism by certain elements in the Palestinian movement, but concluded ultimately that these terrorist acts were acceptable and beneficial to the cause after all, because they made the people of Israel pay 'with their blood for the criminal policy of their rulers'.[46]

The above posture, it must be emphasized, covers all eventualities. It confirms the right to use violence in the name of 'self-determination' and 'world revolution' and does not prohibit the use of terror, but only cautions to avoid it as a 'principal' method. This is, in essence, consistent with Lenin's position on the question.

At the more recent deliberations of the Ad Hoc Committee on the Drafting of an International Convention against the Taking of Hostages, the question of national liberation movements consumed most of the time of the Sixth Committee of the United Nations General Assembly during its thirty-fourth session. It was claimed during those discussions that the acts of national liberation movement fighters were by definition different from those of terrorists. When the Syrian Arab Republic submitted that 'acts perpetrated by criminals under ordinary law could not be placed on an equal footing with the struggle of the national liberation movements which, by their very nature and their objectives, were entirely different',[47] it was enthusiastically supported by the USSR.[48]

The argumentation presented was based once again on the idea of the 'just cause' which we saw earlier in Leninist dogma, and the Soviet delegate went further to encompass all probabilities by supporting the non-aligned countries' claim that one cannot identify national liberation movements with 'the notion of international terrorism which would make it cover the struggle of peoples for national liberation and the struggle of oppressed workers to regain their rights'.[49] The insertion of the word 'workers' extends the applicability of terrorism and justifies its use in countries that do not have a 'liberation' problem in the national sense. Clearly, the parliamentary liberal democracies of Western Europe and the United States fall into that category.

This argumentation appears not only to tolerate but to encourage the epidemic of politically motivated groups self-endowed with a 'just cause' which have been undermining the fabric of these societies. In this instance, as in the concept of aggression, the Soviet Union again separates the revolutionary perpetrators from the non-revolutionary. Since its own argument sees communism in the Soviet Union as irreversible, no hijacker within its borders would or could be considered 'revolutionary' and therefore such a person would fall into the 'terrorist' or criminal category; whereas any act perpetrated in and against 'capitalist countries' would by

Soviet definition be carried out by 'revolutionaries' with a 'just cause', and would therefore not fall into the 'terrorist' definition as used by the Soviet Union.

The Soviet Union has used the terminology 'terrorist' mostly to describe acts by Western states, in repeated attempts to identify the West with oppression and terror and itself with liberation. For example, the raids by Israel into Lebanon as retaliation for Palestinian attacks are always described as terrorist, as was the recent seizure of cargo from the Aeroflot plane in Washington, DC, by the United States government. The Jewish Defence League attacks against Soviet targets in the United States are always called terrorist or criminal and paralleled with Israel's 'terrorism brought to state level' in order to strengthen the Soviet anti-Zionist policy which has been, since 1968, a large element of the Soviet Union's Middle East policy. That labelling of the JDL acts also deprives the group of any political justification, from the Soviet point of view.[50]

The Munich massacre of Israeli athletes by the PLO group 'Black September' was exceptionally termed 'criminal' by Andrei Gromyko in an interview with the *New York Times* on 27 September 1972, and most probably reflected a response to the world indignation and shock at that terrorist act which the Soviet government saw itself bound to echo to maintain its respectable state image.

The attitude more often expressed, however, is that Israel deserves what it gets, thereby exonerating the terrorists and blaming the target - what could be called a process of guilt transference. In an appearance before the United Nations on 22 September 1972 Soviet representative Malik categorically stated that the USSR was opposed to terrorism, particularly violent acts against heads of state and diplomats in foreign countries. The examples of such acts which he cited included, however, not the PLO terrorist activities which had plagued Western Europe in particular between 1968 and 1972, but those acts carried out by 'Zionist activists' in New York against the Soviet mission to the United Nations.[51]

Domestic Policy

Internally, the USSR has taken several steps to protect itself from what it sees as the threat of hijacking. As early as 1966 the RSFSR Criminal Code was amended to include Articles 190-1 and 190-3 to help combat dissidence. A Decree of the Presidium of 3 January 1973 provided a penalty of three to ten years for hijacking, up to fifteen years if a threat of violence existed or an accident resulted, and fifteen years or death if death or serious injury resulted.[52] A few months later, on 9 March 1973, the Principles of Criminal Legislation of the USSR and the Union Republics were revised to include aircraft hijacking.[53]

The USSR also participated in several bilateral agreements on hijacking problems, again reflecting its most immediate internal security needs. One agreement was signed with Iran (7 August 1973), one with Finland (23 August 1974), and an earlier one with Afghanistan in 1971.[54] The agreement with Iran ruled out any political defence by the provision that the return of the accused 'shall apply irrespective of what aims and motives have guided those who have hijacked/stolen the aircraft'.[55] This agreement was invoked in October 1976 when Iran denied political asylum to the pilot of a mail plane and returned him to the Soviet Union.[56]

This exemption of political motive is therefore the *de facto* Soviet position in dealing with its internal problems of terrorist acts. It has consistently been very useful not to use the word terrorist to identify any happenings taking place within its borders. Hijackers and other terrorists are branded 'habitual criminals'. After the bombing of the Moscow Metro train in early 1977, for example, there descended a veil of secrecy on the whole affair. Two years later three Armenians were executed in the basement of the Lubjanka prison after being sentenced at a secret trial. Tass news agency said that Stepan Zadikyan was 'a very dangerous habitual criminal . . .'. In May 1977 an engineer hijacked a Soviet Antonov-24 airliner to Stockholm's Arlanda Airport while on a flight between Riga and eastern Latvia. When Sweden refused to extradite the hijacker, Tass sharply criticized that Swedish government decision on 10 June 1977. The statement was clearly an affirmation of the non-applicability of a political defence. The hijacker was no political refugee, Tass said, but a fugitive from justice.

So the Soviet Union, true to its doctrinaire interpretations of Marx and Lenin, views any incident taking place within its borders as totally devoid of political motive. The rationale applied is simple: the Soviet communism which has been established in the USSR is irreversible; since it is the ultimate goal of mankind, no 'just' political cause can be invoked against it; therefore, any act whatsoever which takes place within the territorial limits of the USSR or against its representatives abroad is criminal by nature and by definition.

Discussion

Internationally, the USSR has, as recently as 1977, continued to argue for a narrow definition of what international terrorism is. Mr Fokine, the Soviet representative at the eighth meeting of the Ad Hoc Committee on International Terrorism of the United Nations,[57] stated that too broad a definition, which would encompass national liberation movements and acts committed for the purpose of resisting an aggressor in the territories it occupied, 'or [apply] to action by workers against the oppression of exploiters', would not be acceptable.[58]

In its insistence on a narrow definition, has the USSR demonstrated a consistently ambivalent position? The answer to this question is both yes and no, or 'it depends'. If one applies the Marxist-Leninist perception of reality which forms the basis of the Soviet decision-making process, it must be concluded that the Kremlin's position is not ambivalent *from its point of view*. Given that by definition it sees itself as incapable of aggression and incapable of suffering acts of political terrorism, its participation in conventions dealing with the problem of curtailing this use of violence must be seen as attempts at achieving two goals:

(1) to bind the hands of 'non-revolutionary terrorists' or what it calls 'counter-revolution';
(2) to achieve an appearance of legitimacy by participating in legal forums with capitalist states.

Both of these goals are not necessarily mere attempts at concealment of other motives or goals, but pragmatic decision-making on the part of the Kremlin. The first assures it of a greater physical safety, at least in the near future, and the second guarantees it the vital trade and credit concessions it might otherwise not receive were it to be regarded as anything but a responsible member of the Society of Nations.

In fact, *a priori*, its very participation *from its point of view* in the international legal systems of the world is seen as a compromise position, an interim behavioural necessity which accords with Lenin's precepts on the necessity of compromise to achieve the success of communism.

The Soviet Union's official behaviour during the Iranian hostage crisis is illuminating on this point. The official Soviet media described the crisis in very ambiguous terms which strongly implied support for the seizure of the American embassy and its personnel in Teheran. Moscow Radio's World Service in Persian language broadcasts asserted that the embassy takeover and the seizing of the American hostages was 'totally understandable and logical' since the embassy was filled with 'agents of the CIA and US imperialists who have not ceased their imperialism against Iran'. While this positive posture on this kind of terrorist act continued on the air and in the press, the Soviet representative at the United Nations, Oleg Troyanosvky, was asserting in the public forum that diplomatic immunity from force or takeovers should be 'adhered to strictly and in all cases in all countries'. Although it can be argued that there was intentional duplicity on the part of the Soviet Union for the achievement of the goals mentioned above, *from its point of view* Marxist-Leninist dogma was being applied to the letter. The embassy takeover was perpetrated by what the Kremlin chose to perceive as a 'revolutionary' group which was therefore entitled to use whatever means it deemed necessary, including terrorism, in its struggle. *Pravda* reiterated that same position when it reported on the United Nations Session on Hostage-Taking:[59]

> the people's right to oppose colonial domination, foreign occupation and racist regimes . . . has been recognized for some time and is enshrined in the UN charter and several other documents of international law . . . *It is necessary to make a distinction . . . between the people's sacred struggle for liberation and criminal terrorist acts by individuals, groups and organizations which have nothing in common with this struggle.* (Emphasis added)

Thus while the Soviet position in the legal forum can be seen as consistent with its ideological doctrine and therefore true to itself, the Western perception in answer to the original question is yes, the Soviet position demonstrates ambivalence. There must be a recognition of all the levels of Soviet argumentation which directly affect Western interests. The tendency has been to take a Soviet word at Western face-value without attributing to it its Leninist values. The questions the West should therefore ask when accepting Soviet rhetoric are: which are the national liberation movements that are to be excluded from the definition of terrorism? and would this definition include both the terrorist groups the Kremlin approves and the groups which might develop within the Soviet Union as well?

The relationship the Kremlin has claimed to have with the national liberation movements around the world has fortified its messianic communist internationalism. The balance which the Soviet Union has had to achieve between the overt diplomatic channels that assure it Western trade and credits, so badly needed for its failing economy, and the clandestine and overt support of what it perceives as revolutionary national liberation movements for the achievement of its expansionist goals worldwide are clearly indicated in its own argumentation which attempts to define the legal limits of violence. The reluctance to define concisely indirect aggression other than on a state-to-state basis reflects the greater emphasis and reliance the Kremlin has placed on non-state entities using this mode of conflict since the Second World War in order to avoid potentially cataclysmic confrontations with the United States in particular and the West in general. As will be discussed later, this is heavily underscored in the strategic considerations expressed by Soviet military writers.

The Soviet legal argumentation has at no time rejected or condemned terrorist activities as a tactic in a greater conflict, as long as that conflict could be defined as 'revolutionary' by 'freedom fighters' or by 'workers' against the 'exploiters', all of which would affect the Western alliance. This has, in fact, been completely consistent with the ideological definitions of aggression, war and peace.

Given the centralized apparatus which governs the USSR, there is a conformity and a consistency between the policy pronouncements made by all the branches of the governing bodies. And, as will be discussed in Chapter 5, Soviet military pronouncements provide us with explicit examples of Party policy which reflect the application of a tactical shift of emphasis towards an increased reliance on intensification of the 'class struggle' within capitalist societies. Given the time element necessary to structure any operational changes in military orientation and organization, the *détente* period leading up to the late 1960s, when international terrorism hit the Western European scene, can be identified as the period when this new political-military emphasis was developed. This new perception by the Kremlin of how to fight on towards the ultimate goal was accompanied by the largest conventional military build-up yet seen anywhere.[60] In the Soviet military view, the aim of this build-up was to achieve military superiority over capitalist armies.[61]

It is of immense interest, however, that the Soviet Ministry of Defence[62] itself perceived as early as 1958 that the non-military violence would be relied upon heavily in the future. The statement provided evidence of the strategic implementation by the military branch of the Khrushchev tactical shift of emphasis towards an increased interest in civil wars - the idea of the conflict *within* capitalist countries, which will be discussed in Chapter 5.

The course of history is determined in the last analysis by economic development and not by violence, and the main motive force of history is the broad masses of the people and not armies. *This, however, is not to belittle the enormous progressive significance of violence* (including violence applied by military methods), if this violence facilitates the destruction of out-dated economic institutions, and if it smashes dead, fossilized, political forms. (Emphasis added)

It is clear from the above statement that the parenthetical comment automatically gives greater emphasis to the use of non-military violence.

However, before reaching the contemporary scene, a historical discussion of the Soviet attitude and behaviour on the question of the use of international terrorism allows the necessary continuity to attempt trend analysis. Given the built-in institutional memory provided by the longevity of service of certain Communist Party members and of the Party structural basis, a certain sophistication has developed in the application of doctrinal policies - a factor which is totally absent from democratic societies which change leaderships periodically.

Notes

1. Resolution 3314 (XXXIV), UNGA, adopted at the 2319th Plenary meeting, 14 Dec. 1974.
2. Bassiouni and Nanda, (eds) (1973) p. 159.
3. See Soviet Association of International Law (ed.) (1979).
4. Schweisfurth (1979).
5. Modzhorian and Blatova (1979) pp. 88-9.
6. Russian dictionaries claim that this word derives from the Latin *aggressio* and is defined as an 'attack *(napadenie)* of one state against another for the purpose of seizing territory, destroying or limiting its independence, suppressing democracy, or imposing reactionary regimes'. There is also another word, *napadenie*, used in connection with aggression, which is perhaps more commonly used. It is defined as a 'rapid, swift action undertaken against someone or something for the purpose of seizure, inflicting losses, damage, etc.' William E. Butler, in 'Soviet attitudes to defining aggression' which appears in Bassiouni and Nanda (eds) (1973) p. 185, states that *napadenie* as defined above is legally and morally neutral, while *aggressiya* as defined above connotes moral or legal disapproval. See also Stone (1958) for an interesting discussion of the etymological origins of aggression.
7. *Slovar' sovremennogo russkogo literaturnogo yasyka*, published by Akademiya Nauk, SSSR, v. 1, pp. 47-8.
8. See P.H. Vigor (1975) p. 75.
9. E.N. Nasinovsky (1968) p. 189.
10. The Soviet Union had earlier signed the Kellogg-Briand Pact of 1928 along with most of its neighbours. Art. 1 renounced war 'as an instrument of national policy' and Art. 2 promised that only peaceful means would be used to solve any disputes or conflicts between the signatories. LXXXIX, pp. 369-75; see

Browlie (1963) pp. 1-65, for his contention that since this treaty was ratified or adhered to by 63 countries and that it has no provision for lapse or renunciation, it is therefore still in force.

11. Report of the International Law Commission, UN Doc. A/C.1/108, p. 9. See also Ferencz (1972) p. 493.

12. *UN Monthly Chronicle*, v. VII, March 1969, p. 42.

13. *Ibid.*; see also Bassiouni and Nanda (eds) (1973) p. 166. GA Resolution 2330, Doc. A/6716. See UN Doc. A/6333, Sept. 22, 1967, for the Soviet proposal and explanatory statement.

14. William E. Butler in Bassiouni and Nanda (eds) (1973) p. 194.

15. '(. . .) a permanent member which has committed or is about to commit aggression, or is in league with the aggressor, can lawfully use its right to veto: it can stop the Security Council from finding there has been an act of aggression. Here, precisely, is one of the fundamental weaknesses of the Charter.' Bentwich & Martin Commentary on the Charter of the United Nations, 1969, p. 13. The reports and subsequent discussion are summarized in *Sovetskii ezhegodnik mezhdunarodnogo prava*, 1968, published in 1969, pp. 355-60.

16. UN Doc. A/AC.134/L.12. Reproduced in *International Legal Materials*, v. VIII, p. 661.

17. See Bassiouni and Nanda (eds) (1973) p. 195.

18. *Ibid.*, Butler points out that Soviet doctrinal views on who may be a subject of international law have changed since 1955; for certain purposes peoples fighting for national liberation are believed to be subjects of international law by many Soviet jurists.

19. Soviet Association of International Law (ed.) (1970) p. 479.

20. *Bol'shaya Sovetskaya Entsiklopedia*, Moscow, 2nd edn, v. 1, p. 350.

21. *Bol'shaya Sovetskaya Entsiklopedia*, Moscow, 3rd edn, v. 1, p. 576.

22. *Ibid*, at pp. 577 and 582 respectively. For a discussion of acts of aggression committed by the USSR even by their own definition, see Vigor (1975) pp. 78-80.

23. UNGA Resolution 3314 (XXIX).

24. Stone (1974) p. 234.

25. Jessup (1948) pp. 184-5.

26. Quoted in Ferencz (1973) p. 420.

27. Butler in Bassiouni and Nanda (eds) (1973) p. 190, points out that there have been divergent translations of the 1933, 1950 and 1953 Soviet drafts, which have led some observers to speculate about the significance of 'curious change in the 1950 and 1953 drafts'. The difficulty in translating *napadenie* and *aggressiya* is again pointed out. See Stone (1974) p. 49.

28. GAOR, 27th Sess., Suppl. No. 19, Doc. A/8719, pp. 14 and 19. The pertinent articles of the Charter of the UN are numbers 2, 39 and 51.

29. See Carr (1950-3), v. 3, Note E: The Marxist Attitude to War.

30. Both these articles appeared in 1916.

31. Lenin, (1958-66) v. 30, pp. 53-4 'The Discussion on self-determination summed up'.

32. Vigor (1975) p. 66.

33. Marx (1871).

34. See Starke (1967) p. 96.

35. For development, see Bartlett (1940) pp. 5-6.

36. 'Declaration of the Inadmissibility of Intervention in the Domestic Affairs of States and the Protection of their Independence and Sovereignty', GA Res. 2131 (XX), 20 UN GAOR, Supp. 14, p. 11, UN Doc. A/6014 (1965). The text of the full resolution can be found in AJIL, v. 60, 1966, pp. 662-4.

37. UN, SCOR, 3, Supp. Jan.-Mar., pp. 34-5, UN Doc. S/696 (1948).

38. See Novogrod in Bassiouni and Nanda (eds) (1973) p. 226. Also Pella (1929) p. 174, for earlier discussions on the question.

39. Convention on Offenses and Certain Other Acts committed on Board Aircraft (Tokyo Convention), 704 UNTS, p. 219.

40. Convention on the Suppression of Unlawful Seizure of Aircraft (The Hague), see AJIL, v. 65, 1971, p. 440.

41. *New York Times*, 16 Oct. 1970 for details of the hijackings by Lithuanians.

42. Resolution 2645 (XXV), 'Aerial Hijacking or Interference with Civil Air Travel', GA, 25th Session, 1914th plenary meeting, 15 Sept.-17 Dec. 1970.

43. *New York Times*, 16 Oct. 1970.

44. Full title being: '. . . and Study of the Underlying Causes of those Forms of Terrorism and Acts of Violence which lie in misery, frustration, grievance, and despair and which cause some people to sacrifice human lives, including their own in an attempt to affect radical change'. This full title appears from the outset to be a justification for the use of terrorism.

45. UNYB, v. 26, 1972, p. 642.

46. *Ibid.*, p. 643.

47. UN Doc. A/32/39, p. 36.

48. *Ibid.*, p. 80.

49. *Ibid.*, p. 32. The Byelorussian SSR used the same phrase, p. 56.

50. Edward Mickolus, *Chronology of Terrorist Attacks against Soviet Interests 1968-1977*, part of 'Appendix A: A Chronology of Transnational Terrorist Attacks', in *Transnational Terrorism: Attributes of Terrorists, Events and Environments*, New Haven, Conn.: Yale University, Department of Political Science, Ph.D Dissertation in preparation.

51. *New York Times*, 23 Sept. 1972.

52. *Current Digest of the Soviet Press*, v. 25, no. 1, 1973, p. 7.

53. Arts. 7(1), 23(1), 30, 44(1), 45(2); *Current Digest of the Soviet Press*, v. 25, nos. 18 and 19.

54. Iran: Dept. of State, Division of Language Series, LS No. 59449, AC/DZ (trans.); Finland: Dept. of State, Airgram, A-174, 9 Oct. 1974; Afghanistan: ICAO Legal Committee, 20th Sess. (special), 9-30 Jan. 1973, 1 Minutes at 12 (1973). See Evans and Murphy (eds) (1978) pp. 55-62.

55. Art. 2(7).

56. *New York Times*, 24 Oct. 1976.

57. UN, GAOR, 32nd session, Suppl. no. 37, 24 March 1977, UN Doc. A/32/37.

58. *Ibid.*, p. 30. The same position was held by the USSR in UN Doc. A/AC.160/1/ Add.1 & Add.2.

59. FBIS, 13 April 1978. On 4 Dec. 1979, the UN Security Council called unanimously for the release of the hostages, and on 13 Jan. 1980, ten members approved economic sanctions against Iran. This resolution was vetoed by the USSR. See Dept. of State, *Current Policy*, No. 179, 8 May, 1980.

60. Collins (1980) for the statistical information on this development.

61. See Dziak (1981a).

62. *Marksizm-Leninizm o Voine i Armii*, Voenizdat, Moscow, 1958, p. 54.

4

Historical Perspective

The First World War brought about immense changes in international relations. The continental European imperial systems collapsed under the impact of war, revolution, and the rising forces of democracy. The Bolsheviks took over in Russia and set out to transform Russia and the world into a new order by revolutionary means.

The new spirit of internationalism in the wake of Wilsonian egalitarianism and the new distribution of power in the world brought with them new requirements for the diplomatic intercourse of nations.

The initial impetus of the successful Bolshevik *coup* saw a repudiation of all that was identified as Csarist-connected and capitalist in structure. The system of international law and diplomacy which up until then had been the structural base of all state relations was struck off the slate by the Bolsheviks.

However, the defeat which the Bolsheviks experienced at the Brest-Litovsk Conference in the winter of 1917-18, the disillusionment with the failure of immediate revolution abroad and the awareness of the necessity of economic interdependence with the 'capitalist enemies', forced a reassessment of the Soviet leaders' utopian goals for the immediate future and a recon-sideration of their general position *vis-à-vis* Western nations. This reassessment was to demonstrate to the West a tactical elasticity and resourcefulness which would remain as permanent attributes of Soviet diplomatic manoeuvring in the years which followed.

The dichotomy of purposes and functions which existed between the overt diplomatic community and the subversive reolutionary arm of Soviet power in overseas operations - the Comintern intermingled with CHEKA operatives - was soon to become a central feature in general Soviet behavioural norms, and one indicative of the balancing act which the USSR had to perform in order to fulfil its oracular ideological goals and yet exploit the capitalist economies.

The Lenin Era

Before taking over the reins of power in November 1917 Lenin and his group relied on terrorist tactics to disorganize the csarist autocracy, and to provoke counter-measures from the government which would be necessarily repressive in nature and, it was hoped, consciousness-raising for the proletariat. After Lenin's *coup* of 1917 he was faced with great problems of power consolidation.

To effect this consolidation, Lenin appointed Dzerzhinsky to set up the CHEKA (Russian initials for Extraordinary Commission for Combating Counter-Revolution and Sabotage), the first secret political police of its kind at the time, and one which would earn the macabre reputation of being the most efficient state terror apparatus of the twentieth century. This political police was eventually to evolve into the KGB, which would prove highly instrumental in carrying out subversive tactics abroad, as well as ensuring effective internal control.[1]

As late as 1922 Lenin's ruthless use of terror as an instrument for 'struggling against counter-revolution', as he termed it, was evident. Counter-revolution was to be fought at home and abroad. He wrote to Kurskii, the Commissar for Justice who was drafting the Criminal Code:[2]

> The Law should not abolish terror: to promise that would be self-delusion or deception; it should be substantiated and legalized in principle, clearly, without evasion or embellishment. The paragraph on terror should be formulated as widely as possible, since only revolutionary consciousness of justice and revolutionary conscience can determine the conditions of its application in practice.

As early as 1918 left-wing attempts to seize power multiplied round the world, with the earliest taking place in Finland. Fervently believing that their own revolution would not survive without other viable revolutions successfully developing abroad, the Bolsheviks set about hastening this 'inevitable' outcome by creating the Third Communist International (Comintern) in March 1919, for the specific purpose of inciting revolts outside their own borders. At the closing of the First Congress of the Comintern, Lenin proclaimed that the 'victory of the proletarian revolution on a world scale is assured. The founding of an international Soviet republic is on its way'.[3]

There was, in fact, a superimposition of personnel on to the Soviet foreign missions. Revolutionaries, diplomats and secret police were all part of the subversive machinery abroad, and diplomatic mail pouches carried dynamite, weapons, currency, or propaganda - all tactical parts of the revolutionary process.[4]

The idea in those early days was to dismantle - or at least attempt to - the European empires, as the first step to the eventual conquest of Europe. The first abortive attempt at seizing power in Europe was in Finland in 1918. The following year there was the eighteen-day attempt to set up a 'Soviet Republic' in Bavaria and the failure of Bela Kun in Hungrary followed by Poland in 1920, and the débâcle at Reval, Estonia, in 1924.

However, with the failure of these spontaneous attempts at left-wing *coups* abroad, the whole concept of world revolution and how it should be achieved by the Soviet Union was to change. The Comintern was now to be regarded strictly as an extension of the Party apparatus solely performing tasks for the advancement of the national interests of the USSR, rather than as a messianic organ of international Marxism at large.

The Third International was far different in structure from its predecessor, the Second. It emerged as a highly centralized and disciplined organization, having authority over the programme and activities of the affiliated parties abroad,[5] its structure much resembling the Bolshevik Party's centralized power core. Having identified the colonies as the weakest points of the Western nations, and in particular of Great Britain, the Bolsheviks set about fomenting unrest and arming what factions they could. The 'national liberation' theme became the principle of the 'just' cause which the movement needed for success.

The *Manifesto of the Communist International to the Proletariat of the Entire World*, written by Trotsky and adopted by a unanimous vote, stated the purpose of the organization:[6]

> We communists, the representatives of the revolutionary proletariat of various countries of Europe, America and Asia, who have gathered in Soviet Moscow, feel and consider ourselves to be the heirs and executors of the cause whose programme was announced seventy-two years ago.

Training camps for 'guerrilla' action were set up as early as 1919-20, for example in Tashkent - precursors of the modern training camps for which evidence is now so readily available. Comintern support for the liberation of the colonies, Lenin argued, would accelerate the victory of the proletariat over capitalism, and on this notion the colonial oppressed peoples' liberation depended.[7] To achieve this revolutionary crusade terrorist tactics were often part of the overall campaign of unrest which Soviet agents were directly instrumental in perpetrating worldwide in those early years. It is noteworthy that when the USPD (German Independent Democratic Party) criticized the use of terror (as opposed to force), Lenin replied that this attempt to make a distinction between terror and force was a textbook argument worthy of a sociology class, but was not in the realm of practical politics.[8]

In 1920 the British government uncovered a mission which had been authorized by Lenin himself: Mohammed Ashur was dispatched to Tashkent along with twenty-eight others for training in 'military' techniques and propaganda work. This took place after the outbreak of hostilities between Afghanistan and the British government, and the graduates of the camp were given money and a hundred bombs to perpetrate a terrorist bombing campaign against the British in India. This particular mission was aborted after a strong note to Chicherin was dispatched by the British government on 7 September, 1920.[9] In August 1921 the same Mohammed Ashur surfaced in Moscow, together with other members of the Indian Revolutionary Association, for special education at a Moscow university, education which has since been given routinely by the Soviet Union to revolutionaries from many parts of the world. At that time, the Indian students in Moscow were supported financially by the Comintern and in addition had direct access to Chicherin himself.

On 22 June 1922 the British Foreign Office reported that the existence of a secret terrorist society had been ascertained. It was called 'Nasrat-ul-Hakh' (Victory of Right) and organized by Abdul Hamid Said and his league to foster terrorism in Egypt, primarily directed against British targets. At a meeting in Rome arrangements were discussed by the terrorist group with Vorovsky, the USSR's representative in Rome at that time. At a later meeting, on 6 August, Abdul Hamid Said discussed with Bolshevik agents the possibility of assassinating Lord Allenby, Sir H. Samuel and Lord Reading.[10] Arms and munitions were promised to the group by the Soviets.[11] Incredibly, perhaps, Chicherin himself attended a further secret meeting in Lavignia, Italy, where he promised the group that in his official capacity as Foreign Minister of the Federated Soviet Republic, '[I] give you my word that we will give you anything you may require towards the attainment of your object'.[12]

It is of interest to note some of the wording of the constitution of the Indian Revolutionary Association of Kabul which the Soviet Union trained and funded in 1922:[13]

1.   . . .
2.   *Aims and objects:*
     a   To work against the English in all possible ways and to

use all possible means and resources which may lead to
the ultimate emancipation of India.

b   To keep well informed the Russian public . . .

3.   . . .

4.   *Distribution of work*

a   Propaganda section:

b   . . . Active section:
To carry on a guerrilla warfare with the English on the
Indian border and to incite and help border tribes to fight
the English Government.

However, India was not the only country in which the Soviets
carried out their revolutionary tactics. In the same year, 1922, an
open letter from the Comintern (signed Bukharin and Radek,
Moscow, 2 July 1922) to the leaders of the Labour Party of England
(Ramsay MacDonald, Tom Shaw and Arthur Henderson) came to
light. Describing the Irish as 'honest, though not Socialist, Irish
revolutionaries who are fighting against the oppression of English
imperialism', the letter went on to condemn the leaders of the
English Labour Party who were 'so shameless as to condemn at a
meeting of [their] party the terrorist act of the Irish Revolutionaries
who fought for the liberation of their country at the risk of their
lives'.[14]

Previously, in April 1922, Karl Radek had sent a letter from the
Executive Committee of the Third International (ECCI) to the
Communist Party of Great Britain in which he stated his conviction
that 'Ireland will form the breach through which the revolutionary
movement will penetrate into England'.[15] This identification by the
Kremlin of the Irish as a good revolutionary tool in spite of their
non-socialist programme (in fact, they were extreme right-wing
nationalists at the outset) was an exemplification of the necessary
policy of compromise - *realpolitik*, opportunism - which the Soviet
Union adopted quickly in the early years after the Bolshevik
revolution. The USSR developed various techniques which
depended not on material strength and power, which it lacked, but
on exploiting divisions and unrest among its opponents. Thus, in
its weakness, the Soviet Union, by manipulating foreign contacts,
developed new forms of revolutionary technique which stronger
countries did not need.[16] The Comintern exemplified one of these
techniques: it was to become the first proxy instrument - surrogate
force - of the Soviet government, set up ostensibly as an
independent organization, to take action on its behalf when that
action was to be more than usually repugnant to international
norms of acceptable behaviour.

At the Second Comintern Congress, which took place on 4

August 1920, the policies concerning the use of 'armed struggle' and illegal organization had already been apparent and served to underscore the tenets set down by Lenin on the subject. To the objection that too much emphasis was laid in the Statutes on these two tactics, Kabakchiev replied: 'how could they shrink from talking of armed struggle at a time when the victorious Red Army was inflicting deadly blows on Entente imperialism and clearing the road for world revolution, and when civil war was raging in a number of countries?'[17]

As part of the balancing act which it had to perform, the Soviet government throughout went to great lengths to dissociate itself officially from the Comintern. Having been accused by the British of 'being' the Comintern, Maxim Litvinov used a somewhat naïve argument which explained that the concurrent membership of some individuals of both the Soviet government and the Third International did not constitute proof or justification for regarding the Soviet government and the Third International as identical.[18] The British government, pointing to the fact that the Comintern included Lenin and Trotsky in its executive refused to accept Litvinov's reply. It had become evident, at least to the British government, if not to the free world at large, that the Soviet government had set up a submissive, subversive apparatus taking actions on its behalf which ranged from 'disinformation' to terrorist attacks.[19]

In 1924 Captain Viscount Curzon asked the Prime Minister in Parliament 'whether he is aware that 100 agitators are being trained in Moscow by a comrade Stuart for active work in Great Britain,[20] and in the same year, a few months later, the Belgian embassy informed the Foreign Office that it had evidence that an active propaganda campaign of agitation was beind organized by the Soviet government in the British, French and Dutch colonies, as well as the Belgian Congo, and that a secret colonial committee had been especially created for the purpose of preparing armed insurrections among the local populations. The head of this committee was named as Manuilsky,[21] the chairman of the Commission for National and Colonial Affairs of the Fifth Congress.

An infamous and mysterious letter which was purported to be a very secret directive from the Executive Committee of the Third Communist International Presidium[22] to the Central Committee of the British Communist Party was the Zinoviev letter which read in part as follows:[23]

armed warfare must be preceded by a struggle against the inclinations to compromise which are embedded among the majority of British workmen, against the ideas of revolution and peaceful extermination of capitalism. Only then will it be possible to count upon complete success of an armed insurrection. In Ireland and the colonies the case is different. There there is a *national question, and this represents too great a factor for success for us to waste time on a prolonged preparation of the working class.* (Emphasis added)

Although the letter was alleged by some to be a forgery, and the matter was never conclusively proved one way or another, the wording did not differ in essence from other documents which had proved genuine. The best confirmation of its authenticity is a note sent in October 1924 to Lord Stamfordham by Nevile Bland of the Foreign Office. Headed *MOST SECRET,* it stated that the letter in question had been obtained from an absolutely trustworthy agent in Russia and its receipt by the British Communist Party had been reported shortly afterwards from an entirely independent source in Great Britain. Bland added, 'it is unfortunately impossible to make this known, as the lives of our informants would thereby be seriously endangered'.[24]

Later events show further continuity in the tactics encouraging the use of international terrorism by the Kremlin. In 1925 Sir P. Loraine, the British representative in Persia, received information that a plot to assassinate him or his military attaché within three days had been organized by Soviet agents. He dispatched an urgent telegram to this effect to Sir W. Tyrrell who transmitted it to the Foreign Office. In a secret reply to Tyrell, the Foreign Office informed him that the threat should be taken seriously in view of certain information it had. This secret reply made the following revelatory points:[25]

(1) Our information is that, whereas the Moscow leaders at first discountenanced terrorism and assassination, as being likely to do their cause more harm than good, they decided at the 5th World Congress, last summer, to sanction resort to such expedients, *provided such caution and circumspection were observed as to ensure that Moscow complicity could easily be disproved.* [Emphasis added]

(2) On the 14th July, Manuilski [Chairman of the Commission for National and Colonial Affairs of the Fifth Congress] stated at a session of the Central Committee of the Russian Communist Party that '*we . . . who dissociate ourselves from terrorism, nevertheless have sanctioned its adoption in the East*'. [Emphasis added]

(3) On the 11th Nov., 1924, the Komintern sent very secret

instructions to the Persian Communist Party stating that: '*Although in principle opposed to terrorism, the RKP recognizes the possibility of punishing by death those enemies of the Soviet system* . . . To the number of such enemies belong the British Mission in Persia, headed by the bitterest enemy of the Persian and Russian Peoples, Loraine . . .' [Emphasis added]

(4)   In continuation of these instructions, the Komintern sent further instructions on the 28th November to Tashkent, stating that a special mission, including Trakman, Mukhtarov and others, had left Moscow for Persia on November 25th, in order to establish contact with the Central Committee of the Persian Communist Party.

(5)   The British Military Attache at Meshed reported the arrival of Mukhtarov in Meshed . . .

(6)   On the 6th of April, Pavlovitch sent a circular to Eastern Communist parties, in which it was stated that: ' . . . There is evidence of the provocative activities of the Ambassador, Percy Loraine . . . The Soviet Commissariat of Propaganda instructs all comrades . . . not to hesitate to take measures to remove *[iikvidatsiya]* these harmful influences'.

(7)   In recent very secret instructions (the exact date of which has not been ascertained) to Semir Zade at Teheran, the Komintern stated: 'Immediately detail from the Militant Section of the Communist Party and from the "Union for the Liberation of Iran" the most important workers for action against the British agents and their spies'.

With regard to the actual plan of campaign, Loraine informed Austen Chamberlain that the Bolshevik Consul General at Tabriz was to organize a 'spontaneous' rising of some sort on 7 November 1925. Mainly Persian subjects were to take part in this uprising. Armed intervention on the part of Russia was not contemplated unless its help was invoked by the insurgents (later parallels to this technique were to be employed in Czechoslovakia, Angola, Ethiopia, Iran and Afghanistan). Loraine went on to inform the Foreign Office that the recent small Shahsavan outbreak could be explained as a result of the alleged distribution among the tribes of a certain quantity of ammunition smuggled across the Russian frontier. The Soviet consulate had apparently also distributed revolvers among the Armenian Bolsheviks.[26]

As early as July 1925 the Foreign Office became aware that the Persian Communist Party had been instructed by the Comintern to form an organization for terrorist activities to be directed against 'the enemies of the Soviet Union in Persian', and primarily against

Loraine. These terrorist activists were to be equipped by the Third International.[27]

The terrorist bomb which exploded in Sofia Cathedral during a funeral on 16 April 1925 created what amounted to an interesting succession of statements by the Soviet press, by the ECCI and by an organization calling itself the Balkan Communist Federation - all of which clearly predicated adherence to the Leninist position on the use of revolutionary terrorism versus individual terrorism, as discussed earlier in this study.

Three weeks prior to that terrorist incident, the Bulgarian government had published the text of an ECCI resolution instructing the Bulgarian Communist Party to start an insurrection on 15 April. There was an immediate denial by the ECCI of the authenticity of the resolution, stating that it was a fabrication intended to justify the repressive executions carried out by the Tsankov government. On 23 April 1925 *Izvestiya* published a statement by the ECCI denying involvement of the Comintern with the terrorist bomb 'by very reason of their objection in principle to acts of individual terrorism'.[28] In May the foreign bureau of the Bulgarian Communist Party denied any plan for an uprising and any complicity in the explosion. It explained, however, that like other terrorist acts, it was an inevitable response to government terror, thereby offering at least a justification for the act. On 1 May 1925 *Izvestiya* published a proclamation by the Balkan Communist Federation, an organization with its headquarters in Moscow, which also denied any complicity but expressed sympathy 'with those who are heroically defending themselves'.[29] There were also denials by Chicherin on behalf of the Soviet government. In March of 1926 the Sixth ECCI Plenum passed the following resolution:[30]

IV The Tasks of the Communist International . . .
    19 . . .
    The Communist International decisively rejects individual terrorism. In rejecting this method of struggle it is guided exclusively by the principle of revolutionary expediency.

It went on to qualify that position, however, as follows:

This has nothing in common with the petty-bourgeois attitude to the revolutionary use of force. Every class-conscious proletarian knows that without the use of revolutionary terror the bourgeoisie cannot be overthrown . . .

The denials of involvement in the terrorist explosion at Sofia Cathedral continued to be emphasized by the Bulgarian Communist Party until 1948. At its Fifth Congress that year, however, Dimitrov all but admitted its involvement when he called the explosion 'an ultra-left deviation . . . by the military organization of the party'.[31]

These public denials of involvement and objections to individual terrorism can be viewed in two ways.

(1) If the explosion was in fact committed without instruction and backing, the disclaimers were clearly reprimands to the perpetrator, and reflected the desire to keep all revolutionary activities under the centralized grip of the ECCI.

(2) If, however, it was part of an insurgency plot organized by the ECCI, then the utterances were merely for Western consumption, and part of the duplicity necessary to the USSR for its balancing act.

In either case, the implication is the same: the statements clearly indicated support for 'revolutionary terror' perpetrated by a centrally controlled group, and an objection to 'individual terror'. The Marxist-Leninist ideology on the question remained the yardstick for permissible revolutionary tactics.

Much more of the same kind of evidence of the use of terrorist tactics abroad by the Soviet government, directly or indirectly, through various proxy instruments, continued round the world,[32] together with other subversive activities reported by numerous foreign governments - which together finally culminated in a crisis of major proportions for the adolescent state.

It is of interest that in 1926 the delegates to the Communist International of the Communist Parties of Chile, Argentina, Brazil, Uruguay, Paraguay, Peru, Venezuela, Colombia, Panama and Guatemala were reported to have severed their connection with the Comintern on the ground that they disapproved of its issuing counterfeit money and its use of terrorist tactics.[33] This was a natural attempt at dissociation, but at the same time it confirmed the Comintern's use of terrorism.

On 12 May 1927 Scotland Yard raided the offices of Arcos Limited in London, a company backed by Russian capital and described by the Soviet Union as an import-export trading company.[34] It had a staff of a thousand people, an enormous number by any standard. The raid, ostensibly carried out primarily to search for a highly secret document which had gone missing from the British War Office,[35] revealed a connection between the Russian Trade Delegation and Arcos Limited which shared the building. Weapons, propaganda films and other subversive material were confiscated.[36]

Had the evidence collected been an isolated instance, the ultimate decision taken by the British government might have been less drastic. But coming as it did, in the wake of the signing of the Rapallo Treaty between the Soviet Union and Germany in 1922, the British General Strike of 1926 in which the government had evidence of Soviet subversion, and the accumulated evidence of Soviet interference abroad, the new evidence was deemed sufficient cause by the British government for breaking off diplomatic relations with the USSR. The decision was announced on 26 May 1927.[37]

The Stalin Era

Up until Lenin's death on 21 January 1924, the foreign policy of the Soviet Union had been principally based on three perceptive phases. The first, and shortest, was based on the euphoric belief that the successful Bolshevik revolution would be copied spontaneously elsewhere, thus guaranteeing the continuation of Bolshevik power; the second was based on Lenin's belief, in light of the rapidly fading hopes of successful revolutionary actions abroad, that his revolution would not survive without the active participation of the Comintern to create those other revolutions; the third phase was based on the realization that Russia's revolution had survived after all without those external revolutions and it could now resume its position as a great power in global politics.[38] For all three phases, terrorist tactics were employed, financed, and organized when they were deemed to be the necessary tactic for the overall Soviet strategy. As the third phase of perception was reached, the only trend which could be identified was a shift towards greater centralization of power by the Party and a duplicity of behaviour in foreign relations dictated by self-interest.

With Stalin's ascendancy, the third phase was to become enshrined, and what has generally been described as a period of isolationism for the Soviet Union (1927-39) was in reality to be a period of tactical revision. The Stalinist conception of 'socialism in one country' accorded absolute priority to the Soviet revolution within the context of the expected world revolution. The Comintern and other communist parties were to be totally subordinated to, and if necessary sacrificed by, Moscow.

The international scene of the 1930s presented a growing anarchy and a declining respect for the customary rule of law. Fascism and nazism emerged in Italy and Germany presenting, together with Soviet totalitarianism, a new form of state power. The

USSR, as a reaction to the manace of the growing fascism, emerged with the United Front policy, an attempt to establish close associations with the democratic states of Europe and a policy of collective security. This policy was a pragmatic view of its self-interest, often conducted at the expense of other communist parties. Thus there was a change of emphasis in favour of diplomacy which would facilitate the trade ambitions of the Soviet Union. This new emphasis, however, did not herald any reversal in the use of terrorism. International terrorism was in fact never abandoned; it simply receded into deeper secrecy.

The Communist International was now directed to penetrate subversive labour movements in 'bourgeois' democratic countries with a longer-term goal in mind. Any identification of the Soviet government with hard-core revolutionary tactics had to be avoided in order to avert the wrath of the West. The new policy was stated as follows: 'It is natural that we have to pursue a path of partial compromise, refraining from an imposition by force, and that we should have been placed under the necessity of cloaking the aims of the Communist International in a nationalist disguise'.[39] At the All-Union Congress of Soviets which met in Riga on 18 April 1927, Rykov, a member of the Politburo, delivered the Soviet government's official report on international relations. It was, he said, impossible and undesirable to restrain 'our sympathies and help for British toilers during strikes and for the Chinese revolutionary movement, and the West should not interpret this as an interference in the internal affairs of other states'.[40] In order to allow the Kremlin a period of respite for consolidation, the era of 'peaceful coexistence' had begun, a creation which was later to be attributed to Khrushchev. This period was still punctuated, however, by evidence of subversion and espionage in the West. The Comintern in fact proceeded with its charter: to bring about unrest and chaos in the West. What Stalin wanted most of all in the West was a state of weakness. To divert the power of Western states from himself, he followed a policy which would exploit any divisions he could perceive among the Western allies.[41]

Stalin was not original in devising this approach, for Lenin had spelt out his policy of compromise much earlier in *What Is To Be Done?*[42] and had carried it out first with the signing of the Brest-Litovsk Treaty and then with the courting of Ataturk and the Shah by officially refusing to back local communists in Turkey and Iran.[43] Stalin, in fact, carried out Lenin's dicta to the letter and showed little originality of approach, for the ideological base provided the necessary flexibility to satisfy his own reasons.

At a meeting of the All-Union Lenin League of Communist Youth on 16 January 1931 it was reported that the Comintern was 'energetically fostering the fighting capacity of the Communist Party abroad' (note the use of the singular).[44] Subsequently, Bolshevik agents visited India to organize a plot for the assassination of the Viceroy.[45] Moreover, a general intensification of terrorist operations against the British Empire was also planned.[46]

Even Nicaragua, which was to succumb almost fifty years later to a bloody civil war, was already burdened by what were then called 'bandit attacks' against private enterprises such as Bragmans Banff Lumber Company near Puerto Cobezas and Chichigalpa. The groups involved in these attacks were reported by Dr Arguello, Minister of Foreign Affairs, to have been well armed and operating under a form of military discipline, thereby giving the impression of some sort of control and organization. Links were established as existing between the groups and a certain Toribio Tijerino who was Communist-affiliated and possibly a Comintern agent [47]

Perhaps the most salient evidence of Kremlin flexibility in the adverse times it was confronting was the information transmitted in a letter in 1931 by Sir H. Rumbold, who was at the British Embassy in Berlin, to Arthur Henderson, MP, at the Foreign Office.[48] The letter informed Henderson that the German Communist Party no longer received any assistance from the Soviet Union. This remarkable confidential information, which had been sent by General Von Schleicher of the German Ministry of Defence, went on to state that the Russians, however, were now supplying the Nazis with funds by indirect channels (*über einem Umweg*). Having reproached the German Communists with their failure to create Communist cells in the police and in the Reichsheer, the Kremlin now concentrated on assisting the National Socialist Party which it perceived as having greater probability of success and in the hope that its victory would ultimately benefit the CPSU. At the same time, however, the Soviets were also supplying monetary funds to Communist newspapers. This alliance with the extreme right was an opportunistic precedent often to be repeated in the years that followed, and should have forewarned at least the British government of the possibility of a future Nazi-Soviet alliance.

Between 1933 and 1936 Stalin embarked the Soviet Union on a whirl of diplomatic activity, mainly in the person of Maxim Litvinov, to woo the Western capitalist states and convince them that the Russians no longer posed a threat to the world. The West proved receptive. Soviet Russia joined the League of Nations and signed mutual assistance pacts with France and Czechoslovakia. Foremost on the agenda of its collective security policy, however, was obtaining recognition from the United States. The key issues involved as the United States saw them at the time were:

(1) Protection against Soviet propaganda and subversive activities in the United States;
(2) Freedom of worship and protection of the legal rights of Americans in Russia;
(3) Satisfactory settlement of Russian debts which amounted at the time to $150 million.[49]

Why the United States failed to utilize properly the lever of recognition was probably due to a misreading of the importance which this lever had for the USSR, although the financial depression which the United States and the West had suffered might have proved more influential in forming the judgement of the policy-makers as trade with the Soviet Union became an attraction, if not a necessity . Be that as it may, the pledges which Litvinov promised to fulfil at the negotiations which took place in Washington, 7-16 November 1933, had regard to the first two issues. The debt question was postponed for discussion at a later date.[50]

It became obvious from later developments that the diplomatic agreements signed by the Soviet Union were incompatible with its covert behaviour, at any rate from the Western perspective. On the occasion of the All-World Congress of the Comintern in the summer of 1935, the plans for developing the Communist Party of the United States (CPUSA) were discussed by American Communists who attended the conference. According to Benjamin Gitlow, a former American Communist leader, the CPUSA had been most concerned about the pledges made by Litvinov in 1933 against subversive activities and the possible effects they might have on the organization. The OGPU (Soviet Secret Police) in the United States arranged a meeting between Litvinov and the CPUSA Secretariat in New York to discuss this question. Litvinov assured the American members that the relations of the CPUSA with the Comintern and the activities of that party would in no way be affected by those pledges.[51]

The apparent lack of worldwide activity by the Comintern in the 1930s and until its dissolution in 1943 did not reflect the realities of the situation. There was, to be sure, only one Comintern Congress held between 1929 and 1943, and even so, the proceedings of the plenary sessions of the ECCI were never published in full. Remarkably, in fact, there were no public Comintern statements made at the outbreak of the Spanish Civil War, the Austrian Anschluss, the Anti-Comintern Pact formation, the Munich Agreement, or the outbreak of the Second World War in 1939.[52]

However, in spite of all these overt indications of a possible change of policy away from fomenting trouble, Stalin still inspired subversive moves abroad. The financial statement by the ECCI actually indicated an increase of expenditures during the early 1930s, rather than a decrease, as one would have imagined for a period of inactivity.[53] And during the same week that Litvinov was negotiating and pledging in Washington, the Comintern official paper announced that in view of the Nazi victory in Germany there was to be a shift of policy, with the Austrian and German Communist Parties having now to work 'secretly and not openly' to create 'cadres of professional revolutionaries' who were to take their pattern for 'conspiratorial work [from] the Bolshevik Party in Russia in the Tsarist days'.[54]

The British Foreign Office also received in the same year, 1933 a telegram containing the following information:[55]

> The Bulgarian Minister telegraphed this morning to his government to say that a recent secret meeting of Communists in Hamburg had discussed a resolution of the Third International ordering a Communist offensive in all countries; attempts were to be made on the lives of prominent persons such as Royalties, and every effort was to be made simultaneously to bring about general disorder.

There was even evidence of Soviet attempts to infiltrate at least one Moscow-trained agent into Egypt later in 1935.[56] Spain was also becoming a most active centre for the Comintern operatives, indicating a continuation by the Kremlin of a policy of duplicity, involving subversion which utilized terrorist tactics when they were deemed expedient for its power projection.

Between 1920 and 1936 Spain had been a bubbling political battle-ground which eventually afforded the Comintern room for manoeuvre. The propaganda activities of the Spanish Communist Party were assiduously implemented, either directly by the Party itself of through the Comintern, and these were sporadically laced with occasional assassination plans and incitement to terrorist acts. The decisions for which activities were to be implemented rested squarely on the men from Moscow. As early as 1931 the Kremlin instructed the Comintern in Spain that the 'crisis should be prolonged in order to prevent the firm establishment of the republican regime, to frustrate the possibilities of effective social revolution, and where possible [to] create soviets'.[57]

To achieve these goals, Vittorio Codovilla, the Comintern agent in Spain at the time, was joined by one of the most experienced professional revolutionaries. His name was 'Stepanov', also known elsewhere as Lebedev, Dr Chavarouche and Lorenzo Vanini.[58] These two men, together with the powerful Anti-Fascism and Popular Front movements which had been gaining momentum during those years, were to have an enormous influence on the still small and weak Spanish Communist Party. And it was at this early juncture that the Soviet Union involved itself in the Basque and Catalan national questions. The Catalans had already been employing terrorist methods through a group called the *escamots*, headed by Miguel Badia; and the Basques, who were staunchly nationalist and Catholic, began their incongruous alliance with the left. Weapons and ammunition were soon landed in Asturias. In retrospect, the uprising which ensued demonstrated all the classical burgeoning signs of a civil war in the making. A substantial co-operation had taken place in Asturias between the Communists, Anarchists, Socialists, the Workers' and Peasants' Alliance and other groups, all of them supported by the ECCI which had been calling for this joint action.[59] This action included terrorist attacks on 'bourgeois' targets: churches, convents, businessmen and priests - all civilian targets.

However, a long war of attrition was more in the interest of the Kremlin than a decisive victory of either side. On 23 August 1936 Stalin in fact signed the Non-Intervention Agreement with Britain and France. This agreement was to bring about a *rapprochement* of these two countries with the USSR which Stalin was most anxious to achieve in view of Hitler's threatening and competitive rise.

The official policy of that agreement forbade any further arms shipments to Spain. However, clandestine shipments by Stalin continued. This demonstrated once again a dual-level policy decision. On the one hand, Stalin did not want the Soviet Union to appear to be against the revolution, as that position would contradict the Kremlin's ideology and weaken its credibility. On the other hand, he did not want to antagonize the French whom he needed on his side. So he took both options.[60]

Alexander Orlov, who defected to the United States and testified to the Senate Internal Security Sub-Committee,[61] confirmed that he had been sent to Spain as an agent for the NKVD (People's Commissariat of Internal Affairs), and that his role there was to advise on 'intelligence, counter-intelligence, and guerrilla fighting'.

Throughout the conflict, Comintern agents never shirked using terrorist methods when they deemed them appropriate. Orlov, in his testimony, named Konev, later to become Marshal of the Soviet Union, as having actually trained terrorists in Spain. In addition, he mentioned another Russian under his command who directed sabotage and guerrilla war in nationalist territory. This was

Eitingon, whose mistress was Caridad Mercader del Rio, a name which was to resound around the world when Trotsky was later assassinated by her son in Mexico. This son was ultimately decorated by the Kremlin for his deed.

During the civil war, the French Communist Party organized big campaigns, demonstrations and collections for 'Aid to Republican Spain', and helped in the clandestine dispatch of arms to the Spanish Republicans,[62] a role which was to be assigned to it many times subsequently.

The Soviet government took a further measure to dissociate the Kremlin from Comintern arms trafficking. An agent for the NKVD, a man called Zimin, went to The Hague for a meeting with Krivitsky, the 'resident' military intelligence officer for the Soviet Union. The aim was, as Zimin presented the case, to set up a separate organization explicitly for the purchase of weapons in Europe. An NKVD member was to be a silent partner controlling the funds of this organization. In this way and through this vehicle arms were gathered from Czechoslovakia, France, Poland, Holland and even Germany.[63] This organizational structure was to be employed on many other occasions.

Concurrently, the Comintern became engrossed in setting up what came to be known as the 'International Brigade'.[64] The recruiting call for the formation of this group was to turn Spain into the graveyard of European fascism - a cause which naturally appealed to young liberals from all over the Western world. The Soviet Union, however, had never abandoned during this time the idea of an alliance with Nazi Germany. In fact, secret meetings exploring that possibility had been taking place between Germany and the USSR since 1934.[65]

One of the most interesting examples, with remarkable similarity to recent events in Central and South America, is provided by the USSR's behaviour in Uruguay and Brazil in the 1930s. On 27 December 1935 the Minister of Foreign Affairs of Uruguay handed a Decree to the Soviet Minister, M. Minkin, severing diplomatic relations with the Soviet government. The cause of the diplomatic break was cited as available hard evidence of Soviet involvement in certain seditious movements which had led to an outbreak of revolutionary violence in Brazil. The violence had apparently been instigated and financed by the Soviet government through the intermediary of the Soviet legation at Motevideo.[66] The Soviet press reaction to this breaking off of relations was exceedingly offensive and at times childish in its language. For example, *Pravda* stated that Soviet public opinion would recognize in the decision of the government of Uruguay a manifestation of forces inimical to the preservation of world peace. The Montevideo press, the paper said, was apparently engaged in rehashing the old nonsense about the 'hand of Moscow' in the revolutionary movements which had been disturbing the South American continent. The real reason for the break, Pravda and Izvestiya both wrote, was the fact that Uruguay was anxious to sell cheese to the USSR and would be willing not to be sensitive to 'anti-Soviet agitation' should such a trade materialize. This the press called an 'odoriferous piece of blackmail!'

However, M. Masanès, the Uruguayan Chargé d'Affaires in Moscow, went to see Viscount Chilston at the British embassy and was able to confirm the evidence which the Uruguayan government had at hand which linked the Soviet Union, not only to the unrest in Brazil, but also in Argentina and possibly to embryonic subversive movements in Uruguay itself. Montevideo was in fact the main focus of Soviet intrigue in South America.[67]

The denials of the Soviet government notwithstanding, the evidence was there. During the Seventh Congress of the Comintern which was held in Moscow in 1935, all speakers were agreed on the adoption of new fighting tactics, which entailed the alliance of communism with other advanced parties, even if they were not communist, to form a united front with the purpose of assisting the cause of international communism. This decision gave rise to what came to be known as the Popular Front. The new tactic would emphasize diplomatic transactions with advanced governments, even if they were not supported by communist parties. This, of course, is indicative of a continuity of thought and policy since the same notions were advanced by Lenin earlier. The Latin American delegates proudly reported on the progress of communist activities in their respective countries and particular mention was made of the Brazilian Communist Party's establishment of the 'Alliança Nacional Libertadora' headed by Luis Carlos Prestes.

The revolt against the government of Getulio Vargas of Brazil was led by Prestes who had recently returned from four years of study and training in the Soviet Union. Evidence of large monetary transfers from the Soviet legation in Montevideo to the Brazilian insurgents was presented as part of the evidence justifying the Uruguayan severing of relations.[68]

The official reactions by the Soviet government to the breaking of relations by Uruguay were virulent. M. Minkin, in a letter to Dr Espalter, denied any responsibility for the Comintern's activities 'as there exists no interdependence whatever' between the Soviet government and that body. He declared as false the accusations of Soviet help, through the Soviet legation in Montevideo, to other communist parties to foment any struggle.[69] However, Mr Millington-Drake, transmitting the details to Mr Eden at the

Foreign Office, referred to several memoranda regarding Soviet agents' activities in Montevideo and generally throughout South America.[70] Viscount Chilston, reviewing the reaction from the Moscow British embassy, pointed out that the general line presented in the Soviet press that 'the Soviet Government have, in the past, yielded out of courtesy to the importunate wooing of the Uruguayan Government', was irreconcilable with the facts. While Uruguayan interests in the Soviet Union had been left in the care of a 'junior secretary with no staff, the Soviet Government have maintained in Uruguay a Legation out of all proportion to the commercial or avowable political importance of that country . . .'.[71]

The Soviet government's official policy of dissociating itself from the world revolutionary movement to favour pragmatic necessities was reiterated by Stalin himself in 1936 during an interview conducted by the *New York Times*. When asked whether the original Soviet plans of bringing about a world revolution had been abandoned, Stalin replied: 'We never had such plans and intentions'.[72] This image, of a friendly peace-loving nation that has given up trouble-making, which Stalin was struggling to create for the USSR abroad was now successfully emerging in the perception of a Western world anxious to avoid war at all costs, and looking for Moscow's support as an ally if war with Hitler became inevitable.

There remained, however, the reality of the Comintern. The French government admitted that it was aware of the fact that Soviet Russia was using the Comintern to fulfil its own military and strategic purposes. The French Ambassador in Moscow, Monsieur Coulondre, urged the American Ambassador, Joseph Davies, to make allowances for the Soviets' need of the Comintern as a military necessity, an interesting notion given the overt tactical shift towards paramilitary emphasis made by the Politburo in the late 1950s and early 1960s. He even suggested that the Radek-Trotsky trial which was under way 'might make it easier for Russia to "cool off" on the Comintern because Trotsky would draw all the radicals'.[73]

Prior to his departure from Moscow, and subsequent to the Soviet-German Pact of 23 August 1937, Ambassador Davies wrote his final report to the Secretary of State, Cordell Hull. This report made a direct reference to the Soviet role in the Comintern. There was no longer any question that the Stalin government used the world revolutionary movement as an expedient agency for its military defence, he said. Stalin showed 'some disposition . . . to minimize its interest in world revolutionary movements'; and then Ambassador Davies went on to add what would become the basis of Western conceptualization of Soviet foreign policy behaviour which totally ignored the credo which propelled it: the fact that the

Stalin government did use the Comintern was 'in direct relation to its apprehensions of danger from military attack of the aggressor nations [referring to Germany]'. In terms of the United States' vital interest, Davies evaluated the Comintern problem as being purely academic.[74]

There are indications that acceptance by the West of the existence of the Soviet insecurity paranoia was in part a carefully cultivated syndrome by the Kremlin. Initially, Pavel Ivanovich Selianinov, alias Edward Alexander Opperput-Upelinz, was in effect an *agent provocateur* who was instrumental in the destruction of Boris Savinkov's anti-Soviet group - the People's Union for Defence of Country and Freedom. In November 1921 he reappeared as an OGPU operative setting up the MOR (Monarkhicheskoe Obedenenie Rossii) better known as the Monarchist Confederation of Russia. Then in 1927, now a defecting member of the CHEKA, he disclosed the tactic,[75] which was initiated by the Kremlin setting up an organization calling itself the Anti-Soviet Group, perhaps an antecedent of what was later to develop into a specialized department of the KGB in the 1960s for the explicit purpose of sowing disinformation (*dezinformatsiya*):

> Further there were employed some forty other Cheke officials who contrived to carry on work between the said organization [Anti-Soviet Group] and foreign intelligence bureaux and genuine anti-Soviet organizations in Russian, which have hitherto not been liquidated, *it being in the interest of the Soviet authorities to convey the impression abroad of the existence of serious anit-Soviet conspiracy* . . . (Emphasis added)

The Kremlin, in fact, had even used terrorist tactics to accomplish this imagery. As an undercover agent, Opperput visited Finland where he got in touch with leaders of anti-Bolshevik groups and stirred them to commit terrorist acts. At least two parties of White Russian terrorists organized by him crossed the Finnish frontier into the USSR where they were caught and shot by Bolsheviks.[76]

The idea of perpetual danger, based on the modern diplomatic conerstone of the notion of self-defence, was to allow the USSR to legitimize any aggressive behaviour which it cared to undertake. This same notion was to be invoked forty years later when Soviet tanks invaded Afghanistan in 1979 'to secure its southern borders', as it had been invoked by Stalin when he went as far as to attribute a defensive nature to Hitler's unprovoked aggressions in 1939-41.

As a final gesture of appeasement to the West, and particularly in the light of Hitler's surprise attack on the USSR in 1941 and his greater need to remove the stumbling block to his treaty ambitions and reach a 'spheres of influence' agreement with the Allies, Stalin officially disbanded the Comintern on 15 May 1943. Ironically, what had been established in 1919 'to organize joint action by the proletariat of the different countries which presume the one goal: the overthrow of capitalism, the establishment of the dictatorship of the proletariat and of an international Soviet republic . . .' was now being dissolved in order to facilitate 'joint action' between the first Soviet state and the very same capitalistic countries it aimed to destroy. And, of course, the mere fact that the Comintern could be dissolved by Stalin automatically implied the control by the CPSU over that organization which it had so consistently denied.

Stalin gave the following reasons for his spuriously momentous decision during an interview by Reuter's correspondent in Moscow:[77]

> The dissolution of the Communist International is proper and timely because it facilitates the organization of the common onslaught of all freedom loving nations against the common enemy - Hitlerism. The dissolution of the Communist International is proper because
> (a) It exposes the lie of the Hitlerites to the effect that 'Moscow' allegedly intends to intervene in the life of other nations and to 'Bolshevize' them. An end is now being put to this lie.
> (b) It exposes the calumny of the adversaries of Communism within the labour movement to the effect that Communist Parties in various countries are allegedly acting not in the interests of their people but on orders from outside. And end is now being put to this calumny too.

Most remarkably, the dissolution of the Third Communist International was not challenged by any of the communist parties, a fact which has been attributed to the extreme control exercised over those parties by the Soviets.[78] In general, the communist parties saw this dissolution as a *ruse de guerre*. There is evidence which suggests that the Comintern merely went underground and was held in abeyance for better days to come. The role of the ECCI was taken over directly, if not publicly, by the Central Committee of the CPSU, in what was eventually to become the International Department, thus allowing the Soviet Party to satisfy and adjust its needs to this high politico-military strategy,[79] and ensuring that it remain monolithic.

The war years saw no change or decline in the use of terrorist tactics by the Soviet Union, and neither did the years which followed the cosmetic dissolution of the Comintern. In 1940 the

British government received information about an international centre for sabotage set up in Moscow which was training individuals for terrorist work in belligerent as well as neutral countries in an attempt to transform the war raging at the time into a civil war in each individual country thus facilitating its eventual seizure by the USSR.[80] In 1941 the Swedish press publicized a report by the Copenhagen police which indicated the discovery in Denmark of an extensive communist terrorist organization directed and subsidized by Moscow.[81] In a follow-up to that information, the leader of the terrorist group was named as E. Wollweber, former Communist member of the Reichstag, who became a Soviet citizen. After his arrest in Sweden the Soviet Union asked for his extradition for fear of his revealing any incriminating facts about Soviet activities in Germany during the Soviet-Nazi *rapprochement* period. Finally, unable to have him extradited, the USSR tried him *in absentia* on a trumped-up charge of forgery and condemned him to seven years' hard labour. The Kremlin then reiterated its extradition demands to the Swedish government on the ground that he was a Soviet condemned criminal, a fugitive from justice. After the outbreak of the Soviet-German war the USSR apparently lost interest in the man.[82]

Although most of the activity undertaken by these groups was part of the overall Soviet war strategy and its takeover plans, terrorism against civilian targets was often part of the preliminaries, as a tactic to achieve a sense of unrest and general panic among the civilian population. The Red Army, however, was the main vehicle for takeovers in Eastern Europe (the Baltic states annexation, Tannu Tuva formally annexed in 1944, the seizure of Carpatho-Ukraine, Poland, Czechoslovakia, and so on).[83] When he could, however, Stalin avoided the use of naked aggressive force and encouraged the use of alternative methods to camouflage his real intentions until the takeover was an accomplished fact.

In the countries of Western Europe the partisans, the *maquis*, which formed to fight the Nazis, were heavily infiltrated and exploited, and the automatic assumption that partisans by being anti-fascist were in fact pro-communist and therefore 'good' - with the opposite corollary that if one was anti-communist that meant one must be a fascist - became the vanguard psychological weapon which was so skilfully exploited that the Western liberal democracies are still saddled with this fatuous notion.

In this connection, the legal position of partisan fighters was presented by Colonel A. I. Poltorak before the Council of the Military Academy of Law in 1949. The theme discussed was consistent with Marxist-Leninist-Stalinist theories of 'just' and 'unjust' wars. Colonel Poltorak described a partisan movement as a powerful weapon in the hands of a people fighting for its independence, and by applying his ideological matrix he further maintained that history had shown that partisan movements only emerged when a nation was fighting a 'just war against an aggressor'.[84] Thus, he reserved that type of paramilitary, or unconventional, approach for the exclusive use of the 'progressive forces of peace', namely, the USSR.

The USSR's short- and long-term strategic goals had been very clearly specified in an agreement with Hitler. These were as follows:[85]

(1) That German troops are immediately withdrawn from Finland which . . . belongs to the Soviet Union's sphere of influence.
(2) That within the next few months the security of the Soviet Union in the straits is assured by the conclusion of a mutual assistance pact between the USSR and Bulgaria . . . and the establishment of a base for land and naval forces by the Soviet Union within range of the Bosphorus and Dardanelles by means of a long-term lease.
(3) That the area south of Batum and Baku in the *general direction of the Persian Gulf* is recognized as the center of *aspirations* of the Soviet Union (Emphasis added)
(4) That Japan renounce her rights to concessions for coal and oil in Northern Sakhalin.

For example, captured documents retrieved by the Finns after the defeat of Russian troops in the Second World War indicated that Soviet hopes for the eventual conquering of Europe formed part of the strategic long-term goals, and garrison roles for Soviet troops were listed, to be effected after the takeover of Finland. The standard of the Red Army 18th Division operating north of Lake Ladoga depicted an embroidered map of Europe with a Soviet dagger reaching into its heart.[86]

How the Soviet Union would go about achieving these goals varied greatly, depending on specific events or conditions at any given time and place. Evidence to suggest that the Soviets never abandoned their policy of using terrorist methods as part of their overall strategy, or instigating others to use such methods for the Soviet Union's benefit, fills the pages of the British Foreign Office declassified documents, and even a brief scanning of the Washington Archives reveals the presence of similar evidence there. These activities were never localized in any particular area of the globe, and as a matter of fact, given the technical difficulties of travel in the 1920s and 1930s particularly, one has to marvel at their global span. However, to the British Foreign Office, at any event, they appeared to be haphazard and disconnected events. The intensity and specific venue changed along the lines of least resistance.

It is important to note that though most of these subversive activities did not always and at all times culminate in the expected revolutions, the incidents did take place nevertheless. In 1925 the USSR sold arms to Afghan tribes[87] and perpetrated terrorist acts in Persia[88] for example. In 1926 there was evidence of a Soviet policy of absorbing Afghanistan, where the Russians were already in control of the air force.[89] In the same year terrorist plans to assassinate various prominent personalities in Bulgaria came to light.[90] In 1928 the Soviet Consul of Ahwaz directly and personally organized acts of violence.[91] munitions were sent to Mexico[92] and Soviet rifles were sent to communists in Persia.[93] In 1929 there were Soviet attempts to instigate a civil war in Yugoslavia.[94]

The years which followed the dissolution of the Comintern and the end of the Second World War did not reflect any alteration in this type of behaviour. The dissolution itself was part of the official policy of duplicity which had been followed by Stalin. In fact, as early as 1944, there were already rumours suggesting that the USSR was about to replace the Third International by the International Labour Organization.[95] And Victor Kravchenko, an important defector to the West, described the continuing functions of the Comintern in the same year.[96] Although none of these activities seems to have been very successful, interest in the technique persisted.

In 1947 Soviet behaviour during the Middle East conflict was to indicate a continuity in multiple-level manipulations which involved the supply of weapons to terrorist groups in both Egypt and Palestine, as well as maintaining diplomatic and commerical intercourse with Great Britain. In a secret memorandum from the British Foreign Office, the Soviet position in Egypt at the time was evaluated as being non-committal and ambivalent. The Soviets presented themselves as the self-proclaimed protectors of colonized peoples and oppressed minorities. At the United Nations, during the heated and emotional developments surrounding the issue of the formation of the State of Israel, the Soviet Union weakly denied rumours which ran through the corridors of the United Nations building that it had in fact undertaken to support Egypt in its appeal against the formation of that state. The USSR subsequently did vote in favour of the establishment of the State of Israel and was the second member, after the United States, to extend diplomatic recognition to it. However, the background to the behaviour of the Soviet Union in that particular conflict provides a picture of both an ambivalent and a duplicitous policy, which closely paralleled the one it had followed during the civil war in Spain just over a decade earlier. Long before the establishment of the State of Israel the decision was taken by the Kremlin to support both the Palestinian Arabs and the Jews in violent rebellion against the British. Czechoslovak weapons were supplied to both the Jewish Agency and the Palestinians.[97] There were at least two practical and immediate reasons which prompted the Soviets in that decision: (1) the ousting of Britain as a colonial power was the most pressing short-term goal they had in the aftermath of the Second World War; (2) by keeping a modicum of input into both, or rather all three, sides of the conflict, they would attempt to establish Soviet influence as a major power in the Middle East area - influence which, up until 1947, had been at a very minimal level. This, in fact, suggests a contradiction of the traditional view which maintains that Soviet official diplomatic pro-Arab policy was not established until 1955 with the signing of the Egypt-Czechoslovakia arms deal. That date more likely established the first successful bid for influence in the Middle East rather than a new direction in its policy. There was evidently already a supplying of Czechoslovak arms to Egypt by 1949 when there was an official complaint on the matter by the government of Israel to the British government.[98]

The Soviet Union's lack of prestige in the Middle East until 1947 did not reflect a lack of activity in the area. As early as 1929 the Russians had actively supported the Mufti's Rebellion and between 1935 and 1939 they had supported other fragmentary groups and were directly involved in political assassinations.[99] Their more recent infiltration into the Mediterranean area of the Middle East had been gradual, initially with the successes in the Balkan states and Albania, and then with attempts at creating disturbances in Greece by supplying weapons to Greek terrorist groups.[100] In the same year, 1947, the Soviets harboured terrorists from Persian Azerbaidjian and gave their leader, Pishavari, facilities to broadcast against the Persian government from a station describing itself as 'Azerbaidjian Democratic Radio'.[101] In 1945 there had been evidence of Russian troop involvement in providing weapons to the insurgents in that same province of Iran.[102] *Izvestiya* had, however, called those reports 'scandalous rumours' spread to conceal 'the real nature of the Democratic movement in northern Iran and to divert attention from Palestine and the uprisings in Egypt'.[103]

None of these events can be viewed in a vacuum, however. While aid was being given to the Greek terrorists, the Kremlin was applying pressure on Turkey to allow the Soviet Union to establish military bases in the Dardanelles Straits; and in Hungary, Bulgaria and Romania, opposition to communist control was being ruthlessly suppressed.[104]

The policy of the Soviet Union in the summer of 1947 was clear: a drive to speed up the assimilation of Eastern Europe to bring it uniformly into the Soviet grip, became intensified, particularly after the introduction of the Marshall Plans. This was, in effect, a 'clearing the decks' operation to enable the Soviet Union to intensify its campaign to bring Greece into the Soviet orbit. The Balkan Commission established by the United Nations Security Council accumulated massive evidence of Soviet and other satellite support for the terrorists in Greece. Gromyko spent thunderous hours at the United Nations delivering vituperative cliches about 'foreign intervention' and using delaying tactics, making it very clear that the Soviet Union would not agree to any effective action which was liable to curb aid to the Greek rebels in practice.[105] That Stalin then made a turnaround decision to stop that support does not negate the former behaviour and only underscores the basic idiosyncratic lack of interest in the 'cause' of the various groups the Kremlin chooses to support at any given time. 'The uprising in Greece has to fold up' (*svernut'*) was the word used, meaning literally 'to roll up').[106] Again demonstrating the flexibility inherent in his foreign policy approach, Stalin made a pragmatic decision. The Soviet Union had no navy to speak of and Stalin had frequently stressed that the United States was the most powerful country in the world and would never permit interference in the Mediterranean. Any confrontation which would now endanger the position already acquired by the Kremlin in the aftermath of the Second World War was to be avoided. At least officially, peaceful respite for purposes of consolidation was to be ensured. However, the unofficial level of Soviet involvements plodded on.

On 2 November 1949 the Norwegian steamer 'Dovro' left Gydnia (Gdansk) bound for Djibouti via the Suez Canal. Its cargo comprised 275 tons of arms and ammunition and 275 tons of machinery and tools, all from the Skoda factory in Czechoslovakia. There had been several earlier shipments from Gdynia in 1948. For example, the SS *Lechistan* left for Albania on 12 January with 300 tons of small arms on board, shipped by the Polish War Department and manifested as 'wire nails'. On 15 January another similar load was put aboard the SS *Opole*, followed by the SS *Oryanfall* with 1,200 tons of munitions destined for Djibouti as well. By the end of the month of April, regular shipments of arms and ammunition were leaving Gydnia for the Eastern Mediterranean on four ships: the *Opole*, the *Lewant*, the *Leschistan* and the *Olsztyn*. All these arms were new and of Czechoslovak origin. While the information received by the Foreign Office indicated that most of these arms were destined for Albania as part of the assistance given to the Greek rebels by the Soviet Union, some shipments were reported to be destined for Kenya (perhaps via Djibouti), Palestine and Egypt. Russian officers working with Albanian labour were seen taking over these arms at the port of Durazzo. Ethiopia, as a sovereign state, had been a regular recipient of Iron Curtain arms on an official trade level, but it was now thought that Djibouti was a contact point for the dispatching of arms to Kenya. There had in fact been confirmation earlier in the year[107] of preparation for a 'rising' in Kenya which ultimately became the Mau Mau rebellion that successfully ousted the British from the colony.

A thread of information on the Czechoslovak connection can be traced through the available declassified information. There were, for example, subversive activities by the Czechoslovak Consul in the Belgian Congo.[108] The subsequent activities of the Soviet Union in that conflict and its official position at the United Nations were suggestive of a multiple-level offensive.

Czechoslovak arms surfaced again in a most incongruous context. This fascinating bit of evidence, for which little elaboration is available owing to the retention by the Foreign Office of the pertinent files out of public view even though the thirty years *de rigueur* are over, shows a shipment of Czechoslovak arms which was destined for the French Communist Party (PCF) and refused transit through Switzerland.[109] At that time, in 1950, the French government was already having problems in Algeria. We saw earlier that the French Communist Party was used as a channel for arms distribution during the Spanish Civil War. Although the answer to the enigma of the Czechoslovak arms shipment may not be revealed for many years to come, we can speculate that the French Communist Party was again used as a conduit by the Soviet Union, although to date there has been no evidence of direct involvement of the Party in the carrying out of actual terrorist acts.[110]

More Czechoslovak arms were reported in Central America. The information, confirmed at the time by the United State embassy in Guatemala, reported that vessels were running Czechoslovak arms from Mexican Gulf ports to Puerto Barrios or its vicinity. It was thought that these arms were destined for the Caribbean Legion, a terrorist group operating from Poptum, Guatemala, in 1950, which was stirring up trouble in that area of the world. The group had in fact planned a *coup* to take over British Honduras.[111]

Soviet behaviour on the official level changed in the immediate aftermath of the war from a relatively co-operative position to a non-co-operative and distinctly aggressive one. Yalta was a political and military victory for Stalin which would allow him this more aggressive an arbitrary behaviour towards the West, his erstwhile allies. He would now overtly move his country to unilateral action. The immediate cause of this official change of policy was the atomic bomb, and the confrontational stand between the USSR and the United States. The disintegration of the European imperial systems provided the power vacuums necessary for more aggressive action and a scramble to assert influence around the world. The USSR thus reverted to official, overt, revolutionary rhetoric and behaviour. What was perceived by the West as a change of policy was in fact merely a change of tactics. It was a continuation of the old with greater emphasis placed on the revolutionary subversive side which had been camouflaged by the dissolution of the Comintern. Until the death of Stalin on 5 March 1953, there was to be no change in that approach.

The Khrushchev Era

Although generally regarded as a period of disengagement from worldwide conflict by the USSR, the Khrushchev era (1953-64) - the era of 'peaceful coexistence' - was marked by several major confrontations between the Soviet Union and the United States. The two Berlin crises of 1958-9 and 1961 were followed by the ultimate crisis over the Cuban missiles in 1962. The first major revolutions of the peoples in Eastern Europe were also to mark this period when Hungary and Poland would both see the Red Army crushing a people's revolution for the first time in the post-war era.

In retrospect, Khrushchev's foreign policy exemplified a seemingly constant typology which can be identified in Lenin's as well as Stalin's leaderships: a 'roller-coaster' approach varying between unexpected aggressiveness and an unexpected retreat to accommodation with the West. To a large extent the emphasis placed on 'peaceful coexistence' was a direct result of an understanding that a nuclear war would mean devastating losses on both sides.

At the Twentieth Party Congress in 1956, perceived by the West as a turning point in Soviet historical development, Khrushchev delivered his famous 'Secret Speech' which appeared to revise the Soviet Communist concept of the inevitability of war with capitalism and accept non-violent parliamentary means to attain power as an alternative method in certain cases. The 'struggle' for the pre-ordained victory of socialism (Khrushchev used socialism and communism interchangeably) was to continue, however, on all levels, including the resort to violence, if necessary. From the

Kremlin's point of view, 'peaceful coexistence' was the prohibition of the West's 'export of counter-revolution'. This was, in essence, the reiteration of the Marxist-Leninist concept of the 'just war' which stated that revolutionary wars were the only 'just wars' and therefore the only acceptable ones.

There was, therefore, nothing in that concept which indicated a major change of policy. 'Peaceful coexistence' was a new semantic deviation used to describe the Party 'line' based on Marxist-Leninist dialectical materialism. Stalin had already presented this burgeoning dialogue, when, in 1952, he announced that the danger of war had diminished and that the likelihood of a war between capitalist countries was greater than between capitalism and socialism.[112]

With the cataclysmic ending of the Second World War, a new perception of future wars and what they would mean in years to come emerged in the Soviet Union and ushered in the new rhetoric, a direct result of the pragmatic needs and fears of the USSR. The damages of the war years and the internal terror and blood-bath the Soviet Union had endured created the necessity for a recovery period.

Moreover, the dimensions of power changed internationally with the splintering of the old colonial empires and the emergence of the Third World as a new contender for power in world politics.[113] In fact, Soviet foreign policy from 1956 onwards seemed to avoid direct confrontations in Europe and concentrated almost exclusively on this Third World, thus extending official Soviet influence from a European dimension to a global one.

Krushchev did not, however, initiate any changes in the concept of Marxist-Leninist global communism. In 1956 he brought the new rhetoric to doctrinal level. The new realities of communist parties freeing themselves from the USSR abroad, such as Tito's broad popular victory in Yugoslavia, were a major contributory factor to the new Soviet definitions of international politics as well. The authority of the Soviet Union over the world revolutionary movement was in question and the strategy for action had to be restated to account for all these changes.

Stalin had based his belief that world revolution would best be achieved through traditional war on his immense successes in establishing communism in Eastern Europe, mainly through the use of the Red Army, although his subversive uses of terrorism were never abandoned.

Khrushchev, even before his famous Secret Speech, argued, on the other hand, that because of the development of weapons of mass destruction, traditional war between the two antagonistic systems was now unthinkable. The concept of 'peaceful coexistence' was therefore introduced as a tactical stratagem to meet the psychological imperatives of the moment. The 'forces of peace' were now seen by Khrushchev as being *within* the capitalist system and not in a confrontational stand from without. Thus, it would be essential to mobilize an armed proletariat to achieve the ultimate goal of global communism and avoid a head-on collision with the United States in particular. In essence, the term 'peaceful coexistence' was interchangeable with 'cold war' and *détente*, as they all reflected the Kremlin's view of international politics: any action on its own part, whether in war or peace (Western concepts of this status), is permissible, including the use of violence, in order to achieve its 'righteous' political goals; no action, on the other hand, is permissible on the part of 'capitalist and imperialist Western nations', for such action is described as counter-revolutionary and therefore inadmissible. In other words, the new semantics deny the preservation of the international status quo since they anticipate the demise of the capitalist system by the sacred advance of communism. As an example of this attitude by the Kremlin, the surreptitious transfer of offensive missiles to Cuba in 1962 was an attempt by Khrushchev to change the status quo, and the ensuing strong reaction by the United States which resulted in the removal of those missiles was attacked by the Kremlin as an agressive act.[114]

The rationale for the seemingly new policy was the immediate pragmatic need for consolidation internally and expansion externally to adjust the balance of power which, in view of the nuclear advantage enjoyed by the United States, was seen by the Kremlin as not being in its favour. The justification for the allegedly new theoretical formulation was Marxist-Leninist dogma.

Stalin had quoted Lenin to justify his own flexible pragmatic decisions which were often carried out at the expense of the immediate revolutionary goals of other communist parties:[115]

> To carry on a war for the overthrow of the international bourgeoisie, a war which is a hundred times more difficult, protracted and complicated than the most stubborn of ordinary wars between states, and to refuse beforehand to maneuver, to utilize the conflict of interests (even though temporary) among one's enemies, to refuse to temporize and compromise with possible (even though transient, unstable, vacillating and conditional) allies - is not this ridiculous in the extreme? Is it not the same as if in the difficult ascent of an unexplored and heretofore inaccessible mountain we were to renounce beforehand the idea that at times we might have to zig-zag, sometimes retracing our steps, sometimes giving up the course once selected and trying various others?

Once again he emphasized, just as Lenin had done, his own abhorrence of individual action as opposed to action initiated and organized by the CPSU. In *The Foundations of Leninism* he argued against what he called the '"theory" of spontaneity'. This, he said, 'actually repudiates the leading role of the vanguard of the working class, the party of the working class', that is, the CPSU or himself, as he chose.

This in no way contradicted what Lenin had said, although the motivations were certainly different. Lenin, obsessed with power and control for himself, devised a centralized power structure which extended to all revolutionary duties. He thus devised a Party apparatus which would ensure that control. Stalin, by all accounts suffering from acute paranoia,[116] found that centralization much to his satisfaction and saw no reason not to reinforce Lenin's notions against 'spontaneity' and 'individual action'.

Khrushchev's policies until his ousting in 1964 reflected a similar approach to compromise and pragmatic decisions while shifting emphasis away from state-to-state confrontations on to internal turmoil, even civil wars. Thus, restating Lenin's views on civil wars which he had always seen as inevitable in a capitalist society because they took place between 'exploiters' and 'exploited', Khrushchev emphasized the dimension of the *armed proletariat*, as Lenin had done, especially in 1917.

Khrushchev's era, in terms of the application of this notion of 'peaceful coexistence', can be viewed in retrospect as a period of transition. His foreign policy, like that of his predecessors, was a multifaceted one which kept all options open and often resulted in the confrontational crises he purportedly wanted to avoid. The ultimate attempt rapidly to shift the balance of power in favour of the Soviet Union with the missiles in Cuba was the closest call to a nuclear confrontation between the United States and the USSR. The resulting failure of that approach caused a tactical shift, with a retreat back to accommodation with the West and a reassessment of procedures in the search for a 'softer' target.

To carry out his new approaches and rapid expansionism, Khrushchev did not alter the internal organizational structure of the Party apparatus, but generally reinforced it, returning it to its pre-May 1941 form.[117] The centralization of power which Lenin had initiated and Stalin had consolidated was to remain as the only working mechanism for decision-making. There was to be no democracy. The Party and its leadership were to have the final decision. The CPSU was to remain the executor and decision-maker in all foreign policy issues. This remained true for the military methodology as well.[118]

This leading hierarchical role of the Party was repeatedly

emphasized. In a *Pravda* article of 6 July 1956, the following appeared: 'As for our country, the CP was, is, and will be the only ruler of thought, the inspirer of ideas and aspirations, the leader and organizer of the people in the entire course of their struggle for communism . . .' In an editorial in *Kommunist*, this was again explicitly stated: 'the CP stands above the USSR government in determining foreign policy . . .'.[119]

The concept of the struggle from *within* began to emerge, in its new emphasis and always within the context of the struggle between the two systems which would no longer lead to war between them. In his speech to the Twenty-first Party Congress, Khrushchev stated:[120]

> We act upon the principle that relations among states with different social systems must be based on peaceful coexistence. We and the ruling circles of the capitalist countries have different views, different outlooks. We shall never change our views and cherish no illusions that out class adversaries will change their ideology. But this does not mean we should go to war because of our divergent views. In each country it is the people themselves who determine their own destiny and choose the direction of their development . . .
>
> Now that a powerful socialist camp exists, now that the workers' movement has great experience in the struggle with reaction and the working class is better organized, the peoples have greater possibilities for blocking the advance of fascism.

The Minister of Defence, R. Ya. Malinovsky, reinforced this notion in his Congress speech on defence policy:[121]

> For the first time in history a social order has come into being in which the working people are the true masters of their destinies . . .
>
> Capitalism is on the wane. The peoples do not want to live under the constant threat of unemployment, poverty and wars . . . They are waging a resolute struggle for their liberation.

And in his speech to the USSR Supreme Soviet, Khrushchev again made the point:[122]

> No state borders can arrest the spread of the communist ideology . . .
>
> Communism will not be victorious in the sense that socialist countries will conquer other countries. No, the people of each country will . . . elect the more progressive form of society.

The KGB presence abroad was increased. Subversive activities abroad continued as before, and although the files at the Washington Archives and the Public Record Office on the Khrushchev era are not to be opened to the public for a number of years yet, there have been various revelations, through both open and intelligence sources, of continued subversive activities, many of these provided by defectors to the West: for example, the revelations by Petrov in 1954 of subversive activities conducted from the Soviet embassy in Canberra, and by Kaznacheev about KGB deeds in Rangoon, Burma.[123] In fact, terrorism had been a major part of Communist tactics in the Indo-China wars, both in the preliminary stages and during the wars. Village heads were murdered and hung in public view labelled as 'traitors' until no one was willing to take on the job of headman. Recruits for the guerrillas were also gathered by terrorist tactics of intimidation.[124] South-East Asia was in ferment in those years and terrorist activity was a daily occurrence in Laos, Siam (Thailand) and Vietnam before the devastating 'wars of liberation' were initiated. Although most of those terrorist tactics failed to achieve the victories which were expected, the policy of using such tactics was not abandoned when the conditions for their use were seen as favourable or expedient by the Kremlin. In fact, they often set the necessary conditions for the escalations which were to follow.

An example of duplicitous behaviour on the part of Khrushchev which differed little from his predecessors' was provided when the establishment of the new Provisional Government of the Republic of Algeria (GPRA) was declared. Khrushchev's policy was once again and predictably to follow a course which would allow him to keep his options open. Officially he remained aloof from the bloody revolutionary war which was raging against France. His calculations were pragmatic: there would be more to gain from not upsetting de Gaulle by extending such a recognition to the GPRA and exploiting the growing potential for disruption in the Western alliance. In 1958 the Kremlin was officially cool to the first delegation of the Front de Libération Nationale (FLN), but it was nevertheless received. The FLN, it might be remembered, was a nationalist, and not a Marxist, liberation movement. Surreptitiously, and contrary to the official posture, arms were shipped regularly to the FLN by the Soviet Union, although never at a level sufficient to turn it into an army. And the Algerian Communist Party (PCA), which was eventually disbanded on orders from Moscow, was mostly absorbed into the FLN in 1956, some of its members making the shift in membership secretly.[125] Terrorism was to become the effective technique of the FLN in the Algerian War.[126]

It was in connection with the FLN that the activities of Henri Curiel were first in evidence. Curiel, although illegally residing in France, conducted clandestine support operations for the FLN. He was one of the original founders of the Egyptian Communist Party (PCE) in the 1940s and would be seen again the context of international terrorism in Europe in the 1960s (as will be discussed in Chapter 5 of this study).

The Party programme adopted in October 1961 at the Twenty-Second Congress - the first such programme to be adopted since 1919 - emphasized the avoidance of a war between the superpowers and the use by the working class of both 'peaceful and non-peaceful, parliamentary and extra-parliamentary' means to achieve the victory of the revolution. Of the CPSU tasks in the field of international relations, three are worth quoting in this context:

(1)   To use, together with the other socialist countries, peaceful states and peoples, every means of preventing war and providing conditions for the complete elimination of war from the life of society,

(2)   To contribute in every way to the militant solidarity of all contingents and organizations of the international working class which oppose the imperialist policy of war,

(3)   Steadfastly to pursue a policy of consolidating all the forces fighting against war. All the organizations and parties that strive to avert war, the neutralist and pacifist movements and the bourgeois circles that advocate peace and normal relations between countries, will meet with understanding and support on the part of the Soviet Union.

This appeal to a wider public, to include the non-communist public, was to be greatly emphasized in the Brezhnev era and would indicate the application of a more sophisticated approach to the export of international communism, most probably a product of long institutional experience and a maturing leadership.

The increasingly large peace movement which has developed in the West recently alongside the plague of international terrorism must be assessed with Khrushchev's policies in mind. In a speech to the World Congress for General Disarmament and Peace held in Moscow on 10 July 1962, Khrushchev stated the Soviet perception of what the interrelationship between 'the struggle for disarmament and peace' and the 'struggle for national liberation' was to be:[127]

The Soviet attitude is clear and precise. There must be no people shackled with the chains of colonialism in Asia, Africa, Latin

America or any other area of the globe. All peoples must be free! There is a close interconnection between the struggle for national liberation and the struggle for disarmament and peace. The struggle for general disarmament facilitates the struggle for national independence. The achievements of the national liberation movement, in their turn, promote peace and contribute to the struggle for disarmament.

Conclusions

Although the historical evidence presented in this chapter is certainly not exhaustive, partly because a large quantity of material evidence has most certainly been weeded out of the files, and mainly because much information is still not available for public scrutiny, it does nevertheless provide sufficient evidence to support the description of ideological doctrinal structure and policies which shaped the realities of the Soviet state between 1917 and 1964. During that time the Soviet Union has displayed a continuity of attitude to the use of international terrorism, with shifting degrees of emphasis on its use as an instrument for the ultimate attainment of world revolution. These shifts have been in direct relation to its pragmatic needs at any given time and to its conceptualization of the power position it has held.

None of the writings of Marx, Lenin, Trotsky, or Stalin on the question suggests any abhorrence for the use of terrorist methods; for 'individual terrorism', yes, but not for organized and centrally controlled terror methods and groups. These are specifically encouraged. Western perceptions have more often than not erroneously interpreted this repugnance towards individual action as a repudiation by the Kremlin of all terrorism in principle. The individual act is anti-communist from the Soviet point of view and it is therefore logical that it would receive condemnation from above.

However, at no time between 1917 and 1964 did the Kremlin ever renounce the use of terrorism as a matter of principle and it was often seen to initiate, support and participate in revolutionary and sub-revolutionary terrorism. The Marxist-Leninist ideological matrix provided the legitimacy and flexibility it required for this behaviour, and vice versa. The structural apparatus necessary for the deployment of the terrorist approach was provided for, in the absence of a reliable and organized military structure of the new state, by zealous members of the CHEKA's Foreign Department, soon intermingled within the organizational set-up of the Third Communist International, which provided the necessary alternatives for Soviet power projection.

Lenin had set the seeds of an obsession with the concept of a paramilitary auxiliary which was to be controlled by himself. He had, in fact, viewed terrorist tactics as part of military strategy when he wrote very early in 1901 that 'we have never rejected terror on principle, nor can we ever do so, for that is one of those military actions which can be very useful and even indispensable in certain moments of battle'.[128]

In this respect, the Lenin, Stalin and Khrushchev periods can best be described respectively as:

(1) Lenin: period of initiation.
(2) Stalin: period of consolidation.
(3) Khrushchev: period of transition.

In direct relation to international challenges and shifting patterns of power politics abroad, the historical evidence presented here - on both official and unofficial levels - indicates a conscious shift of emphasis away from confrontational issues which might lead to nuclear devastation and towards an increased reliance on unofficial levels of activity. The ideological justification for this shift was presented by Khrushchev in 1956 and was to form the basis for the international behaviour of the Brezhnev era which followed. The growing interdependence of the world in general and the pressures of failing economies within the Eastern bloc were to be contributory factors in sustaining this policy.

The increased competition for raw materials was likely to be an important factor as well. High technological development in both armaments and the media was to increase the potential impact of a small group of terrorists with no concomitant risk of increased superpower confrontation. Combined strategies aimed at cumulative gains were to be implemented. Hence the Brezhnev era was to usher in a period of 'roller-coaster' diplomacy similar in tactics to the ones which preceded it even though Brezhnev lacked the bombastic style that characterized Khrushchev's approach. There was to be a marked emphasis on the exploitation of local conflicts through the use of surrogate forces. The main thrust of Soviet foreign policy in the Brezhnev era was to be a continuation of a global search for influence. Coincidental with this Soviet lateral strategic shift, the Western liberal democracies were to experience an unprecedented level of terrorist attack which, if analysed within the context of Soviet ideology and practice, does not prove contradictory to any previous orientation but, on the contrary, follows a certain logic.

Notes

1. For a comprehensive history of the CHEKA, see Leggett (1981).
2. Lenin, (1935-7) v. 27, pp. 296-7. See also seven telegrams by Lenin all of which advocate terror, Aug. 1918, in (1946-50) v. 35, pp. 287-293. For a more detailed discussion of the CHEKA in this connection, see Wolin and Slusser (eds) especially at pp. 3-9, 31-3, 373; also see Leggett (1981).
3. Quoted in Claudin (1975) p.35.
4. Von Laue in Craig and Gilbert (eds) (1953) p.246.
5. 6 March 1919. Degras, (ed.) (1956) p. 162.
6. *Ibid.* p. 38.
7. Gruber (1974) p. 252.
8. Degras (ed.) (1956) p. 167.
9. Secret letter from M. Hodgson, British Consular Section in Moscow to Foreign Office Marquess Curzon of Kedleston, FO 371/8170, N 476, 1922. Marquess Curzon of Kedleston was Parliamentary Under-Secretary of State for Foreign Affairs from June 1895 to Oct. 1898, and acted as Secretary of State for Foreign Affairs from Jan. 1919, during the absence of Mr Balfour, later the Earl of Balfour, at the Peace Conference in Paris, and was appointed to that office in Oct. 1919.
10. FO 371/8170, N 9302, SIS 2 Aug. 1922.
11. FO 371/8170, N 9302, SIS 22 June 1922.
12. FO 371/8170, N 9302, 12 Oct. 1922.
13. FO 371/8170, N 9302, Appendix A.
14. FO 371/8170, File 123, 1922. This letter indicates clearly approval of the terrorist act in the context of Ireland.
15. FO 371/8170, *ibid.*
16. Von Laue in Craig and Gilbert (eds) (1953) pp. 279-80.
17. Degras (1956) p. 162.
18. FO 371/8170, N 9302, SIS 19 May 1922. 'The Communist Party (of the Soviet Union), at any time in the future can cancel a treaty signed by the Soviet Government, terms of which are contrary to the principles of Communism. Moreover, the CP itself can be forced by the Third International to annul a treaty.' This statement by Vorovsky to Abdul Wahid, the Indian Revolutionary, indicates the hierarchy of power which existed at the time.
19. Russian reply, 27 Sept. 1921, in *British Government Blue Paper,* Cmnd. 2895 Russia No. 3 (1927), 'A Selection of Papers dealing with the relations between his Majesty's Government and the Soviet Government (1921-1927)', pp. 12-13.
20. FO 371/10478, N 5323, 25 June 1924.
21. Memorandum from the Belgian Embassy to the Foreign Office, FO 371/10478, 5 Sept. 1924.
22. The election of the Presidium of the ECCI was reported in Moscow on 10 July 1924. G. E. Zinoviev's name stands first on the list. MacManus figures as the English member. O. V. Kuusinen is first on the list of the organizing bureau. FO 371/10478, 29 Oct. 1924.
23. *British Government Blue Paper,* Cmnd. 2895, pp. 30-3.
24. FO 371/10478, 27 Oct. 1924.
25. FO 371/10841, E 4206, 1925.
26. No. 8 Archives, Persia Confidential, FO 371/10841, E 6935/81/34, 1925. Although this document does not specify who these Armenian Bolsheviks were, they were presumably Communists from Armenia who were assisting the Bolsheviks in their anti-British work. George Leggett mentions that there were Armenian Bolsheviks members of the Vecheka operating in Azerbaijan, Baku, and Armenia, (1981) p. 444.

27. FO 371/10841, E/4494/G, 31 July 1925.
28. FO 371/10666, C 5658/1142/7, 1925.
29. Also mentioned in a letter from William Peters of the British Mission, Moscow, to Mr. Austen Chamberlain, MP, 6 May 1925, FO 371/10666, C 7338.
30. Degras (ed.) (1960) p. 257.
31. *Ibid.* p. 212.
32. See for example FO 371/10478, 16 June 1924; also FO 371/10841, War Office, with reference to SIS reports No. CX 1722/1, dated 18 Dec. 1924 and 5 Jan. 1925.
33. Reported in *L'Avenir*, 10 April 1926. US Dept. of State, 1910-44, Sub. 403, 12 April, 1926, National Archives, Washington DC.
34. *The Times* (London), 13 May 1927.
35. *The Times* (London), 16 May 1927.
36. *The Times* (London), 14 May 1927.
37. *British Government Blue Paper,* Cmnd. 2895 Russia No. 3 (1927). Also see *The Times* (London), 26 May 1927.
38. Degras (1956) p. vi.
39. Eliava, 5 July 1927. Report to the Central Committee of the Third International, reproduced in *British Government Blue Paper,* Cmnd. 2895, p. 5.
40. *The Times* (London), 19 April 1927.
41. Kennan (1960) p. 253.
42. Lenin (1958-66) v. 6, pp. 1-192.
43. Claudin (1975) pp. 86-87; see also Gaucher (1974).
44. Sir. E. Ovey to Mr. A. Henderson, FO 371/15600, N 764/84/38, 1931.
45. FO 371/15600, N 3024 and N 3686/1970/38, 1931.
46. FO 371/15592, N 3435/4/38, N 3440/4/38, N 3793/4/38, 1931.
47. FO 371/15072, 1931. See FO 371/16332 for information regarding Comintern propaganda activities in 1932.
48. FO 371/15213, C 1740, 19 March 1931.
49. US Congress, *House Foreign Relations of the US 1933-39, Soviet Union,* Washington, 1952, pp. 25-37.
50. See Beloff (1947) v. 1, p. 126.
51. The comments by Gitlow are discussed in Browder (1953) p. 150. Cordell Hull mentions the incident in his *Memoires* (1948) p. 305.
52. See Degras (ed.) (1965).
53. For example in 1929: £167,600, and in 1930: £392,000. FO 371/15619, 1931. Also *Manchester Guardian,* 25 April 1931.
54. Extracts from the Soviet and White Russian Press, 1 Dec 1933, in FO 371/17246, N 9038/7/38, 1933. Regarding the Bolshevik record of terrorist activities in the Czarist period, Boris Souvarine mentions that 'while Lenin was penning his treatise on "partisan war", the terrorist phase of the first Russian revolution was reaching its peak. In October 1906 alone, 121 terror acts, 47 clashes between revolutionaries and the police, and 362 expropriations were reported.' See Souvarine (1935), p. 92.
55. Telegram from Sir E. Phipps, Vienna, 21 March 1933, FO 371/17247, N 1991/46/38, 1933.
56. FO 141/532. This document entitled 'Attempts by Soviet Union Government to introduce trained agents into Egypt' and appearing as J 8378/81/16 in FO 371/19067, was cut out from this last mentioned file. A second copy was found after some search in the files of the Home Office. The agent in question was named as Shaaban Hafex or Youssef Hamdan.
57. See Thomas (1979), pp. 120-1.
58. *Ibid.* p. 123
59. The ECCI was now comprised of Dimitrov, Togliatti, Manuilsky, Pieck, Kuusinen, Marty and Gottwald.

60. See Claudin (1975) p. 209.
61. Orlov defected to the US and gave evidence after Stalin's death during spy trials and to the Senate Internal Security Sub-Committee of the US, *Hearings,* Part 51, 1957, p. 3422.
62. See Claudin (1975) pp. 208-9.
63. Krivitsky (1963) pp. 103-5.
64. Longo (n.d.) p. 44.
65. *Documents on British Foreign Policy 1919-1939,* Second Series, v. V: 1933-34, London 1957, pp. 875-77. See Shirer (1960) pp. 513-44, and Schapiro (1970) pp. 479-92, for the detailed machinations of the Stalin Government.
66. FO 371/20342, 5360, 1936.
67. Confidential report by I. Chilston to Mr Eden 3 Jan. 1936, *Ibid.* Uruguay had granted *de jure* recognition to the USSR in 1926, and in 1933 had agreed to set up diplomatic representation.
68. For the Soviet denials, see M. Minkin's reply to the Uruguyan Government, FO 371/20342, N 47/47/38, 1936. The accusations were described as 'pure inventions'.
69. FO 371/20342, N 137/47/38, 28 Dec. 1935.
70. Confidential Memorandum from E. Millington-Drake, Montevideo, 30 Dec. 1935. He refers to despatch No. 23, 15 Feb. 1932 from Montevideo to London; despatch No. 21, Confidential, 14 Feb. 1933; despatch No. 311, 4 Sept. 1935 from Santiago to London.
71. Confidential Memorandum from Viscount Chilston from Moscow to Mr Anthony Eden at the Foreign Office, 31 Dec. 1935, FO 371/20342, N 61/47/38.
72. Stalin interview with Roy Howard, *New York Times,* 6 March 1936.
73. Davies (1943), Moscow Diary, 15 Feb. 1937, p. 51. This notion might require some reassessment of the whole relationship between the Trotskyite groups and the Soviet government, particularly in view of some indications of collaboration. See US Congress. Senate, Committee on the Judiciary, SIAIS, Hearings, *The Trotskyite International,* 94th Congress, 1st session, 24 July 1975.
74. Final Report, Strictly Confidential, No. 1342, 6 June 1938, Davies (1943) pp. 255-6.
75. Letter from Mr Rennie to Mr Gregory at the Foreign Office, regarding Cheka dissolution of 'Anti-Soviet Groups', FO 371/1840-2187, N/2131/G, 1927. See also Kennan (1960) pp. 251-2, where he states that Stalin intentionally confused Trotsky with Hitler in the nightmarish inventions of the purge trials as part of this cultivation; and Leggett (1981) pp. 297-8, where he elaborates on this question of *agents provocateurs.*
76. Letter from Mr Rennie, British Legation, Helsingfors, Finland, to C. M. Palairet, Foreign Office, 15 Dec. 1927, FO 371/1840-2187, N 6223.
77. In Degras (1965) p. 476. Also FO 371/37019, N 3086, N 3248, 1943.
78. *Ibid.* p. vii. Stalin in fact announced the dissolution as a *fait accompli* before the Presidium of the ECCI had collected the perfunctory 'yes' votes necessary to dissolve itself.
79. Claudin (1975) p. 32.
80. FO 371/24842, N 538, 1940.
81. From Mr Mallet, British Legation, Stockholm, to the Rt. Hon. Anthony Eden, Foreign Office, 10 July 1941, FO 371/29695, N 3922.
82. FO 371/29695, N 3923, 16 July 1941.
83. See Peters in Hammond (ed.) (1975) p. 275.
84. Article by Colonel A. I. Poltorak in *Soviet State and Law,* No. 11, 1949, as summarized in FO 371/86721, NS10115/1, 1950.
85. Dispatch by German Ambassador to Moscow to Hitler, Shulenberg, 26 Nov. 1940, NSR, pp. 258-9. In Shirer (1960) p. 809. For detailed study of German-

Soviet relations, see *Documents on British Foreign Policy 1919-1939*, Second Series, v. VI, 1933-34, London 1957; and *Nazi-Soviet Relations 1940-41*, Documents from the Archives of the German Foreign Office, ed. by Raymond J. Sontag and James S. Beddie, Washington DC, 1948.

86. FO 371/24794; also cited in Tolstoy (1981) p. 149.

87. FO N277/N284/130/97, 1925.

88. FO 371/10841, E 7186/E 6504/E 16441/E 103/81/34, 1925.

89. FO N 2376/43/97 and N 344/43/97, 1926.

90. FO 371/11221, C 10886/10671/7.

91. FO 371/13058, E 2079/49/34, 1928. Folios 136-224 still retained by the Foreign Office under Sec. 3(4) of the *Public Records Act*, 1958.

92. FO 371/12783, A/8803, 1928.

93. FO 371/13058, E/2079/E/1087, 1928.

94. FO Green Papers, C 2717/2717/92, 1929.

95. FO 371/43325, N 3732, N 4156, 1944.

96. FO 371/43407, N 2093, 1944.

97. FO 371/566294, N 2370, 1947, *Secret Report on Soviet Tactics;* The fact about the Czechoslovak weapons provided to both sides before the establishment of the State of Israel was confirmed to this author in two separate interviews: Isar Harel, former Chief of the Israeli Mossad, in May, 1979; and Ephraim Ilin, one of the participants in the Czech arms deal and presently an Israeli industrialist, in June 1979. The fact is also mentioned in Lapierre and Collins (1971) p. 69.

98. FO 371/73561, 1949.

99. Personal interview with Isar Harel.

100. FO 371/66418, 1947. Document N 12448 entitled 'Soviet aid to Greek Rebels'. See also FO 371/72293, 1948, 'Communist International Brigades in Greece'. This document is still retained by the Foreign Office under Sec.3 (4) of the *Public Records Act*, 1958.

101. FO 371/66294, N 1011, 1947.

102. Fatemi (1980) pp. 80-5.

103. *Izvestiya*, 19 Nov. 1945.

104. There was evidence that a coordinated plan by the Soviets was being carried out as the measures taken in all three countries were so very similar. See FO 371/66296, N 8755, 1947. Also see Hammond in Hammond (ed.) (1975) pp. 1-45, for a more detailed discussion of the blueprint theory.

105. FO 371/66296, N 8755, 1947; and SCOR, First Year, Supp. No. 1, Annex 3, p. 73. See also Truman (1956) v. 2, p. 121, where he writes: 'Under Soviet Direction, the (intelligence) reports said, Greece's northern neighbors - Yugoslavia, Bulgaria and Albania - were conducting a drive to establish a Communist Greence.'

106. Djilas (1962) p. 181. See Kousoulas in Hammond (ed.) (1975) p. 301, where he argues that another Soviet motive for these actions in Persia, Turkey and Greece, was to test the resistance quotient of the Western world. This would explain the eventual abandonment of that particular strategy in face of the determined opposition from the Americans and the British at the time. The support for the terrorists was abandoned for tactical reasons only.

107. FO 537/5117, 1949. Information relayed from the British Embassy, Warsaw, on 2 Sept. 1949.

108. FO 371/80337. Files 1903/1, 1903/3, 1903/4 retained in the department of origin under Sec. 3(4) of the *Public Records Act*, 1958. See also *Middle East Record* (hereinafter referred to as *MER*), Shiloah Center for Middle Eastern and African Studies, Tel Aviv University, v. 2. 1961, where the Congo representative to the United Nations accused the United Arab Republic (UAR) of acting as the conduit for those Czechoslovak arms, p. 637.

109. FO 371/86791, NS 1193/1.

110. The PCF played a crucial role during the Second World War by supporting Stalin's ally Germany. Nikolai Tolstoy suggests that it may have therefore been a large contributor to the destruction of the French will to resist the Nazis (1981, p. 114). The full extent of the French Communist Party's subservience to Moscow is in need of careful reassessment given the presence of CP members in the Mitterand Government; see Gaucher (1974), also Montaldo (1979), where the author exposes the Banque Commerciale pour l'Europe du Nord/Eurobank as having share capital which is 99.7% owned by two Moscow banks: Gosbank and Vneshtorgbank. The Soviet Union itself keeps several accounts in the bank, as does the PCF and various individual members of that party, *L'Humanité* and several of its journalists, the Cuban Embassy in Paris, the German Democratic Republic and Eastern bloc countries, and organizations which depend on PCF funds. Regular reports are sent to Boris Ponomarev, head of the International Department. The Banque Commerciale pour l'Europe du Nord also served as bankers to several of Henri Curiel's contacts, as well as board of director members of Solidarité.

111. FO 371/81102, A 1071/1, 1071/13, 1950. Regarding the evidence on Central America, FO 371/81404, AG/1016/6 and AG/1016/15 for example are retained in the department of origin under Sec. 3(4) of the *Public Records Act*, 1958.

112. cf. Stalin (1973) pp. 469-73.

113. Between 1944 and 1964, 52 new nations emerged in the Afro-Asian areas.

114. See *Documents on International Affairs*, 1962, Royal Institute of International Affairs, 1971, for the official exchanges between President John F. Kennedy and Nikita S. Khrushchev during the Cuban Missile Crisis.

115. Stalin (1945) pp. 41, 65-6, 78, 162.

116. Cf. Souvarine (1935) and Kennan (1960) for biographical details.

117. Schapiro (1970) p. 559.

118. General-Major S. N. Kozlov, *The Officer's Handbook*, Translated and published by the USAF, *Soviet Military Thought*, No. 13, p. 13; see Dziak (1981a) for a discussion of the military perceptions and structural basis of the USSR.

119. *Kommunist*; 14-18 Nov. 1959; see also Colonel Slavko N. Bjelajac, 'Unconventional Warfare: American and Soviet Approaches', in *Unconventional Warfare*, The Annals of the APSA, May 1962, p. 78.

120. *Current Digest of the Soviet Press*, v. XI, no. 4, 4 March 1959.

121. *Pravda*, 14 Feb. 1959; also in *Current Digest of the Soviet Press*, v. XI, No. 12, 22 April 1959.

122. *Pravda* and *Izvestia* both 15 Jan. 1960; also in *Current Digest of the Soviet Press*, v. XII, No. 2, 10 Feb., 1960.

123. See Royal Commission on Espionage, Report and Transcript of Proceedings, Sydney, Australia, 1955, and Kaznacheev (1962).

124. See Crozier (1965).

125. Horne (1977) pp. 405, 547. Horne mentions that the PCA members were never fully trusted by the FLN and were often sent on violent 'suicide missions' (p. 138).

126. Horne (1977) p. 125, mentions an interesting incident regarding Albert Camus, the French writer, and a former Communist who had been labelled a 'renegade' by the French Left led by Sartre, Simone de Beauvoir, etc. when he criticized the repressions of the Stalin regime. Simone de Beauvoir, commenting on Camus' attempts to stop the murderous character of the growing unrest in Algiers, said that his language 'never sounded hollower than when he demanded pity for the civilians. The conflict was one between two civilian communities.' The shift of emphasis from state to state

confrontations to the 'struggle' of an armed proletariat are clearly reflected in her comments.

127.   *Soviet News*, 11 July 1962; also in *Documents on International Affairs*, 1962, p. 361.

128.   Lenin (1958-66) v. 5, p. 7 ('Where to Begin?').

5
Contemporary International Terrorism

At a formal meeting held at the Bolshoi Theatre in Moscow in 1964, B. N. Ponomarev, Secretary of the CPSU Central Committee and head of the International Department of the CPSU, took to the floor to deliver a report entitled 'Proletarian Internationalism is the Revolutionary Banner of our Era'. The Party hymn - the International - rang out. The event commemorated the centennial of the First International. The speech he delivered stated a policy which indicated little departure from previously enunciated and attempted goals, but reflected a shift of emphasis in tactical approach. Through the vehicle of the banner of peace, that is, 'peaceful coexistence' and *détente*, the fears of nuclear confrontation and the importance of building up conventional forces to 'defend' peace, Ponomarev described the era of the 1960s as follows:[1]

> Peace is not a pacifist fairy tale or an abstract ideal for us. We are all aware that the danger of war has not yet passed. Striving to save mankind from irreparable calamities, we are maintaining our defence capabilities at a level that makes it possible to defend peace. In the thermonuclear age the defence of peace and the struggle for socialism and not two different causes but one great common revolutionary cause.
>
> Finally, we understand our internationalist duty as consisting in support for all the revolutionary, democratic movements of modern times . . .
>
> In observing the 100th anniversary of the First International, we Soviet Communists call upon all the fraternal parties and all the revolutionary forces to close their ranks more tightly, to overcome all difficulties, to rally under the banner of Marxism - Leninism in the name of the triumph of the working class . . .

This doctrinal speech set out what was to remain the Soviet position and policy in the international arena in the rapidly changing atmosphere of the 1960s. Its full intent was later to be revealed by General Jan Sejna of Czechoslovakia's military intelligence who defected during the Prague Spring of 1968.[2] In files he took with him to the West, covering over twenty years of intelligence knowledge, he documented a Politburo decision taken in 1964, to the effect that spending for terrorist enterprises should be increased dramatically.[3]

In fact, the Brezhnev era saw an intensification of the use of the 'peaceful coexistence' concept, which the West for a time accepted in its own sense. This greatly facilitated official Soviet support of national liberation movements, and covert support of certain terrorist groups which were to start in the Western liberal democracies during the late 1960s.

Neither the Politburo decision nor the official rhetoric contradicted the continuing Soviet application and interpretation of Marxist-Leninist ideology which was heavily relied upon as justification. An editorial on the subject in *Kommunist*[4] was explicit:

A situation of peaceful coexistence creates favourable conditions for the further development of the national liberation movement. In such a situation, the Soviet Union and the other Socialist countries are in a position to give the national liberation movement broad moral, political, and material support . . .

In 1965 the same concept was even more clearly elucidated by Alexandr Shelepin, chairman of the KGB from 1958 to 1961 and a full member of the Presidium since November 1964.[5] He noted that 'for the successful fulfilment of the great plans for building communism . . . in fraternal countries . . . we need peace, and in our foreign policy we shall, as always, consistently and unflaggingly fight for the realization of the principles of peaceful coexistence.'

Kosygin, in a speech on 3 July 1972, was more specific about the avoidance of state-to-state confrontation:[6]

The policy of peaceful coexistence . . . proceeds from the inadmissibility of the application of force in solving disputed questions among states. But this in no case means the rejection of the right of peoples, arms in hand, to oppose aggression or to strive for liberation from foreign oppression. The right is holy and inalienable and the Soviet Union without fail assists peoples . . .

The shift of emphasis, which Khruschev had introduced, towards internal turmoil - attack from *within*, the idea of the armed proletariat - was asserted once again in 1972 by a lecturer for the CPSU Central Committee, Yu. Molchanov:[7]

> Peaceful coexistence applies only to relations among states and does not include the ideological struggle between the two systems, the class struggle in the capitalist states, or the nationalist liberation movement of the oppressed peoples.

And again, by A. Bovin, political commentator for *Izvestiya*:[8]

> War can and must be banned as a means of resolving international disputes. But we must not 'ban' civil or national liberation wars. We must not 'ban' uprisings and we by no means 'ban' revolutionary mass movements aimed at changing the political and social status quo.

Soviet military thought echoed this foreign policy strategy. But before this can be reviewed, a brief discussion of the Soviet military establishment's philosophy and structure is necessary for the analysis of Leninist thought on types of war and how international situational changes affect the typology to be emphasized.

The Soviet brand of the military, which derives its strategic orientation from Party policy, must be given due emphasis if the international terrorist phenomenon which has developed primarily in the West is to be understood.

First, it cannot be overemphasized that Soviet concepts of war and peace differ greatly from Western concepts. Soviet doctrine, which bases itself on Clausewitz as applied by Lenin, sees all wars as part of a political process. Lenin had emphatically stated over and over again that war is a continuation of politics by other means, and central to Moscow's ideology is the assumption of perpetual conflict between classes and between communism and capitalism. It could thus be argued that the converse is also true: that a state of non-war between the superpowers, that is, the Soviet definition of peaceful coexistence or *détente*, is a continuation of war by other means.

Secondly, the Soviet military has always placed a large strategic emphasis on the use of unconventional warfare and special purpose forces. Lenin's insistence on the use of partisan warfare, for example, is a case in point which has been repeatedly applied by the USSR. Both the KGB and the GRU plan and execute Soviet unconventional warfare operations for the military branch of the apparatus. The special purpose forces *(spetznaz)* are used as deep cover units normally to be deployed in advance of conventional military action by the armed forces, as in Afghanistan in 1979.

Penkovsky informed the West that the GRU, dominated by the KGB, is involved not only in military, political, economic and scientific intelligence, but also in terroristic acts and sabotage, as well as propaganda activities, provocations and blackmail, mainly through its Fifth Directorate.[9] The hierarchical dominance of the KGB over the GRU was indicated by Penkovsky when he stated that KGB approval is necessary for a GRU officer to be stationed abroad, for example.[10]

The KGB is thought to be targeted primarily against the civilian sector.[11] The aim is generally to disrupt civil government and public utilities through the application of various methods, as has been discussed. Within the context of international terrorism, it is the KGB personnel who are most likely to be directly involved in exploiting indigenous terrorist groups or at times creating such groups as part of their duties.

The military writings published mostly for a military public in the Soviet Union reflect the various stages of development of Soviet society in general and the military in particular, as well as the major doctrinal and strategy positions emphasized by the CPSU.

Marshal A. A. Grechko, Minister of Defence from 1967 till his death in 1976 and who also held the position of member of the Politburo of the Central Committee of the CPSU, was a major contributor to Soviet military thought. In a book published in 1975, *The Armed Forces of the Soviet State*, and under the heading 'V. I. Lenin's principles of creating an army of a new type', he presented very clearly the same flexibility of approach which has been evident in all doctrinal statements of the Party since 1917. Grechko enunciated the Soviet view of military development as one application of multiple instrumentalities which are not all strictly military in nature and of which the paramilitary one is given particular emphasis. The partisan movement is heavily underscored as an important form of combat operations and is seen as part of the 'concept of total war'.[12]

Soviet military doctrine comprises the following elements:[13]

> Marxism-Leninism, military science, and to a certain degree, branches of social, natural and technical sciences related to the preparation and waging of armed struggle as well as other forms of struggle (economic, ideological and diplomatic).

By again emphasizing the historical determinism which automatically blames the 'enemy' for having the only aggressive aims, thereby exculpating the Soviet Union from any wrongdoing ever ('and the truth is that the source of wars is hidden in the aggressive nature of imperialism'), Grechko falls back on Lenin to explain that war is a continuation of politics and emphasizes that bourgeois military theoreticians wrongly view war as ' "simply" an armed engagement of sides - a rivalry involving the use of weapons -'.[14] This underscores the necessity for Western analysts to place literal value on this criticism, implying as it does the presence of other methods of conducting war which have perhaps been overlooked.

Soviet military doctrine, by their own definition, is a state's system of views and instructions on the nature of war under specific historical conditions, the definition of the military tasks of the state and the armed forces and the principles of their development, as well as the means and forms of carrying out these tasks, *including armed combat.*[15]

Moreover, Soviet military writers have clearly echoed the foreign policy emphasis enunciated by the CPSU. The lateral shift of emphasis towards the conflict from *within* based on the proletariat was justified by predictably reverting to the analysis of Leninist thoughts on war and peace. In these military writings the Soviet Union is always portrayed as 'peace-loving' and 'progressive' while the United States and the West are 'aggressive' and 'imperialistic'. For example, in a book published by the Military Publishers in Moscow and intended for a military public, the rationale presented for the shift of emphasis to conflict from *within* is obviously the nuclear stalemate:

Lenin's thesis on the correlation between a war and its era is of fundamental methodological significance for analysis of the genuine substance and political content of each war in any historical period . . .[16]

Lenin always proceeded from the leading and growing role of the masses of history, from the fact that the worker class stands at the center of our era, a class which is uniting, consolidating and leading other revolutionary and democratic forces. The *worker class*, affecting the transition to socialism, *is compelled to resort both to peaceful and non-peaceful* means of struggle.[17] (Emphasis added)

The typology of wars - all falling under 'just' ('progressive') and 'unjust' ('reactionary') classifications - which is presented in relation to a particular era, provides an interesting reinforcement of the emphasis on the struggle from *within*:[18]

In the era of imperialism the second relationship was dominant [two oppressing nations, i.e. England Germany 1914-17] engendering World War I . . . In addition there existed and developed conflicts between the bourgeoisie and proletariat, constituting the basis for the third type of war characteristic of the era of imperialism - civil wars between the bourgeoisie and the proletariat.

The approval of civil wars is specific and described as achieving 'progressive aims, gaining total suppression of the exploiters'. Civil wars are considered 'just', but their use to achieve revolution must be determined on the basis of the specific situation. Individual communist and worker parties are thus instructed to choose peaceful or non-peaceful paths of transition to socialism, depending on circumstances.[19]

The distinction is further made between different types of civil war. And here the categorization of international terrorism as presented in Chapter 1 of this study - revolutionary and sub-revolutionary - applies, as will be seen from the Soviet distinctions made on civilian unrest. Two types of civil war are presented by the military thinkers, mainly differing in goal:

(1) Civil wars between proletariat and bourgeoisie during the course of a socialist revolution.
      (This type would fall under the revolutionary classification of this study).
(2) Civil wars between people and reactionaries in power. The aims are generally democratic and might result in the preservation of the bourgeois democratic republic.
      (This type would fall under the sub-revolutionary classification of this study).

Interestingly, among the examples included for the second type is the 'struggle presently being waged in Northern Ireland'.[20]

The growing emphasis placed on civilian combat as opposed to conventional army confrontations was further elaborated in 1970, in an article by the then Chief of the General Staff, Marshal M. V. Zakharov:[21]

> The appearance of nuclear weapons and other modern weapons of war have caused a total revolution in military affairs . . . even the question of the strategic target of war has been raised in a new way. Whereas in past wars the armed forces as a whole were such a target, now *one should add the economy of the warring countries, industrial regions and communication centers, and the system of state and military control.* (Emphasis added)

This shift of emphasis was to provide the justification for finding common ground with the rising radical nationalist countries in the Third World by channelling the 'national liberation struggle' into a general 'anti-imperialist' struggle against the West, and in particular against the United States, and limiting the degree of confrontational issues between the two superpowers. In other words, the tactical elasticity of the ideology was to be applied in a manner which would enable the USSR to conduct an offensive policy towards the West through the use of proxy parties, while emphasizing for itself an image of peacemonger.

The preoccupation with the disastrous potentials of a nuclear confrontation led to a multiple-level and multi-pronged policy, a consistent feature of Soviet power projection since 1917. This was exemplified by an increase in overt diplomatic activity to secure from the West both limitations in the arms race (i.e. SALT), and trade concessions necessary for the failing economy of the USSR which was so heavily burdened by the dramatic increase in conventional forces build-up; but at the same time an intensified exploitation of local conflicts worldwide.[22]

The thrust of Soviet foreign policy was to increase the possibilities of causing strategic losses for the West in general and the United States in particular, rather than to achieve immediate *de facto* gains for the USSR. As part of the global search for influence, a Soviet alliance system emerged with the signing of several bilateral treaties, the establishment of close ties with Cuba, and the extension of massive support to various national liberation movements in Third World countries.[23]

The side which was less visible, but always a part of Soviet foreign policy behaviour, was to be heavily emphasized - the covert side of its operations abroad. To implement this policy, both the GRU (Intelligence Directorate of the General Staff) and the KGB have been actively involved in clandestine operations abroad in one way or another. The importance of the intelligence community's role in the application of Soviet foreign policy needs to be stressed. The KGB in particular has more often than not been considered by the West as strictly an espionage and information-gathering agency for the USSR, whereas in fact it has many different paramilitary functions.

The KGB, controlled from the Politburo, resembles its predecessors, the CHEKA, OGPU and GPU in many ways. Made up of various directorates, each specializing in one policy application, the KGB not only has a 'sword and shield' role for the CPSU but also operates within and throughout the Soviet military.

The First Chief Directorate is entrusted with clandestine activities abroad.[24] Its duties are numerous and include, not only espionage on government, media, academics, the military and industry, but also, through its Disinformation Department, Service *A* - renamed from the original 1959 Department *D* (for *Dezinformatsiya*) - which received adverse publicity in the early 1960s, systematic attempts to demoralize foreign countries and prepare the ground for future selective disorder. This it does through actively exploiting the 'peace movement' in the West, for example, and forging documents to sow discord among the Western allies.[25]

For its police functions at home, the Second and Fifth Chief Directorates are empowered to carry out counter-intelligence, which involves both the attempted subversion of foreign diplomats and the control of the expression of ideas in the Soviet Union.

The Third Directorate performs similar functions within the Ministry of Defence. Here KGB officers wear military uniform and have 'special detachments' with exclusive powers. The chief function of this directorate is to maintain ideological 'purity' within the military. In the context of this study its hierarchical ascendancy over the GRU is of particular interest.[26]

All these functions are multiplied in the subject intelligence communities of satellite countries such as East Germany, Bulgaria, Czechoslovakia and Cuba.[27]

The GRU, which is the sister service to the KGB, and which together with it carries out destabilizing activities including economic disruption, labour strikes and assassinations, also involves itself in the training of local groups of the target countries for terrorism, guerrilla warfare and 'national liberation struggles'.[28] Its present chief, General P. Ivashutin, is in fact a former KGB deputy chief and also former chief of the KGB Third Directorate.

The chain of command for decision-making provides a politico-military integration which conforms with expressed Leninist ideology, endowed with the necessary flexibility in applying policy both in war and peace.

The pinnacle of power, as stated earlier, is the CPSU, and more specifically the Politburo of the Central Committee of the Party. This fact is repeatedly emphasized by Soviet military writers. Within the Central Committee, the International Department is the most likely formulator of foreign policy and political strategy generally.[29] This department, as was seen in the historical part of this study, dates back to 1943, the year of dissolution of the Comintern, and it is generally agreed that it took over the functions of the ECCI. Boris N. Ponomarev has headed the International Department since the 1950s, having previously been an official of the Comintern, providing the necessary continuity in Comintern activities. It appears that the International Department is the orchestrating arm of the CPSU for the activities of the GRU, diplomats and related personnel abroad, and even KGB residencies abroad.[30] (See Figure 5.1 for the structure and chain of command of the Soviet intelligence community.)

The KGB, created in 1964 in its present structural form, was to increase its role as an instrument of support and organization to terrorist groups and guerrilla movements.[31] In fact, Yu. V. Andropov, chairman of the KGB until 1982, when he became a Politburo member and most likely successor to Leonid Brezhnev,* was elected as far back as June 1967 as a candidate member of the Politburo, a move which in itself indicated the greater importance the secret police have been acquiring in policy-making. The appointment in October of the same year, of S. G. Bannikov, the deputy chairman of the KGB, to the Supreme Court of the USSR, ensured a tight control on sentencing, and is a sign of the concern of the Party over the ever-growing dissent.

Several world events in the years 1965-68 were decisively to influence Soviet perceptions and decisions. The major troop commitment by the United States in Vietnam in 1965 was a boon to the Soviet Union, as it diverted United States concentration from the Middle Eastern and European theatres, allowing the Soviet Union a greater opportunity for penetration, in the Middle East particularly. The Chinese Cultural Revolution effectively removed China from the competition with the USSR for leadership of the world revolutionary movement. The British withdrawal from Aden in 1969 provided the Soviet Union with unexpected opportunities. Now called the People's Republic of Yemen, Aden was to become a close associate of the USSR. Yemen, in fact, was to provide large training camps and asylum for terrorists and guerrillas of various kinds and origins.

The year 1966 also saw the fall of Syria's government to a *coup d'état* which put a more extreme Ba'athist regime in power. The Soviet Union was to take this opportunity to establish a much closer relationship with this Middle Eastern country, which itself sponsored Palestinian *fedayeen*. The United Arab Front, which the Soviet Union had repeatedly called for, was formed. All this gave the Kremlin hope that an 'anti-imperialist' and definitely anti-American Arab bloc might now at last be fashioned.

In addition, the decision by de Gaulle to pull France out of the North Atlantic Treaty Organization (NATO) was to indicate to the Soviets a potential ineffectiveness of that organization and a general lack of consensus among the Western allies which might be

---

*Andropov was, of course, elected as Secretary-General of the CPSU in November 1982.

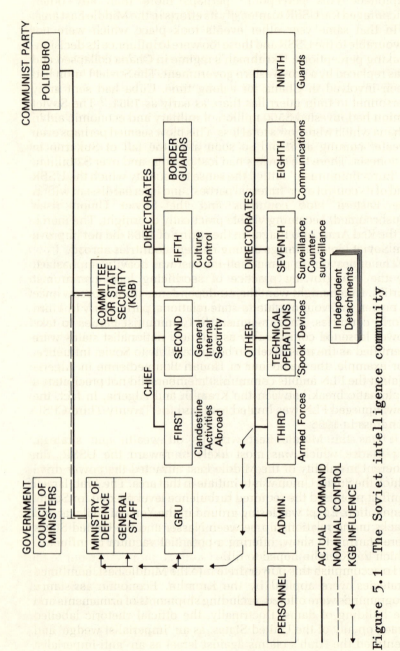

Figure 5.1 The Soviet intelligence community

Source: Collins, 1980.

exploited. This perception, perhaps more than any other, encouraged the USSR to intensify its efforts in the Middle East area.

In that same year other events took place which were not favourable to the USSR and these too were to influence its decision-making perceptions. Nkruhmah's regime in Ghana collapsed and was replaced by a pro-Western government. The Soviet Union had been involved in Ghana for a long time. Cuba had sent army personnel to train guerrillas there as early as 1961.[32] The Soviet Union had invested $500 million of military and economic aid in Ghana which were now a total loss. This blow seemed perhaps even greater coming as it did so soon after the fall of Sukarno in Indonesia. There the Soviets had lost prestige and over $2 billion.

'Eurocommunism' rattled the sense of security which the USSR had of its control over 'fraternal parties', and internal dissent within the Eastern bloc countries and the Soviet Union itself mushroomed, becoming visible practically overnight. The march of the Red Army into Prague in the spring of 1968 did not improve the Soviet Union's image among nascent countries abroad.

The endeavour to pursue self-interest was heavily emphasized by the ever-growing practice of sacrificing local communist parties, which might want their independence from Moscow once in power, in favour of state-to-state relations, particularly in Third World countries. Encouragement to Communist Parties to take power lessened considerably as the new nationalist states were identified as the most likely to be susceptible to Soviet influence. For example, the behaviour of Houari Boumedienne in Algeria against the FLN and its communist members did not precipitate a diplomatic break between the Kremlin and Algeria. In fact, the newly purged FLN was invited to attend the Twenty-Third CPSU Congress in 1966.

It was the Middle East with its oil wealth and strategic importance which was most likely to reward the USSR, the inherent instability of the Middle East attracted the power drive which the Soviet Union was to initiate in that area. The Arab-Israeli conflict promised the required turbulence level needed for Soviet penetration. Egypt was losing ground in the Yemeni civil war and cracks in the relationship between Nasser and the United States were starting to show, offering a potential vacuum of influence which the Kremlin hoped to fill.

To accomplish this power drive into the Middle East, combined strategies were applied by the Kremlin. Economic assistance programmes were offered, including shipments of armaments and the building of dams. Doctrinally, the official rhetoric labelled Israel, on ally of the United States, as an 'imperialist wedge' and identified the Arab's claims against Israel as an 'anti-imperialist struggle'.

Apart from these official policies, there was a concurrent covert one. The KGB mounted its biggest subversive operation up to that time, endeavouring to lay the foundations for a long-lasting Soviet influence, if not dominance, in the area.[33] This subversive operation entailed several kinds of activity, of which penetration into various governments was one. For example, Sami Sharaf, the intelligence adviser to President Nasser, was a controlled KGB agent, feeding information to Nasser which was intended to erode the links he had with the West. Sharaf, for instance, planned the November 1964 mob demonstration which resulted in the burning of the USIS Library in Cairo.[34] On 22 May 1971 Anwar Sadat was to arrest Sami Sharaf, along with Aly Sabry and ninety others, for planning an imminent *coup*.

A part of the covert strategy was to organize various terrorist groups. The oilfields of Saudi Arabia were the targets of the Front of Liberation of Saudi Arabia, for example, and smaller sheikdoms south of Kuwait were 'targeted'. Also, urban terrorism, including kidnappings and assassinations directed against Turkey, was to be organized. The Turkish operation was apparently set up early in the 1960s with a few agents recruited in Ankara by the KGB and sent for training in the Soviet Union and later in Syria, where training camps were set up and supervised by Soviet personnel.[35]

In the Kremlin's attempts to penetrate the Middle East, the PLO was to form the fulcrum of the Soviet Union's strategic approach. That group, for various reasons, was to emerge as a terrorist organization above all others, the initiator of the terrorist recrudescence which was to plague Western democratic societies from the late 1960s on, and the central co-ordinator of logistical and material support to a vast network of terrorist groups worldwide.

The Soviet Official Position on the PLO

The PLO was officially founded at the Arab Summit Conference of January 1964. Up until the 1967 Six-Day War and the massive defeat of the Arab armies by Israel, there were few direct contacts between the Soviet Union and the PLO, although at least one high-level meeting is known to have occurred. In May 1966 there was a meeting between Ahmad Shuquairy, the leader of the PLO at the time, and Kosygin.[36] The content of the meeting can only be guessed at but the meeting itself would indicate an interest in the group which predates the official shift of interest, generally seen as occurring after the Six-Day War.

At the time of the first terrorist act carried out on Israeli territory by al-Fatah, in January 1965, the Soviet media made no mention whatsoever of its occurrence. This position, or rather avoidance of a public position, was then gradually replaced by comments which alleged the non-existence of the *fedayeen* groups - what *Izvesitya* called 'the activity of mythical diversionary groups'.[37] There were, however, a number of scholarships granted by Bulgaria, Czechoslovakia and East Germany to the General Union of Palestinian Students - a PLO affiliate.[38]

During those years the main thrust of Soviet policy in the Middle East stressed state-to-state normalization which resulted successfully in closer ties with Syria, Iraq, Yemen and the Sudan, and in a growing Soviet military presence in that whole area. Coincidentally, between 1964 and 1967 the PLO opened branch offices in many of the same states: the UAR, Syria, Lebanon, Iraq, Kuwait, Qatar, Libya, Algeria, Morocco, Sudan and Aden.[39]

Immediately after the Six-Day War, the USSR, attempting to consolidate an international front of Soviet bloc states with Arab and 'non-aligned' countries at the United Nations, shifted the emphasis of its policy from the strengthening of Arab 'progressive' forces to one stressing all-Arab unity. 'The war showed . . . Imperialism [to be] the enemy of all Arab countries . . . not merely of the progressive republics.'[40] To justify this new approach, the Marxist-Leninist doctrine was to be interpreted with great flexibility so that military dictatorships might become acceptable allies.[41] Since states such as Egypt, Syria and Algeria did not have a dictatorship of the proletariat and had no national bourgeoisie, these lacunae were explained as being specific problems of that area and the path to be followed in order to transform these societies had to be a flexible application of Marxist-Leninist doctrine.[42]

In the immediate aftermath of the war, some Soviet statements advocated an 'Algerian' strategy to be adopted against Israel. It was said that there was a need to prepare the Arabs for protracted guerrilla warfare and a 'real people's war'.[43] However, on the whole, the call for the liquidation of Israel was sharply criticized and the PLO's use of that 'absurd slogan' was called 'hysterical'.[44]

With the overthrow of the first chairman of the PLO, Ahmad Shuqairy, at the end of 1967, the Soviet Union used the opportunity to criticize, not the organization itself, but the man, and this mainly because of his past reliance on Chinese assistance.[45]

In 1968 the USSR initiated a campaign of approval and justification, in the media and at the United Nations, for the 'partisans' struggle against the 'occupier'. The immediate aim of Soviet policy in the Middle East was to isolate Israel and the United States by establishing Soviet influence and exploiting the on-going conflict to gather and unite the Arab world as much as possible.

The strategic choice to achieve this end was, however, uncertain, especially after the humiliating defeat of the USSR's clients during the Six-Day War, with its own loss both of prestige and of expensive weaponry.

After the severing of relations with Israel in 1967 a tentative shift away from military confrontations, at least in the immediate future, was initiated. This shift was in fact reflected in official pronouncements which were at first vague, but which gradually, in the second part of the year, indicated growing approval of unconventional methods of warfare. The Soviet media began the publication of detailed descriptions of terrorist activities. The image these publications were creating was that there was a growing struggle by 'partisans' from within which was gaining support among the local population in Israel.[46]

The growing approval manifested itself in other ways as well. The first conclusive evidence of some Eastern bloc support for the terrorist organizations was reported by Muhammad Jabih, president of the Palestinian Students' Association of which Arafat had been the first president. In April 1968, upon his return to Cairo from a trip to Eastern Europe, he reported the promise made by the USSR, Bulgaria, Czechoslovakia, Hungary and Yugoslavia, to supply 'light equipment and medicaments' to the terrorist groups and to offer study grants as well.[47] Radio Cairo had reported a year earlier that East Germany had offered to supply arms to the PLO.[48]

In July 1968 Yassir Arafat secretly visited Moscow as part of the UAR delegation. The purpose of the visit was to establish contact with the Soviet leadership and arrange for the supply of arms.[49] Subsequently, Soviet embassies in the Middle East made several approaches to the *fedayeen* groups with the view to establishing some co-operation,[50] and the Jordanian Communist Party was regularly employed as a go-between to maintain contacts between the Soviet Union and the PLO. There was approval and even praise of the Arab terrorists in an article by Georgii Mirskii in *New Times*[51] in which he called al-Fatah the 'dominant force' in the resistance movement, having both moral and political influence, and declared that the 'very existence of this patriotic organization waging a dedicated struggle against the invaders is a source of inspiration for the Arabs'.

The singling out of al-Fatah for specific approval - a practice which was to be frequently adopted by the Soviet Union - and the visit by Arafat to Moscow might even suggest a concerted attempt at organizing the centralized type of group preferred by the USSR, which would greatly simplify the application of Soviet influence on its activities and would be a mirror image of Lenin's concept of the 'professional' terrorist group. Yassir Arafat appears to have been singled out as a focal point to effect that centralization.

However, the intrinsic lack of cohesiveness of the various groups was repeatedly criticized by the Kremlin, and a call was made for a unification of 'all national Palestinian forces'.[52] The adoption of a programme for the liberation of Palestine was praised.[53] The official Soviet position was indicated at the United Nations, by the Soviet Union's asking for a political solution to the problem.

During the same year of official Soviet hesitation and gradual shift towards the Palestinian terrorists, the various *fedayeen* groups were themselves undergoing a reorganization, in terms of both structure and ideological adherences. The PFLP (Popular Front for the Liberation of Palestine) came into existence in late 1967 and was made up of three principal groups: one set up by George Habash in the aftermath of the Six-Day War (The Vengeance Youth), one made up of PLO anti-Shuqairy members (The Heroes of the Return) and one formed in the early 1960s by Ahmad Jibril and Ali Bushnaq, Palestinian ex-officers of the Syrian army. Raids into Israel by this last group began in 1965. The need for the adoption of a strict Marxist-Leninist revolutionary ideology was emphasized in their own publication.[54] PFLP publications included the same terminology which was used by the Soviet Union, which called Israel a 'bridgehead for old and new Imperialism'[55] led by the United States, and linked Zionism, racism and world imperialism into one expression. 'The war for the liberation of Palestine', the PFLP said, 'is a war against Israel and all those who stand behind Israel, particularly American Imperialism.'[56] It also identified itself with the 'world liberation movement'. Although the PFLP declared that it would only direct its strikes against military and strategic targets, this was qualified by one of its commanders who stated that they might attack civilian targets in reaction to 'Israeli terror'. He explained his position in cost-effectiveness terms thus: 'Attacks on Israeli military targets cost us effort, weapons and people - while attacks on civil targets and concentrations are not so costly.'[57]

The PLO equally directed most of its activities in 1968 to reorganization and unification of the various *fedayeen* groups. Although amalgamation and control by the PLO over all the other groups was not achieved in that year, the slogan for unity was heavily emphasized by the PLO leadership. 'To unify the Palestinian *fedayeen* forces, the PLO has called for co-operation, co-ordination, and unification . . . The achievement of this aim is essential for the escalation of the armed struggle.'[58]

The major effort made by the PLO to secure its position as the controlling umbrella body was to reconvene the Palestinian National Council (PNC). At the Cairo meeting held between 6 and

15 January 1968, the PLO publicly called for 'every Palestinian organization that takes part in the armed resistance to co-operate with the PLO in order to unite this struggle and escalate it'. A subcommittee was formed for that purpose composed of members of the Executive Committee 'which will have direct revolutionary contacts with all the Palestinian organizations'.[59]

Yassir Arafat,[60] who had been one of the founders of al-Fatah in 1958, explained that unity would be achieved 'on the battlefield forged by guns and sealed with the blood of martyrs'.[61] This extremist terrorist position was the rallying cry of the PNC which adopted an amended National Covenant reflecting the new outlook which had developed as a consequence of the Six-Day War. The terrorist groups were seen to be gaining in influence within the PNC, as exemplified by the term 'Palestinian revolution' and the definition of the 'armed struggle' as the 'only way to liberate Palestine' which were incorporated in the new Covenant but were absent from the 1964 Covenant.[62] Moreover, the new Covenant also specifically and totally rejected a political solution. To unite all the various groups and help them to ignore the differences which divided them, 'armed action' was made the rallying cry - the essential requirement for co-operation.

The Soviet Union, in 1969, continued to demonstrate an increased, albeit still cautious, official approval of *fedayeen* activities. The main thrust of its foreign policy in the Middle East was still directed towards state-to-state relations and an attempt at establishing its influence through those recognized channels. Concurrently, however, the terrorist groups were praised more strongly and more often by the Soviet press and officials of the government. This shift of emphasis became more apparent as the possibility of a four-power settlement receded. Alexandr Shelepin, a member of the Politburo, speaking in Budapest, compared the activities of the *fedayeen* to the partisan resistance against the Nazis, and identified the 'Palestinian patriots'' struggle for the liquidation of the consequences of Israeli aggression' as a 'just anti-imperialist struggle and we support it'.[63]

The Kremlin encouraged the use of violence by these groups hoping perhaps that a quicker withdrawal by Israel from the territories occupied in the Six-Day War would ensue. In a broadcast in Arabic, for example, Radio Moscow stated that the 'resistance movement had become a part of the general struggle of the Arab people against the Israeli aggression' and that it was therefore 'natural' that the Palestinian refugees should carry arms to defend their rights usurped by the aggressors.[64]

This position was reiterated by F. A. Tabeev, leader of the Soviet delegation to the Second International Conference in Support of the Arab Peoples in Cairo, and a member of the Presidium of the Supreme Soviet. He stressed the Arab peoples' 'right to resist' and that the USSR 'has provided and will continue to provide active support'.[65]

In 1969-70 the USSR tried with difficulty to establish some influence over the *fedayeen* groups, enough at least to prevent any interference by them with the Kremlin's official manoeuvrings. In fact, the Soviet Union timed a renewal of diplomatic initiative in the Middle East with the inauguration of the Nixon administration. The Kremlin presented a peace proposal which would permit a return to a four-power participation based on UN Resolution 242. No doubt the Soviet Union at the time saw this type of initiative as the best vehicle for the re-injection of its influence into the area. However, the representatives of al-Fatah rejected this step in no uncertain terms, calling the Soviet Union 'the slave of the Israeli *fait accompli*. - It supported the 1947 Partition Plan: it now supports the 1967 Partition Plan'.[66] Stung by this public criticism, the USSR in turn responded with a strongly critical article in *Sovetskaya rossiya*. The criticism, however, mainly attempted to bring al-Fatah to a more acceptable position on the issue of the existence of the State of Israel, and was not directed at any *fedayeen* activities. 'It is clear that the aims which al-Fatah and some other organizations have set for themselves, which amount to the liquidation of the State of Israel and the creation of a "Palestinian democratic State", are not realistic . . .'[67]

As the likelihood of a political solution receded, the USSR increased its official expressions of support for the PLO - al-Fatah and other groups, but still showed its unhappiness with the fragmentary and non-cohesive character of the Organization. *New Times* published for the first time photographs of *fedayeen* in training in August 1969 (the site of the training camp is not identified), and in September it described al-Fatah as the leader of the groups, and the PLO as a 'growing political and military force'. The article went on to say that in spite of the 'highly favourable' conditions for guerrilla warfare, the PLO was 'badly hindered in its activities by the lack of co-ordination among the guerrillas'.[68] In short, the Soviet position encouraged violent action but wanted this action to take place under a unified command.

Plans for a second visit to Moscow by Arafat - this one more nearly official than the first, but not quite - were revealed in November 1969. The shift of the Soviet Union's official policy towards the PLO, it was said, was to provide it with 'active aid'. It would permit 'popular organizations' to provide aid to the *fedayeen* in the same way as they supplied 'aid to Vietnam', and other East European countries would also supply aid.[69]

Still exhibiting official caution in its overt approaches to the PLO (which now included al-Fatah), the USSR arranged for Arafat and his delegation to be hosted by the Soviet Afro-Asian Solidarity Committee.[70] The arrival of the delegation in Moscow coincided with the presence there of a PFLP representative. The visit was given minute attention in the Soviet press, but nevertheless the coverage indicated a more amenable official attitude by the Soviet Union towards supporting and recognizing the PLO as a potential positive force.

Although there was yet no official indication of a promise of arms as an overt policy at the time, the report of the Executive Committee of the PLO which Arafat submitted to the Seventh Palestine National Council in Cairo in May 1970 did mention that the USSR had promised 'certain military support to the PLO'. *Pravda's* Cairo correspondent, Evgenii Primakov, referred to the PLO in a radio interview as a 'now important military factor'.[71]

During the same interview, which Primakov gave on Radio Moscow, he broached the subject of terrorism and presented a position which the Soviet Union has consistently maintained on the issue. He stated that after three years of Palestinian struggle, two approaches to the problem had emerged. First differentiating between 'individual terrorism' and the terrorism connected to 'the general popular struggle, the struggle of the whole people', he said that the Palestinian groups had on the whole adopted an 'organized popular struggle for the liberation of occupied territory' as opposed to choosing 'individual terror'. Second, and at the same time, he hinted at a possible shift in the PLO position which would abandon the extremist demand for the destruction of the State of Israel, which would bring it more in line with the Soviet position.

Neither of these points represents any departure from former official postures or unofficial behaviour on the part of the USSR in regard to the use of terrorism as a strategic weapon when deemed expedient. They seem to indicate more Soviet anxiety to achieve the same sort of centralized infrastructure necessary to support terrorist activity; in essence, the same concept of organization which Lenin had expounded, as was discussed earlier - the 'professional revolutionary' as opposed to the 'amateur' or 'individual' terrorist. The Primakov interview, in particular, seems to hint at a greater degree of acceptability for the PLO by the Kremlin, based on this point about organization. Also, the Soviet attempt to legitimize their own position in relation to the PLO and its activities, and to exploit the groups through greater control, is seen in their efforts at harnessing the Palestinians into the Soviet Union's 'world liberation movement'.

The Soviet reaction in 1969-70 to terrorist incidents which were perpetrated by the PLO unequivocally endorses these points. Following the terrorist attack on the El Al airliner in Zurich in February 1969, for example, the blame for the 'bloodshed' was placed on 'the adventurous policies of the rulers of Israel'.[72] Further sympathetic approval was published in *Pravda* on 28 February 1969, in an article which again blamed Israel's 'abominable provocations' as being the cause, and exonerated the terrorists because they were 'patriots defending their legal right to return to their homeland'.

In February 1970, following the mid-air explosion of a Swiss airliner over Switzerland in flight from Zurich to Tel Aviv, the Soviet media absolved the *fedayeen* of the crime completely. TASS claimed that the Americans and the Israelis had used slanderous propaganda by accusing 'Arab guerrillas' as a 'diversion' to detract attention from 'the atrocities of the Israeli military',[73] and that there was a 'false communiqué involved at any event'.

Soviet reactions to the spread of hijackings by the PFLP in September 1970 present their position on the question of terrorism quite clearly, if the reactions expressed are placed in the proper chronological perspective. On 6 September 1970 three civilian airliners were hijacked: a Pan-American Boeing 747 on a flight between Amsterdam and New York was hijacked to Beirut and then to Cairo; a TWA Boeing 707 on a flight from Tel Aviv to New York was hijacked after a stop-over in Frankfurt; a Swissair DC8, flying from Zurich to New York, was hijacked and forced to fly to a desert airfield near Zarqa', outside Amman in Jordan.[74] Two days later a BOAC VC-10 flying from Bombay to London, was also forced to land near Amman, as was the TWA flight.[75] The PLO, having congratulated the PFLP on their success once all planes were in Jordan, ordered the PFLP to transfer the passengers and crew to Amman on 10 September 1970. This fact alone is of interest, establishing as it does the organizational and hierarchical supremacy of the PLO over other so-called 'splinter' groups. In fact, that order was at first acquiesced to by the PFLP hijackers, but was subsequently defied.[76] It is not until several days *after* the defied order that the USSR called the hijackings 'regrettable'[77] and criticized 'the Palestinian guerrillas' for their use of 'hijacking of civilian aircraft as a method of struggle'. The lapse of time might indicate a criticism of the lack of control and discipline revealed after the multiple hijackings rather than criticism of the terrorist acts themselves. Moreover, *New Times*, reporting the events late in the month of September, commented more on the destruction of the airplanes (they were blown up on the airfield) than on the actual terrorist act of hijacking and, at any event, it blamed that on 'extremist elements'.[78]

These hijackings came in the aftermath of a cease-fire agreement which was initiated by the United States and agreed to by Egypt and Israel. The disruption caused by the hijackings, it could be argued, might well have been welcomed by the Kremlin as an attempt at keeping its influence in the area alive. Moreover, there was evidence of Soviet involvement in Egyptian cease-fire violations, indicating a reluctance by the Soviet Union to accept the Rogers initiative as a peaceful solution.[79]

The immediate aftermath of those hijackings was the Jordanian-PLO confrontation and war which ended with the massive defeat of the *fedayeen*. The Soviet Union's conspicuous lack of activity during this conflict tends to reinforce the notion that the Kremlin hoped to curb or do away with insubordination in the ranks of the PLO which might result from the fighting, and that the defeated group would thus emerge as a more cohesive unit, albeit weakened. The massive defeat of the *fedayeen* in 1970 no doubt provided an immediate opportunity for the Kremlin to exert greater influence on the organizational structure and leadership of the PLO.

As a result of the defeat, minor organizations were in fact liquidated. Moreover, Yassir Arafat's leadership was accepted by the various remaining groups and resulted in a greater unification of *fedayeen* activities. The consolidation of the Organization contributed to the transformation of the Palestinian problem from one of refugees to a national one. This enabled the Kremlin gradually to shift towards greater public endorsement of the PLO.

This official transition reflected the changed conditions which developed for the Soviet Union in the Middle East, particularly in the aftermath of Nasser's death on 28 September 1970. Egypt, which up until then had formed the cornerstone of Soviet policy in the region, now presented the Kremlin with uncertain prospects. The choice of state-to-state relations on the official level was an obvious one for the Kremlin until the death of Nasser, given the unprecedented growth of military and naval presence in Egypt and the Mediterranean. Because of this inordinate success for Soviet state-to state relations in the Middle East, contacts with the PLO continued to be channelled through the Soviet Afro-Asian Solidarity Committee, which is controlled by the International Department. By December 1970 Boris Ponomarev, Secretary of the CPSU Central Committee, was supporting the 'Palestinian liberation movement' and stating that the USSR 'will support it in the future', adding that 'every assistance' was rendered to it by the Soviet Union.[80]

In direct contrast to the official sympathetic response to the PLO hijackings, the Soviet Union was quick to call the Lithuanian hijackers of a Soviet AN-24 airliner on a domestic flight from Batum on 15 October 1970 'criminal murderers'[81] and to demand that the Turkish authorities extradite them for trial in the USSR.[82] In fact, Ambassador Grubiakov submitted the official request for extradition to the Turkish Foreign Ministry on 24 October.[83] Three days later, on 27 October 1970, a second hijacking occurred, much to the embarrassment of the Kremlin. A twin-engine Aeroflot on a domestic flight from Kerch in the Crimea to Krasnodar was hijacked by two students who asked for political asylum in Turkey. On this occasion, the Soviet government chose to ignore the event. A Soviet Foreign Ministry spokesman stated he 'knew nothing' about that hijacking.[84] The Soviet media in general were silent on this second hijacking. The sudden flurry of interest which the USSR exhibited at the United Nations in an anti-hijacking convention was, as we saw earlier, an immediate response to these two events. In neither hijacking was there any political demand made on the Soviet Union by the hijackers, nor was there the organizational infrastructure of the classic terrorist groups which have plagued the Western liberal democracies.

The following year, 1971, saw the Soviet Union gradually losing ground in its state-to-state relations in the Middle East.[85] A renewed interest in the local communist parties of the area was initiated as one of the possible means to help to arrest the anti-Sovietism which was building up. The Communist Parties of Jordan, Syria, Iraq and Lebanon, which had established their own terrorist group, Al-Ansar, in November of 1969,[86] were encouraged into greater activity. Al-Ansar was supported by the PFLP, the Marxist-Leninist faction of the PLO. Possibly to stop the pro-Chinese trend in the PLO or to attempt greater control over the organization, it would appear that at the time of Arafat's visit to Moscow in February 1970 Moscow made its assistance to the *fedayeen* organizations conditional upon their acceptance of Al-Ansar to their ranks.[87]

With the expulsion of the Soviet Union in 1972 by Egypt's Anwar Sadat, which marked the lowest ebb of Soviet influence in the Middle East, there was a proportionate increase in the official acceptance of the PLO as a political factor by the Kremlin. In retrospect, one can see where the Soviet Union's position in the Middle East was markedly improved after the Munich massacre of Israeli athletes. The increase in Israeli-Arab fighting which immediately followed that tragic incident renewed Arab reliance on Soviet weapons supplies, thus helping to re-establish Soviet influence in the region. The deterioration of United States and West German relations with the Arab States was an unexpected bonus. Moreover, the stated elements of Soviet policy towards the

West and Israel were very similar indeed to those enunciated by the 'Black September' sub-group of the PLO* which killed the Israeli athletes.[88] After the deed, a spokesman for the group said: 'The operation was aimed at exposing the close relations between the treacherous German authorities and United States imperialism on the one hand and the Zionist enemy's authorities on the other.'

The Munich massacre appears to be the starting point of an official Soviet policy attempting to create a public image for the PLO which would eventually endow it with political acceptability in a broad sphere. Repeatedly over the years, the Soviet Union, through its press, radio and representative officials, has attempted to dissociate the PLO from its terrorist activities, particularly those taking place outside the Middle East area. Thus, the Munich murders were credited to the 'extremist terrorist group "Black September" '.[89]

At the United Nations Soviet representative Y. Malik, reacting to the Israeli raids into Lebanon and Syria which immediately followed the massacre, expressed sympathetic understanding for what he called 'Palestinian rebels who became themselves victims of non-stop Israeli aggression in the Middle East'.[90] A few days later, an announcement by the PLO Executive Committee disclaiming any connection with 'Black September' was given very wide coverage by several Soviet publications.[91]

This policy of legitimization of the PLO was further endorsed and emphasized with direct Soviet arms supplies in 1972.[92] It is noteworthy that this date coincides with the shift of emphasis towards civilian conflict which has already been discussed, and is not in contradiction with this military doctrine.

Following the Khartoum invasion of the Saudi Arabian embassy by the PLO's 'Black September' which resulted in the murder of the American Ambassador, his deputy and the Belgian Chargé d'Affaires, Radio Moscow quoted: 'Yassir Arafat, Chairman of the Executive Committee of the PLO, in a cable to President Numeiri, said that his organisation has nothing to do with the Khartoum incident.'[93] On the same day, in its English broadcasts, Radio Moscow described 'Black September' as uniting a few extreme groupings of Palestinians, suggesting links with non-Palestinian extremist interests. A few days later, however, *Pravda* quoted a telegram from Arafat to Sadat in which he attacked the United States for its campaign against the Palestinians and their *armed insurrection*[94] (emphasis added).

---

*Black September was a sub-group of al-Fatah, created after, and named for, the month when King Hussein's loyal forces fell upon the fedayeen, killed thousands of them, and drove them from his kingdom. It was formed to revenge the fedayeen. It's first act was to murder Wasfi al-Tal, sometime Prime Minister of Jordan.

The growing official reliance on the PLO by the USSR and the latter's image-creating efforts can also be seen in the technique often used by the Soviet media of quoting the PLO as the authority rather than the officials of a given country where a terrorist incident occurs. Thus, after the destruction of the oil refineries in Lebanon, Radio Moscow, in its Arabic broadcast, quoted the PLO as accusing Israel of the deed which took place on Lebanese soil. Presumably the oil refineries belonged to Lebanon, but no comment by the Lebanese government was given.[95] And, moreover, *Pravda* called the Israelis 'terrorists' . . . 'raising violence to the status of state policy'.[96]

In August 1973 *Radio Moscow*[97] quoted the weekly *Falastin Ath-Thawrah* of the PLO as sharply denouncing 'the act of terrorism staged by two unidentified persons at Athens airport on 5 August'. It went on to stress that the 'Palestine resistance movement is against all forms of terror'.

This systematic and uniform denial of involvement by the PLO after every incident was consistently published and quoted by the Soviet media. The size of the articles, the extent of coverage of any particular terrorist incident and the languages in which Radio Moscow was beamed all helped this process of 'politicization'. Often particularly brutal terrorist acts (although it is difficult to define what would make one act of terrorism more brutal than another) are either ignored by the Soviet media or given very small attention. For example, the attack by the PLO (Jibril's group) on the Israeli town of Kiryat Shmona in April 1974 in which eighteen Israelis died was reported by TASS in four sentences.[98] Those four sentences blamed the attack on 'Israeli Arabs', thus giving a brand of approval and a legitimation of the act by attributing it to 'local partisan resistance' - which in itself attributes to the 'resistance' a political label that endows it with a 'justifiable' cause. In other cases an attempt was made to place the blame on 'unknowns', as mentioned above, or on Israel itself, as the Soviet response to the Rome and Athens terrorist attacks at the end of 1973 indicated.[99] These attacks, coming as they did just before the reconvening of the Geneva Conference and after the Yom Kippur War which the USSR had tacitly and materially supported,[100] must be viewed in that context. Moreover, a few months earlier the official relationship between Arafat and the USSR was upgraded with Arafat's invitation in August 1973 as an honoured guest to the World University Games in Moscow and with the PLO being allowed to open an office in East Berlin in the same month.[101] *Pravda*, in fact, trying to place the blame elsewhere, stated that in view of the forthcoming Geneva Conference it was unlikely 'that the criminals were Palestinians'.[102] Radio Moscow in Arabic broadcasts to the Arab world stated that the terrorists had to be non-Palestinian as 'such deeds arouse anti-Arab feelings'. Given the negative position of influence the USSR had at the time of the reconvening of the Geneva Conference, it could be argued that the anti-Arab feelings which were, in fact, aroused by such deeds, would prove to be beneficial to the overall Soviet position. By presenting itself as the only friend of the Arab states in general and the PLO in particular, the Kremlin probably hoped that these anti-Arab feelings would push these parties to place greater reliance on the USSR for material and moral support, and lead to greater cohesion on the 'anti-imperialism' posture pursued by Moscow.

The opening statement by Soviet Foreign Minister Gromyko at the Geneva Conference on 21 December 1973 called for the 'participation of representatives of the Arab people of Palestine', but did not specifically mention the PLO as such a representative. Thus the official Soviet policy in the Middle East appeared to be hesitant at this juncture, or at the very least displayed the habitual multiple-level considerations of a pragmatic attitude adopted by the USSR while attempting to rally the Arab states around it and against the United States. To achieve its ultimate objective of re-establishing its influence in the area, the Kremlin would allow the Geneva Conference to open without the PLO if necessary.[103]

When Naif Hawatmeh, leader of the PDFLP (Marxist Popular Democratic Front for the Liberation of Palestine) wing of the PLO attacked an Israeli school at Ma'alot which resulted in the death of many children, there was no condemnation of the act in the Soviet official media, although *New Times* reported 'international condemnation'.[104] The article, however, placed the blame for the murders on Israel and in particular on Moshe Dayan, whom it called a 'Palestinian Eichmann'. This label appears to be a part of the general polarizing attempt by the Soviet Union of the 'left' (pro-Soviet) and 'right' (pro-USA) positions which could be exploited within Israel as well as outside it. And the 'international condemnation' referred, therefore, to the Israeli actions rather than the terrorists. The Soviet press once again dissociated the PLO from the deed, and the Soviet Union could now broadcast a general condemnation of terrorism in a radio communication to Western audiences.[105] In fact, in Russian language publications and Arabic language broadcasts, Hawatmeh was repeatedly referred to as a moderate only a couple of months after Ma'alot, which in itself was an encouragement for future similar terrorist action. Hawatmeh was on friendly relations with the USSR* on his own merit and was possibly being groomed as an alternative leader to Arafat or as a leverage against him to ensure that there would be no change in the serving of Soviet interests.[106]

The cultivation of the PLO as a 'political' alternative continued. And it could be argued that the increased official recognition of the PLO by the Kremlin at that time indicated an exploitative use of that group as a vehicle for imposing itself in the Middle East and elsewhere, rather than reflecting any real interest in its 'cause'. It must be recalled that until 1961, the date of the Khrushchev doctrine, there was in fact no interest in the 'Palestine liberation' issue expressed on an official level by the USSR or any other country. At the United Nations only the Palestine refugee problem was discussed.[107] Arafat created al-Fatah in 1958 and it is unlikely that he would have escaped the attention of the Kremlin until 1966. One of the primary factors leading to the Sinai campaign of 1956 had been daily terrorist attacks in Israel.[108] So it is safe to state that it was not the 'cause' which grasped the imagination of the Politburo in the case of the PLO.

The very strong objections to PLO participation in the Middle East peace process and the Soviet Union's insistence on its inclusion in that process would, at any event, guarantee, at least for the near future, a continuing exacerbation of the local conflict and the increased probability of Soviet success in gaining influence in the area.

In the Kremlin's general attempt to harness the Palestinians and the Arab states in a globalized 'anti-imperialist drive' it applied the same distinctions to terrorist actions as it had consistently applied previously in other contexts in its efforts to consolidate a 'national front' position which could use terror when deemed expedient. The distinction was made between the use of terrorism and the use of violence to further the struggle of national liberation movements. As an example, in July 1974 a 'political observer' for *Izvestiya* wrote an article which condemned terrorism but approved the intensification of 'Palestinian partisans' action against the aggressor'.[109] A month later, Alexandr Ignatov presented a sympathetic picture of the use of terror by the Habash and Jibril groups of the PLO.[110] Quoting the *Novosti* news agency,

---

*Hawatmeh's PDFLP had the longest and closest ties with the USSR of all the PLO factions. It was Hawatmeh who introduced the idea of a 'stages' policy - that the PLO would accept a part only of the claimed Palestinian territory, as a first step towards 'recovering' it all. Al-Fatah and al-Saiqa, the Syrian-controlled group also accepted the idea, which was against the principle of the Covenant to accept nothing less, ever, than the whole of the former mandated territory of Palestine. This slight concession was accepted by the 12th PNC, in June 1974, when the Soviet Union was eager for peace talks at Geneva in which it would participate. It is likely that Hawatmeh proposed the concession at the behest of the USSR, and it might be seen as a compromise between the PLO's position of holding out for the total destruction of Israel, and the Soviet Union's of accepting Israel's existence.

the Voice of Palestine (Clandestine) in Arabic to the Arab world explicitly described how the USSR viewed the Palestinian issue: 'The Soviet Union and the socialist countries . . . consider this movement a *combat* unit of the *world movement* for national liberation, as well as a unit of the Arab and world democratic forces' (emphasis added).[111]

Radio Moscow in Arabic usually carried a more aggressive and encouraging line than, for example, Radio Moscow in English. Furthermore, in a very interesting article on 'international terrorism and the struggle against it',[112] the USSR described terrorism as being 'most frequently . . . the actions of individuals not of groups', once again paraphrasing Lenin's rejection of *individual terrorism*. This was another attempt to dissociate the PLO from any terrorist incidents by attributing the acts to 'splinter groups', and also as a condemnation of the apparent lack of cohesion among the groups - a fact which continued to trouble the Kremlin. The article went on to define what it called the 'theory of so-called state terrorism' as 'Israel's policy toward the Arab population . . . and the barbaric methods of the Portuguese colonialists in Africa . . . the bloody outrages of the fascist junta in Chile'. It then made the following statement:

> The Soviet Union, proceeding from a position of principle, opposes any attempts to use the question of international terrorism perpetrated by *individual elements* in order to harm this [Palestinian] patriots' struggle . . . whose justness and legitimacy has been recognized, in particular by the United Nations . . . (Emphasis added)

In addition, the incorporation of the Palestinian National Front into the PLO* drew warm praise from the *New Times* correspondent, Victor Bukharov. This group, mainly made up of West Bank Arab Communists, gave the USSR added influence on the PLO. It was very active in terrorism.[113]

With the appearance of Yassir Arafat, gun-holster on hip, before the Twenty-Ninth General Assembly of the United Nations in the autumn of 1974, the Soviet propaganda campaign of legitimation and politicization of the PLO saw its first major success. Arafat, addressing the Assembly, spoke once again of the PLO's wish to destroy Israel and warned that it would continue its terrorist attacks if it could not achieve this. Five days later the PDFLP killed four Israeli civilians and wounded nineteen in a terrorist raid on the town of Bet Shan.[114]

*The PNF was founded in 1973, by the Jordanian CP. Some of its leaders, when exiled by Israel, were appointed to high positions in the PLO.

It was at this time that the Soviet Union shifted its official position even more strongly towards the PLO, and in particular, towards the idea of a Palestinian state to exist alongside the State of Israel.*[115] One day before the United Nations General Assembly debate on the Palestinian issue, Vladimir Volgin, in a radio commentary to North America, called the PLO 'the legitimate representative of the Palestinian people' and 'the sole representative'.[116] This was, however, not an abrupt decision taken by the Soviet Union but part of a gradual process. A few months earlier the Soviet Union had already begun to use a new terminology when referring to the PLO: 'legitimate national rights', an expression which carries within it the idea of statehood.[117] Although there was reticence on the part of the PLO to declare for a state, eventually a year later it fell in line with the Soviet position. Moscow Radio made the announcement on 28 November 1975 in its broadcast in Arabic. By that time the civil war in Lebanon was raging and although Moscow tried to explain the PLO's acceptance of the Soviet position as a sign of maturity and realism,[118] it probably more accurately reflected the growing dependence the PLO had developed in that civil war.

The advocacy of the destruction of the State of Israel, which the PLO still maintains as its foremost goal, was never seriously considered as a possibility by the USSR. To endorse that extreme position must have been seen as too strong a confrontational issue with the United States. However, it can also be argued that the continued existence of Israel would provide the necessary and possibly only catalyst for a certain amount of cohesiveness among the Arab states in general, and within the PLO in particular, and could thus facilitate the extension of Soviet influence in the Middle East area through either, or both.

Whatever the reasons - and the deteriorating relationship with Egypt, together with the concomitant growth of United States influence in the post-October War period (in spite of massive Soviet help in that area), must not be ignored as major influencing factors - the official relationship between the USSR and the PLO was strengthened and could now be used more aggressively and openly by the Kremlin.

From 1974 onwards official meetings between Arafat and Soviet leaders became more frequent and the continued practice of exonerating the PLO from any terrorist involvements featured widely in the propaganda efforts. A series of articles in *Izvestiya* in April 1975 by Victor Kudryavtsev categorically denied PLO involvement in any terror whatsoever, thus passing no comment

*For further details see ed. note p. 119.

on the Fatah attack on the Savoy Hotel in Tel Aviv on 6 March 1975. That attack was ignored by the Soviet media in general, which in itself can be interpreted as a sign of acceptance, if not of outright approval. A few months later, when al-Fatah took credit for the terrorist attack in Nahariya, the Soviet Union passed over the incident once again. This time the PLO behaviour departed from its habitual mimicking of the Kremlin's myth-creating insistence that all attacks on Israeli territory emanated from the local resistance movement and not from outside. Fatah claimed to have perpetrated the act.[119] The silence of the USSR on the event could indicate embarrassment - rather than any disapproval of the death of civilians. In August 1975 Radio Moscow in Arabic went so far as to quote 'PLO spokesman Shafiq Hut' who said that the 'PLO is prepared to sign an international agreement to combat terrorism'.[120] The statement in fact juxtaposed the PLO with Japan which had submitted an anti-terrorist treaty proposal, thus endowing the PLO with a sovereignty of equal standing to Japan, and here one can clearly find the growing emphasis on legitimizing the PLO as if it were a government-in-exile rather than treating it strictly as a national liberation movement.

The successes which resulted from the USSR's efforts in the Far East during this same period, with Vietnam and Cambodia falling to the communists, together with the stronger alliances enjoyed with Libya and Syria, must have been contributory factors to the Kremlin's ever-increasing reliance on a 'political' PLO for its official manoeuvres. When, in that year Kissinger's peripatetic step-by-step diplomacy failed, the USSR stepped up its diplomatic gestures to reconvene the Geneva Conference in a further attempt to extend its influence.

The importance which the Kremlin attributed to the PLO as an alternative 'political' instrument was particularly evident during the Lebanese civil war. Although the 1975-6 crisis presented the Soviet Union with difficult dilemmas of policy decision-making, its general position was one of offical support of the PLO-Lebanese leftist front against Syria.*

Syria, which had drawn closer to the USSR as a result of the Egypt-Israel disengagement agreement in Sinai, had assumed a leadership role of the 'anti-imperialist' bloc of Arab states. However, Libya and Iraq - both allies of the USSR - were financially

---

*Syria and the PLO were both allies of the USSR; and when Syria, which had armed, supported and sponsored the PLO in order to use it as a surrogate to overthrow the Lebanese government, turned against its own proxy in 1976, it was not with the approval of the USSR. Syria's own faction in the PLO, al-Saiqa, fought for its masters against its fellows.

supporting the leftist Muslim groups aligned with the PLO. And there were indications that the USSR made it known that it would look favourably on the overturn of the Lebanese Christian government which would have as an immediate result a considerable loss of influence for the West.[121] The pragmatic choice of supporting the PLO even at the expense of the favourable state-to-state relations the USSR enjoyed with Syria can only be viewed as a strategic long-term option choice, having direct bearing not only on the Middle East, but on the larger world policy goals of the USSR.[122]

It was in fact at the height of the Lebanese civil war that the Kremlin stepped up its official support for the PLO, again insisting on statehood and Geneva participation. In June 1976 the PLO opened its office in Moscow. That same month, on 27 June 1976, an Air France airliner was hijacked to Entebbe in Uganda by a mixed group of terrorists made up of PLO and Baader-Meinhof (RAF) members. There was no Soviet statement on the hijacking until several days later. Radio Moscow in English condemned the hijacking by quoting the Arab League and referred to 'the international convention on the prevention of illegal seizure of aircraft and hijacking of airliners' which regards such a seizure as 'a criminal act of air piracy'.[123] The articles covering the hijacking did not identify which terrorist group perpetrated the hijacking, preferring to call them 'a group of armed persons'[124] and, predictably and consistently with previous reactions, exonerated the PLO of any terrorist connection.

The condemnation of the act of hijacking must, however, be interpreted in the light of another hijacking which returned to the news a few days before Entebbe and was one on which the USSR had taken a strong legal condemnatory position: the escape from Turkish jails of the father and son Soviet hijackers (the Brazinskas) of the AN-24 Soviet airliner on 15 October 1970. It triggered an angry and vituperative response from the Soviet authorities who had renewed their request for the extradition of the pair of 'murderers for trial in the Soviet Union'.[125] In view of the proximity of the two events, the Soviet condemnation of the hijacking act was understandable and necessary if that legal position was to be maintained. The Entebbe raid by Israel which resulted in the release of the hostages, on the other hand, was given far more extensive coverage in the Soviet media and, while the terrorist act was indirectly condemned by quoting a foreign source, the raid by Israel was directly condemned by the Soviet Union which characterized it as 'a vivid example of terrorism . . . elevated to government policy' which should be condemned more than the act of air piracy.[126] On the same day, on Radio Moscow in English to

Africa, citing the OAU (Organization of African Unity), Kurt Waldheim and Idi Amin as all condemning the raid, the Soviet Union made propaganda value out of it, attempting to inflame the Arabs with anti-American and anti-Western emotion. Israel was identified as the aggressor and the Palestinians as victims of aggression: 'It is Zionist brigandage and terror brought to the level of state policy by Israel that reaffirms the justice of the stand taken by those who consider Zionism a form of racism.'[127] That comment in itself was an indirect admission that the PLO had been involved in the hijacking. A few days later TASS political news analyst Vladimir Goncharov was quoted on Radio Moscow explaining that any 'similar terrorist actions [such as the hijacking] are a direct result of Israel's refusal to reach an agreement that would respect the legitimate national rights of the Palestinian Arab people, the rights which are provided for by UN resolutions'. And the argumentation continued thus: 'Who then has created and continues to create this terror? Is it the Palestinian people or the aggressive usurping Israel?'[128]

This is, of course, consistent with the doctrinal position which the USSR has adopted on the concept of 'aggression'. As was seen earlier,[129] the Soviet position on defining aggression follows the dicta of Marx and Lenin which declared that 'aggression' is peculiar to 'class' societies only and therefore that only those societies are capable of aggressive behaviour. The removal of blame for any aggressive act, including a terrorist one, from the 'Palestinian people', is therefore consistent with that position which maintains that every form of struggle is permissible against the 'aggressor'. It also indicates an automatic approval of the act. Confirming this consistent position, Soviet Deputy Foreign Minister Vasily Kuznetsov, speaking at the General Assembly's 145-nation Main Political Committee, argued for a special treaty making the renunciation of the use of any kind of force 'an iron law in international life'. He qualified that request, however, by adding that the treaty 'should accept force in defence against aggression or its use by national liberation movements'.[130]

The years 1977-8 were to see the Soviet Union coming ever closer to a formal recognition of the PLO. Within the context of global foreign policy objectives and events, the Soviet position on the PLO, at least in the first half of 1977, indicated apparent official inconsistency in Soviet enthusiasm towards the PLO. This was governed by fluctuating international relations having a direct bearing on Soviet national interest, and formed a part of the multiple-options programme which was and has been characteristic of Soviet foreign policy decision-making.

The goal of Soviet policy in the Middle East, as elsewhere,

remained first and foremost one of opposition to United States policies and initiatives. However, several pragmatic considerations were to influence these fluctuations of emphasis in what concerned the PLO connection. For example, the SALT 1 agreements were due to expire in October of 1977. In retrospect, the renewal of Soviet diplomatic peace initiatives in the Middle East which culminated with the 1 October joint United States-Soviet declaration appear to have been, at least in part, a tactic of accommodation with the United States which would facilitate the resumption of the strategic arms limitation talks that Moscow viewed as a focal point in its foreign policy objectives. In addition, a lifting of the trade restrictions imposed by the United States in the aftermath of Soviet involvement in Africa was an immediate short-term goal which the Kremlin must have hoped to achieve. Brezhnev's repeated calls for an amelioration of United States-Soviet relations were accompanied by an apparent Soviet official shift away from the PLO's radical position, with suggestions of several points for a Middle East settlement which did not include the PLO at all and were aimed specifically at pleasing the United States and Israel. These points (secure borders for Israel based on the pre-1967 boundaries; timed withdrawal by Israel; a United Nations presence in a demilitarized zone) were presented along with renewed demands for the reconvening of the Geneva Conference, which would have ensured Soviet participation in any Middle East peace settlement.[131]

On the other hand, calls to reconvene the Geneva Conference with PLO participation were made several times throughout the year. Arafat paid several high-level visits to Moscow during 1977, even meeting Brezhnev himself during his April visit - a first meeting for the two, which in itself was one more step in the creation of a political image for the PLO. Soviet concern over an Egyptian-Syrian *rapprochement* might have been the immediate cause of Arafat's further promotion, but it was not inconsistent with the Kremlin's previous endorsements of the PLO. In a *Pravda* article of 4 May the Kremlin quoted Farouq Qaddoumi, head of the PLO's political section, as saying in an Arab magazine interview that the USSR regarded the Palestinian delegation which had recently visited Moscow as representing a sovereign state.

The meeting between Brezhnev and Arafat was splashed on the front page of *Pravda* in a report which included a photograph of the two men.[132] The importance of creating an independent state was once again emphasized by Brezhnev and made an inseparable part of any peace settlement, and Arafat reconfirmed his position and the position of the PLO as the leaders in the fight against 'intrigues of imperialism and reaction'.

The election of Menachem Begin in May 1977 provided the Soviet Union with propaganda material which it exploited in an attempt to revive the anti-imperialist Arab bloc, though ultimately with little success. Rather than exploiting the disagreements which quickly developed between the Carter and Begin administrations, the Soviet government sought to present United States-Israel relations as being very close, thus allowing the Kremlin to place itself squarely in opposition to any United States peace initiative. The joint United States-Soviet declaration of 1 October 1977 indicates in retrospect only a very brief shift in that policy. But, as it reintroduced the USSR into the Middle East peace process, it was an understandable pragmatic decision.[133] The joint statement made no mention of an independent state, nor of the PLO. However, this apparent moderation of the Soviet position was to disappear rapidly. Only a few days after the signing of the declaration, the Soviet Union rescinded those concessions and once again emphasized the need for a Palestinian state and PLO participation at the Geneva Conference.[134] In a strong position statement, Vadim Sergeyev, in a commentary in English to North America, once again presented the Palestinians as 'victims of aggression' and therefore as having the 'right to defend their interests using armed strength as well as peaceful means'. This, the commentary stated, should not be termed terrorism, but a 'just struggle for liberation'. Although reiterating the consistent line that the acts of terrorism were perpetrated by extremists - in itself a contradiction of the previous statement - Sergeyev encouraged further violence by stating that 'without a doubt the Palestinians will continue to respond with violence as long as Israel continues to suppress the rights of the Arabs'.[135] A few days later the Soviet representative to the United Nations, Oleg Troyanovsky, officially re-emphasized Soviet support for the PLO, which he now called 'the sole lawful representative of the Palestinian people'.[136]

By December 1977, and certainly because of the Sadat peace initiative a month earlier, the PLO was being described in more emphatic terms and its 'political' importance was spelt out. Emphasizing the recognition of the PLO by the Arab heads of state 'as the sole legal plenipotentiary representative of the Palestinian people' at the 1974 Rabat Conference, the Korshunov commentary which appeared in *Izvestiya* on 31 December 1977 presented a clear position statement of its position:

> The Soviet Union and the other socialist community countries take a clear and plain stand with regard to the PLO. They recognize it as the sole legitimate representative of the Arab people of Palestine, advocate the participation of its

representatives in the Geneva Conference on a basis of equal rights with the other participants and believe that there can be no genuine or comprehensive settlement in the Near East without implementation of the inalienable rights of the Palestinian people, including their right to self-determination and to create their own state.

The murder of Youssef el-Sebai, the Egyptian representative at the meeting held in Nicosia by the Soviet-sponsored Afro-Asian Solidarity Organization, was described in a TASS headline as an 'Act of Terrorism in Nicosia'. During the terrorist attack the Soviet delegation to the meeting, which included *Pravda's* correspondent, was taken hostage along with the rest of the participants, as were members of the PLO. This in itself was an unusual event and one which would presumably trigger negative reactions in Moscow. The murder was in fact called 'perfidious'[137] and said to have been carried out by 'criminals', and Arafat's denial of involvement was predictably broadcast in Moscow to the Western world.[138] The condemnation of this terrorist act indicated the Soviet impatience and discontent with the renewed and growing signs of fission within the PLO groups, warning of a potential loss of control by Arafat. The indications that this was probably so came right after Arafat's visit to Moscow in March.

To ensure his continued popularity among his members and the Arabs, Arafat proclaimed his intention to make 'war to the end'.[139] In an apparent attempt to reunify the PLO - which, as mentioned earlier, could only be achieved by a show of extremism - Fatah itself carried out the terrorist attack on a civilian bus in Herzlia outside Tel Aviv just one day after Arafat's return from Moscow. The action, which killed the largest number of civilians up to that time, including many children, took place on 11 March 1978. The Soviet response was immediate, an unusual timing for the Soviet Union which habitually delayed reactions to terrorist events. This in itself indicated perhaps a preparedness on the part of the Kremlin. In spite of the espousal of the act by the PLO, the official response by the Soviet media ignored its admission.* It called the terrorist act 'Incident near Tel Aviv',[140] and supported the action by attributing to it military characteristics. TASS, in fact, described it as an 'armed clash between a detachment of Palestinian guerrillas and Israeli army units' and the casualties were described as 'soldiers'.

A few days later Vladimir Kudryavtsev[141] blamed Israel once again and one can detect a certain amount of incitement to further

---

* Arafat himself was visiting the USSR at that time, and he denied prior knowledge of the attack

violence in his statements. First, he blamed Israel for conducting a policy of genocide in Lebanon, then went on: 'The "incident of 11 March near Tel Aviv" was not the product of malevolence but the result of Israel's own brutality and intransigence.'[142]

It is difficult to assume that Moscow had not been cognizant of the plan for the Herzlia terrorist attack, and the suggestion that the Soviet Union might have co-ordinated it [143] is not an extravagant one. Even without hard evidence of collusion between the Kremlin and the PLO, there are several overt circumstances which would tend to suggest it. The timing of the terrorist attack, which had the highest civilian casualties within Israel since the Six-Day War, coming as it did immediately after a Brezhnev-Gromyko-Arafat meeting in Moscow, is the most incriminating aspect. Brezhnev had, after all, met Arafat on 9 March and reaffirmed the USSR's unwavering support for the 'staunch struggle' of the Arab people of Palestine for freedom and independence, for which 'just struggle' they could always count on the USSR's support.[144] And Gromyko had noted 'an identity of views and attitudes . . . on the issues discussed'. The presumption that the imminent attack would not have been discussed at all between the parties is therefore difficult to accept. Both the timing and quality of the immediate reaction by the USSR which has already been mentioned also point to such a conclusion. In fact, the timing of the terrorist act itself would seem to have had at least three immediate goals, all of which were paramount for short-term Soviet policy goals.

First, it was an attempt to consolidate the PLO, a point of concern for the USSR, through perpetrating an extremist action. In view of the erosion of Soviet influence in the Middle East from 1973 to 1978, the PLO had come to represent the most reliable and dependent foothold for Moscow in the Middle East. Arafat would have needed this sort of extreme action to rally his members around him. A month after the attack there was a major crackdown by Arafat on the dissidents in the PLO.[145]

Secondly, it was aimed at torpedoing the Sadat peace initiative by impelling a predictable Israeli retaliatory raid on PLO bases in Lebanon, thus polarizing the 'left' and 'right' factions in the Middle East. It has been suggested that goading Israel into retaliation was an important factor in the Soviet policy of encouraging PLO activities.[146] An example of Soviet media incitement to violence had come a few months earlier in the immediate aftermath of Sadat's trip to Jerusalem. Radio Moscow broadcast the following message on 29 January 1978:

Who could imagine that the PLO would agree to such a defeatist agreement concluded behind its back? Who could imagine that

Fedayeen warriors, who were educated from childhood on the strength of the struggle for the liberation of their homeland, would sit with their hands clasped and watch the betrayal which is unfolding in front of their own eyes?

The third goal was consolidation of the 'left' rejectionist front* in an anti-United States and anti-imperialist mould, thus facilitating and justifying Soviet influence-seeking in the Middle East.

What must also be taken into consideration when looking at Soviet position statements on the PLO is the fact that Soviet tactical support to the PLO in the form of weapons and training was continuing and increasing at that time and was not ill-affected by the attack. None of this support has been denied by either the PLO or the Soviet Union. In fact, meetings between the various leaders of the PLO and Soviet officials continued throughout.[147]

Whether the March 1978 attack was actually co-ordinated in fine detail by the Soviet Union or not does not in itself alter the overall Soviet position on the question of terrorism and its use by the PLO. The attribution of a military scenario to that attack would even indicate an increased interest in the PLO itself. Even though the Soviet Union did demonstrate its concern for the apparent splintering and dissension within the PLO, and was perhaps ambivalent in regard to Arafat's future as its leader, the repeated meetings with various other leaders with greater Marxist tendencies, such as Naif Hawatmeh (PDFLP), could in themselves have accentuated this dissension. At any event, they did not indicate a shift away from the PLO or from its terrorist activities. On the contrary, the statements issued by Hawatmeh in May 1978, for example, denote a shift of emphasis towards a concerted revolutionary policy with greater global appeal - a position more in line with the Kremlin's overall policies in the area. Hawatmeh called for the PLO 'to mobilize all the popular masses behind a plan of action opposed to . . . Zionist imperialism, Arab reactionaries and defeatists'.[148] The same terminology has been emphasized to date by the Soviet media and by other members of the PLO: George Habash (PFLP), for example, in an interview of April 1973, made the following statement:[149]

> We emphasize a firm and clear stand against imperialism and its interests in the region and affirm that imperialism - *primarily American imperialism* - is our principal enemy. Therefore, the interests of the US in the area should be crushed, and any

*The Rejectionists were those PLO factions which did not accept the 'stages' policy introduced by the 12th PNC in 1974 (see ed. note p. 119). The author is using the words 'rejectionist front' in a looser sense to mean all the left-wing Arab groups and states in the Middle East, the so-called 'progressives'.

thought that that country could be neutral in our conflict with Zionist enemy should be abolished and rejected. (Emphasis added).

Arafat's deputy Abu Iyad, asserted that:[150]

American interests in the Middle East and elsewhere in the world are well known to us, and we will hit them because we realize the enormity of the animosity that the Americans harbour for us, Palestinians . . .

There have been over the years many official expressions of Soviet interest in the PLO terrorists which would tend to underline the support the Kremlin has demonstrated for the Organization. For example, when Abu Daoud, leader of the PLO terrorist wing 'Black September', was condemned to death by King Hussein for the Khartoum murders, the Presidium of the Supreme Court of the Soviet Union issued the following appeal for his release:[151]

Guided by humanitarian considerations, the Presidium of the USSR appeals to King Hussein to spare Abu Daoud, a prominent leader in the Palestine resistance movement and other Palestinians arrested . . . This humane act would be in keeping with the interests of uniting the patriotic forces of the Arab people in the struggle against Israeli aggression and would meet the approval of all friends of the Arab people.

There are at least three points which can be made about this statement. (1) 'Humanitarian considerations' were never alluded to by the Soviet official channels in any terrorist attack on civilians in Israel or the West, (2) The identification of Abu Daoud as a 'prominent member of the resistance movement' not only emphasizes approval of his deeds, but also serves to confirm that the murders at Khartoum and elsewhere were in fact carried out by the PLO, and not by 'splinter' groups over which the PLO had no control. This point at any event is only a contentious issue from the Soviet point of view, (3) Thus it follows that, had the terrorist attacks truly been perpetrated by 'dissidents' and not acceptable to the Kremlin, the Soviet Presidium would have at best remained silent on the imminent execution of Abu Daoud, content to get rid of such an unruly element. And again, when the French government released Abu Daoud several years later with unseemly haste, ignoring both German and Israeli extradition requests for the terrorist, the Soviet government praised France for that decision.[152]
Since 1979, build-up of the political image of the PLO by the

USSR has acquired intensified momentum. The official recognition of the PLO as the 'sole representative of the Palestinians' has been followed by a consistent series of appearances by Arafat or other PLO leaders in diplomatic roles. And it would appear that the PLO was persuaded by the Kremlin to join in a diplomatic offensive in addition to continuing its terrorist activities - a strategy the Kremlin had been encouraging for some time.*

The first such occasion was during the Egyptian embassy seizure in Ankara by the terrorist group calling itself the 'Eagles of the Palestinian Revolution', actually members of the Al-Saiqa Syrian-backed faction of the PLO. The terrorists' request was for Turkey to recognize 'the Palestinian State'. The PLO once again disclaimed any responsibility for the attack, but on this occasion offered its services as mediator. The rapid success of this PLO mediation was seen by local observers as a conclusive indication of the PLO's authority over the 'Eagles'.[153] Not only did the PLO preserve and improve its political legitimacy by presenting itself as a moderating force, but the outcome of the mediation provided the PLO with Turkish permission to open an office in Ankara and the safe-conduct of the 'Eagles' out of Turkey.

On 18 February 1979 the *Daily Telegraph* (London) published a picture of Khomeini and Arafat in a friendly grasp of hands. Arafat had arrived in Teheran to celebrate Khomeini's victory and to set up PLO training bases in Iran. A month later the USSR entrusted Abu Mazin, one of Arafat's closest aides, with negotiations on its behalf with Khomeini.[154] Other incidents, if correctly reported, showed the Kremlin utilizing the PLO increasingly as its agent. For instance, when the Iraqi Communists suffered a major crackdown, Boris Ponomarev, head of the International Department of the CPSU, is said to have appointed Abu-al Zain of the PLO to organize help and escape where possible for these Communists.[155]

After the takeover of the American embassy in Teheran, Chedli Klebi, Secretary-General of the Arab League, is reported to have stated that the siege 'could be solved overnight' if the United States would negotiate directly with the PLO.[156] This was once again an attempt at presenting the PLO as a mediator, this time through the auspices of the Arab League. It also implied at least considerable power of persuasion by the PLO, if not outright involvement. Since then American intelligence sources confirmed the participation of

---

* Diplomatic and political means to attain a Palestinian state, in addition to the 'armed struggle' which the Covenant laid down as the only means to that end, were agreed to, along with a second endorsement of the 'stages' policy (see ed. note p. 119) by the 13th PNC of 1977. Not all the PLO factions accepted either of these two concessions even then.

Palestine terrorists in the capture of the American hostages in the United States Embassy. A few months later, on 18 July 1980, Arafat was reported to be in Moscow, not only to seek new arms, but to pave the way for a possible meeting between the Soviet leaders and President Assad of Syria who at the time had difficulties in Lebanon with which he needed help.[157] In addition, Arafat was an official guest at the Moscow Olympics, an honour usually accorded only to state representatives. From Moscow, he flew to Managua, Nicaragua, where he was accorded to hero's welcome by the Sandinista government and official thanks were given for the help the PLO had extended to the Sandinistas in the training of guerrillas.[158]

In 1981 the Soviet Union faced several major problems in its foreign relations. The quagmire in Afghanistan had by now proved to be a major blunder of strategic miscalculation. The massive unrest in Poland was causing grave concern to the Kremlin and embarrassment abroad. And in the Middle East, Iran and Iraq were at war. Perhaps to detract attention from its own massive problems, and consistent with its previous diplomatic behaviour when it perceived itself in a delicate position *vis-à-vis* the West, the USSR initiated a new round of diplomacy with the expressed purpose of achieving peace in the Middle East. In that process the PLO, in the person of Arafat, was placed at the service of the Kremlin. In April 1981 the USSR dispatched Arafat to Holland where he was received by the Dutch Foreign Minister, Christoph van der Klaauw. The purpose of this trip was to present this new Soviet initiative for a Middle East peace plan and the PLO acted as spokesman for the Kremlin.[159] Farouq Qaddoumi, head of the PLO's Political Department, quoted by the Palestine News Agency WAFA in Beirut, stated very recently that the Soviet leaders had praised 'the active and effective resistance of the PLO and the Palestinian people to the Zionist occupation and to the United States imperialist plans, in the Middle East and *outside it*' (emphasis added). He stated that Moscow was now seriously considering giving the PLO full ambassadorial status.[160] This statement not only indicates the growing Kremlin interest in the PLO, but does so with the direct implication that the Kremlin approved the PLO's terrorist activities both in the Middle East and elsewhere in the world.

This ever-increasing overt endorsement and reliance on the PLO by the Kremlin in 1979-81 was very much aided by the inordinate diplomatic success the PLO enjoyed in Europe during those years. The invitation to attend the Socialist International meeting in Vienna extended to Arafat by the Austrian Chancellor, Bruno Kreisky, in 1979, marked the beginning of a boost to the 'respectable image' which the Soviet Union had been nurturing for years for the PLO. Moreover, Italy, itself plagued by terrorism, extended political recognition to the PLO in 1980 - and this in spite of evidence accumulated by the Italian security services and the government of PLO material support for Italian terrorism. In the same year the European Economic Community (EEC) was considering the adoption of a formal stance in favour of the PLO.[161] The initial move, led by France in the person of Giscard d'Estaing, was quickly followed by Lord Carrington, then Britain's Foreign Secretary, who on 17 March 1980 stated that the 'PLO as such is not a terrorist organization'.[162] This European initiative to endorse the PLO culminated with the Venice Summit Declaration of June 1980 and must have been viewed with some degree of satisfaction by Moscow, for not only was its ward becoming more useful to the Kremlin in the political arena for its Middle East initiatives, but it was also helping to create a schism between the Western European countries and the United States, which still supported Israel. Thus, the isolation of Israel and the United States, long a declared objective of Kremlin foreign policy, was becoming a reality.

Arafat had already paid official visits to Spain and Turkey in September 1979 and October 1979 respectively. In November he met Portuguese leaders during a Lisbon conference on the Palestinian question. In March 1980 India extended recognition to the PLO. This was seen as part of India's policy of supporting, or at least not opposing, the Soviet Union's invasion of Afghanistan. Throughout the year renewed demands were made to the Security Council for a Palestinian state. And in October 1980 Arafat addressed the UNESCO General Conference at Belgrade with all the ceremony normally reserved for heads of state.

The fifteenth meeting of the PNC, held in Damascus in April 1981, reaffirmed the PLO's hard-line statements and renewed the commitment to armed struggle. Vladimir Kudryavtsev, now a member of the Supreme Soviet, told the 'Palestinian Parliament' that the Soviet Union supported the Palestinian people and Syria, which now occupied most of Lebanon, 'in their struggle against American Imperialism and Zionism'.[163] On 20 October 1981, during a visit to Moscow by Arafat, Leonid Brezhnev announced the upgrading of the PLO office in Moscow to full diplomatic status.[164]

This full recognition of the PLO was extended in the immediate aftermath of the assassination of President Anwar Sadat of Egypt - a deed which had been hailed by Arafat as 'the beginnning of the failure of the Camp David Agreement'.[165] In effect, this move reflected the Kremlin's interest in assuming a larger role in the Middle East in view of the uncertainty regarding Sadat's successor's policy. Brezhnev praised the PLO as the 'political avant-garde' of the Palestinian people, emphasizing that it had won 'wide international recognition' as the Palestinians' 'sole legitimate representative'.[166] Here, once again, Brezhnev reiterated the overall Soviet policy of 'strengthening of the unity of action of Arab states, of all patriotic forces of the Arab world, as one of the decisive factors in the struggle against the intrigues of imperialism and Zionism, and for the establishment of a genuine peace in the Middle East'. A few days later the newly elected Greek Socialist Government followed the Soviet initiative and raised to ambassadorial level the PLO's official status, a higher diplomatic representation than that enjoyed by Israel in Greece. The country only accords *de facto* recognition to Israel.

This full endorsement by the USSR as has been seen, was the culmination of a steady shift in favour of the PLO, and was extended in spite of the totally unchanged extremist position held by that group. The PLO had not indicated any softening of its radical line, either on the question of the existence of the State of Israel, or on its continued use of terrorist tactics. In fact, 1981 was marked by several terrorist attacks by the PLO on Jewish civilian targets in Western Europe, and a continue policy of terrorism within Israel, mostly on the West Bank and in the Gaza Strip, where many Palestinians were killed.[167]

In a long interview on the recognition by the USSR, PLO executive Abu Iyad was quoted by Voice of Palestine Radio as stating that this endorsement 'signifies recognition of the State of Palestine before its birth'. He proceeded, in an apparent public relations effort for Moscow, to entreat the conservative Arab states to extend diplomatic recognition to the USSR:

> Will this initiative be met by another initiative, in that some Arab states, in which to this moment the Soviet Union does not have an embassy, take the intiative of announcing the opening of Soviet embassies? . . . [We should] not consider the Soviet Union only as a source of arms but also as a political and military power, and [should] ally ourselves with it as an answer to the US-Zionist alliance.

He also went on to emphasize that the mutuality and support was not limited itself to the Soviet Union alone, but included 'the Socialist bloc and all the world liberation movements'.[168]

The question of a Palestinian state headed by the PLO has been on the agenda of Soviet policy since 1974. Although the initial official interest shown by the USSR in the PLO was not accompanied by simultaneous interest in a state entity for that group, this interest gained in importance in the immediate aftermath of the USSR expulsion from Egypt.

Since 1974 the Kremlin has not always appeared to be in agreement with the PLO, particularly on the latter's aim of destroying Israel. However, the culmination of its policy of political endorsement, the bestowing of diplomatic honours, confirms the *de facto* nullifications of any real objections Moscow might have expressed on this question and certainly indicates no abhorrence for the terrorist activity systematically undertaken by the PLO. This point can be clearly seen in Soviet official statements.

In view of the very strong opposition by Israel and the United States to the inclusion of the PLO in any peace negotiations, this Soviet endorsement, and insistence on PLO participation ensures a confrontational atmosphere which is detrimental to all parties concerned except the USSR. Furthermore, it has allowed the Kremlin to keep a foothold in the Middle East in an otherwise unreliable area of Soviet influence and has enabled the Kremlin to present itself as more moderate than the PLO itself. Moscow, in fact, has kept several options open in its Middle East dealings and particularly with regard to the Palestinian issue. Its diplomatic manoeuvring has included, as previously discussed, the possibility of dropping the PLO completely in the official domain of negotiations, were such a move to prove more beneficial to Soviet interests at any given time. The absence of territorial perimeters for the PLO has, at any event, been beneficial to the Kremlin as it has kept that group in a dependent position *vis-à-vis* the USSR and thereby more prone to control by the Kremlin. It has also allowed the PLO to maintain its radical position and to continue in its use of terrorism, both of which it would have found more difficult to do had it been endowed with the more responsible behaviour expected of state entities. The initial hesitations by the Kremlin in the official endorsement of the PLO were thus the product of rapidly changing international positions and the Kremlin's view of how best to realize its goals and interests, and not in response to PLO objectives or methods. It is important to note that Soviet official statements, as has been seen, have consistently demonstrated approval of and even incitement to violence.

The overriding goal of the Soviet foreign policy, of maintaining itself always in a tense and confrontational position to the United States, has been the determining factor in its choice of options and, it can be argued, the consistent political endorsement of the PLO has successfully kept it in that position not only in the Middle East but also elsewhere. At minimum expense to itself, the Kremlin has greatly benefited in political and psychological terms from its 'anti-imperialist' strategy.

The successful political image-building of the PLO has enabled the Soviet Union to use that group as one of the vehicles for obtaining privileges and opportunities within the Third World, as well as elsewhere, in its quest for worldwide influence.

Should the Palestinian issue result in the establishment of a state headed by the PLO, the Soviet Union would naturally be the immediate beneficiary. For a certain time at least, such a state would be fully dependent on Soviet arms and international diplomatic support. Should the Palestinian issue, on the other hand, be resolved in some way which would ultimately exclude the PLO, the Organization might by kept alive to foment conflict. The Soviet Union would still need it as a tool for its overall global and specific regional policies. In either case, the use of terrorist methods would have to be continued if the PLO were to maintain any degree of cohesion and if Arafat were to remain as its leader. *
The fulfilment of its covenant would remain the ultimate goal.

The Soviet Unofficial Position on the PLO

That the Soviet Union should have an unofficial relationship at all with a group with which it has been in a strong official partnership is interesting in itself, and would tend to indicate that official statements made by the USSR about the PLO have not always asserted either the reality of the purpose or of the affiliation. In fact, it would indeed tend to confirm at least three points which have been argued so far:

(1)   that the USSR has consistently managed its foreign policy on multiple levels since 1917 while seeking the most pragmatic way to attain advantage for its interests;
(2)   that by finding it necessary to carry on an unofficial relationship with the PLO, the Kremlin has in fact been indicating an interest in all its activities, which have at any rate been primarily terroristic;

* Such agreement as the factions could reach in 1968 was made possible by all of them agreeing to 'the armed struggle' being the only method by which Palestine could be 'recovered' and Israel destroyed. The idea was that all differences, however wide, would be set aside while the urgent business of battle claimed their necessary collaboration. Nevertheless, the PLO was not cohesive - the component groups were constanly in conflict with one another. 'Unity' was maintained as a front for the outside world only. Arafat was good at public relations, and particularly successful with West European foreign ministries and press correspondents. To this he owed his being allowed to continue as 'leader', that is to say front-man, right up to 1983. The USSR too, presumably, appreciated the good impression he made on West European governments.

(3) that the Kremlin decided to make the PLO a politically respectable entity, although it was fully aware of the Organization's terrorist activity (an awareness which the covert nature of the relationship confirms).

The fact of this unofficial relationship has already been established[169] and is no longer a contentious issue. All the details of this relationship are, by their very nature, difficult to come by, and the complete picture may not be known for some time to come. There has, however, been enough information surfacing to establish its existence.

The exact date of the initiation of the covert relationship is not a precisely available fact, and if it were clearly established it might prove to have greater significance in the global context of international terrorism than the PLO-Israel context.

As has already been pointed out, the first known contacts between the PLO and the USSR were made through Bulgaria, Czechoslovakia and East Germany granting a number of scholarships to the General Union of Palestinian Students of which Arafat had been the president.[170] There was also a report of an East German offer to supply arms to the PLO in 1967.[171] The earliest link this author has been able to trace is one which started in 1966 and came to light in August 1968, at the time of an al-Fatah demand for the release of one of its colleagues held in an Israeli prison. The demand noted in passing that the man had been trained by the Viet Cong in Vietnam in 1966.[172] The known role played by the Soviet Union in the Vietnam War, through training and logistical support of the Viet Cong, leads to the speculation that the interest in the PLO by the USSR pre-dated its official statements of support which began to appear after the Six-Day War and after the replacement of Shuqairy. The *Izvestiya* article of 6 May 1966 which described the *fedayeen* as 'mythical diversionary groups' would then have to be viewed slightly differently, particularly in view of the Gromyko-Shuqairy meeting which took place in the same month, and might be indicative of a lack of readiness for support on the part of either the group or of the Kremlin.* Possibly there was a disagreement with Shuqairy rather than a lack of interest. The ambivalence of the Kremlin at that time would at least indicate a hesitation, perhaps, to place all its support in the PLO when it was enjoying successful state-to-state relations with Syria, Iraq, Yemen and the Sudan.*

In March 1969 a Kuwaiti paper quoted Arafat as stating that the Cuban army commanders had visited *fedayeen* bases in Jordan.[173] The Cuban connection with the PLO and active support extended

---

* The PLO was not a fedayeen group at this time, nor were any fedayeen groups yet part of it. The fedayeen took over the PLO in 1968.

to it with the training of PLO terrorists caused talks to be held in Havana between Israel's envoy and Cuban Foreign Ministry officials who predictably denied the reports.[174] However, during a lecture given in Kuwait a year later on 13 April 1970, Hani al-Hasan, an al-Fatah leader, mentioned that a number of Fatah members had just graduated from the military academy in Havana.[175] Cuba, in fact, has been a major supportive surrogate for the Soviet Union in its foreign operations since the middle 1960s.[176]

The Soviet Union established a school for sabotage in Prague, specifically for the training of Fatah men, the very group which it went out of its way to politicize and dissociate from any terrorist activity. The course, taught by Russian and East German instructors, lasted six weeks, after which the men were transferred to a camp in Kosice, Slovakia, where they stayed for a further four and a half months.[177]

The USSR has traditionally provided training in unconventional warfare methods since it first opened camps in Tashkent shortly after the Bolshevik *coup* was discussed in Chapter 4. The Central Committee of the Communist Party controls the Lenin Institute and Patrice Lumumba University where instruction is given in all methods of psychological warfare and subversive use of the media, as well as in Marxist-Leninist ideology.[178] From there the students move on to training camps dotted around the country as in Baku, Tashkent, Odessa and Simferopol in the Crimea. Other camps exist in Karlovy Vary, Doupov and Ostrava in Czechoslovakia; Varna in Bulgaria; near Lake Balaton in Hungary; in East Germany near Pankov and Finsterwalds.[179] Other countries such as Cuba, North Korea, Lebanon, South Yemen, Libya and Algeria also have camps which are used for this kind of training. East Germany, because of its geographic position, has served as a link-up station for these students once the courses are completed.

The first concrete evidence of this specific training of PLO personnel and others emerged during the Israel's Litani operation in Lebanon in 1978. The Israel Defence Forces captured important documents which included maps in Russian attesting to the nature of the training received by PLO members in East Germany, together with graduation certificates issued by the USSR Ministry of Defence's Command and Staff College, and propaganda material. The graduation certificates attest to completion of specific courses and entitle the bearer 'to practise in the acquired discipline'.

Another revelation of direct involvement by the Soviet Union in

---

* The PLO was under the control of President Nasser of Egypt, between 1964, when he founded it, and 1968 when the Syria-supported fedayeen took it over. The Syrian regime was in rivalry with Nasser and hostile to him.

the training of PLO terrorists as well as European ones came in the aftermath of the Hebron terrorist attack on 2 May 1980, which resulted in the murder of six Jews. The four-man terrorist squad arrested by the Israelis was led by Adnan Abu Jaber who admitted to having had several months of advanced training in the Soviet Union near Moscow.[180] The quality of the training is of particular interest for it concentrates mainly on the production of incendiary and explosive devices, the preparation of electrical charges, the study of exploding metals and special training in chemical and biological warfare. The PLO took credit for the terrorist attack in Hebron and Yasser Arafat even praised it the following day when he said: 'This is the answer of our people who decided to carry on a strong fight, and who completely reject the Camp David conspiracy.'[181]

In the same year, 1970, George Habash (PFLP) confirmed in an interview with Italian journalist Oriana Fallaci that Arab terrorists had been receiving arms from the Soviet Union.[182] It should be recalled here that the USSR had presumably not yet officially endorsed the PLO and the meetings were still being held only between Arafat and the Soviet Afro-Asian Solidarity Committee. However, in 1970 Arafat did meet secretly with Mazurov and with Ponomarev.[183]

At this juncture, there are two important points to be emphasized.

(1)   As has been seen, the so-called splinter groups of the PLO all operate under the control of al-Fatah headed by Arafat* and therefore Soviet official and unofficial material support to the PLO is *a priori* an endorsement of all its terrorist activities.

(2)   As will be discussed later, the links of the PLO with all major terrorist groups operating in Western liberal democracies, and some Third World countries, have allowed the Soviet Union a means of having global impact. This reflects an increasing reliance on destabilizing terrorist tactics. This shift towards the PLO and its use of terrorism coincides with Soviet military thinking and foreign policy statements which have emphasized the need to promote civil wars *within* the capitalist countries, as has already been discussed, and placed increased emphasis on the paramilitary use of unconventional forces.

With regard to the PLO, the provision of arms on an official level alone would be sufficient to indicate an endorsement of the PLO's

* Al-Fatah was the largest and most powerful group in the PLO. Such real power as Arafat had in the Organization derived from his leadership of al-Fatah and his shop-window authority as Chairman of the whole Organization. His actual control over the member factions was negligible. This does not, however, invalidate the point that to support the PLO was to endorse its terrorist activities.

terrorist activities, but the secret meetings and the training camps only serve to underline that the relationship between the Kremlin and the PLO was not based on support of a purely political group, as the USSR has systematically asserted. The policy overtly followed by the Kremlin is more indicative of an attempt at obfuscation directed at the Western world, and does not represent the reality of the relationship. Although the Western media, and some Western governments, have also lately dissociated the PLO from terrorist deeds, Abu Daoud himself long ago admitted, in a broadcast over Amman radio, that 'Black September', for example, did not exist as a separate organization and that all its activities were carried out by the intelligence branch of Fatah.[184] During that broadcast he mentioned that Arafat's chief lieutenant, Abu Iyad, had planned the Munich massacre. Whether that massacre was planned by Abu Daoud or Abu Iyad is irrelevant to the case, as both are and were at the time, executives of the PLO.

Moreover, at the time of the murder of United States Ambassador Cleo A. Noel, Jr, the US Deputy Chief of Mission George Curtis Moore, and the Belgian Consul Guy Eid, by 'Black September' terrorists, it was reported that Arafat was present in the command centre which gave the death order.[185] The perpetrators of the Rome massacre of thirty passengers in December 1973 were eventually handed over to the PLO by Kuwait for trial. The four men were never tried and eventually were reportedly allowed to live in Cairo.[186] The PLO had denied responsibility for the attack and had even denounced the terrorist acts for 'hurting the Palestinian cause'.[187]

The extent of Soviet interest can ultimately best be pointed out if one examines the kinds of weapon which have been provided by them. In the Litani operation of 1978 the first massive quantities of Soviet and Soviet-bloc materiel were first discovered. The arms included a wide variety of anti-tank and anti-aircraft missiles - SAM-7s, such as those found in the possession of Daniele Piffani and two Palestinians in November 1979 in a Rome apartment - and Soviet-made artillery: guns, mortars and Katyusha rockets together with a wide array of small arms. In addition, the PLO is the only terrorist group to have received ultra-modern, sophisticated weapons, which have often not been available even to state clients of the USSR and these in turn have been made available to other groups.*

Underlining the relationship on the unofficial level there are the weekly meetings which took place in Beirut between Arafat and the

---

* It is now known that the USSR did not supply its newest and best weapons to the PLO.

Soviet Ambassador Soldatov to Lebanon, confirmed by reliable sources in Israel. Soldatov was posted to Beirut from Cuba and is generally regarded as a leading expert on urban guerrilla warfare. It is unlikely, therefore, that these regular meetings did not discuss co-operation in regard to the undermining of the peace process.

In summary, the decision to endorse the PLO on an official level was influenced by many variable factors which might have delayed that decision further than 1967, or even altered the policy completely, if those factors would have brought different results. Ultimately, the choice of the PLO as the main emissary for Soviet power projection, in both the regional and global contexts, was conditioned by several factors which amplified its appeal.

(1)   The endorsement and financing of the PLO by the oil-rich states made it a cost-effective paramilitary tool for Soviet foreign policy.

(2)   The absence of any territorial perimeters allowed the PLO to set up training camps in many countries and endowed it with a larger potential for unacceptable behaviour without the possibility of any retribution from the Society of Nations. The United Nations calls Security Council meetings for state actors only. The result has been that the PLO has not been called to answer for its actions by that or any other world body. There has therefore accrued a distinct advantage for future support and sponsorship of such non-state actors under the present framework of the United Nations.

(3)   The latent anti-semitism which exists in the West must have been an added factor which was not overlooked by the Kremlin in its selection of the PLO. It was, in fact, certainly the only such group which could have that potential for harnessing 'anti-Zionism' in a worldwide context.†

(4)   The backing of the PLO by the oil-wealth of the Middle East provided the added attraction of a clash of interests within the Western alliance, caused by European states fearing to be starved of oil.

(5)   The PLO, in its extremism, ensured a continuity of conflict in the Middle East area, thus allowing the Soviet Union to have some influence in that region.

(6)   There is in fact no evidence to suggest that, had Moscow *not* opted to back the PLO on the diplomatic front, it would also have denied the unofficial support.

---

† It might also be said that the Soviet Union could have expected the Western support for national self-determination to be translated into support for the Palestinian cause and hence for the PLO. It was perhaps to reinforce this predisposition that the PLO adopted its policy of concentrating rather than dispersing the refugees, so emphasizing - and worsening - their plight.

In the *Washington Post* of 28 November 1974 there appeared a photograph of Arafat accompanied by KGB officer Samolenko at a wreath-laying ceremony in Moscow. It would appear that the first connections and regular contacts between Arafat and Samolenko began in the 1950s[188] Should this information be conclusively corroborated sometime in the future when more classified information will be declassified and made public, it would underline the fact that the interest the Kremlin had in the PLO was a subversive one from the beginning.* The political endorsement progressed steadily as the volatile situation in the Middle East changed, and as the Soviet Union failed to maintain reliable ties with the existing states. It was also influenced by the political success obtained by the PLO in the West and in the oil-rich Arab states. It saw a strong possibility of the establishment of a Palestinian state, which would naturally gravitate towards it, at least in the short term.

International Links

SUB-REVOLUTIONARY TERRORISM

This section will examine principally the type of terrorism which has been prevalent in the Western liberal democracies since 1968 and which, within the definitional framework of this study, is classified as sub-revolutionary in nature.

As previously mentioned, the clandestine support given by the Soviet Union to the PLO indicates that the Soviet Union found them useful far beyond the Middle East. In the last few years, the links established by the PLO with practically all the major and the minor terrorist groups operating in the West and countries allied to the West have become now a matter of record. For example, a link which is often overlooked is the one al-Fatah maintained with Eldridge Cleaver and the Black Panthers movement in the United States. On 27 December 1969 Arafat met Cleaver in Algiers where Cleaver had been given asylum after fleeing the United States, and both Cleaver and Arafat participated in the First International Congress of Palestine Solidarity Committees.* Less than a month later Abu Bassam, al-Fatah representative in Algiers, admitted that his organization was in fact training Black Panthers.[189] As reported

---

* Arafat had no connection with the PLO until 1968. Nevertheless, it may indeed have been KGB knowledge of Arafat in his student days in Cairo, or his years in Kuwait, which made them interested in him as a potential activist. However, if they had known much about him they might have doubted the reliability of a Muslim fundamentalist and nationalist, whose sympathies were always more naturally with the 'conservative' than the 'progressive' Arab states and parties.

in the 1976 *Yearbook of International Communist Affairs*, the close connections have indeed extended in Europe, to Carlos, Henri Curiel, the Red Brigades, the IRA, ETA, the TLA (Turkish Liberation Army), the RAF, the JRA and the JCR (umbrella organization for South American terrorist groups from Argentina, Bolivia, Chile, Paraguay and Uruguay). As will be seen, all of these groups have had links with other groups, assisting one another with weapons, safe-houses, passports and targets.

The more recent evidence which has emerged presents a picture of a conglomerate of groups, having little to do with ideological labelling, some of which are only just coming on to the scene of international terrorism, so that an increase in the use of this mode of conflict in the future may be predicted. The web appears in fact to be very thick, and it is difficult to discuss one group without bringing many others into the picture. For example, on 23 May 1980 it was established that links existed between the Dutch 'Red Resistance Front' and ETA. Four ETA members were arrested in Amsterdam after a training period of four months in the People's Democratic Republic of Yemen in a PFLP camp. Both before and after that date, on 17 March and 27 June 1980, remote-control explosive devices were detonated for the first time by ETA members who had likewise been trained in Yemen. Such devices were used by the PLO in the early 1970s and it is a justifiable assumption that those acquired by ETA came through the auspices of the PLO. The 'Red Aid' and 'Red Resistance Front' groups themselves underwent training in South Yemen in PFLP camps earlier in 1976.[190] They, in turn, collaborated with the RAF of West Germany.

Moreover, there has been a multitude of co-operative ventures by terrorist groups, often initiated by the PLO, such as the Air France hijacking to Entebbe in 1976 which was carried out by both German RAF members and the PLO; the hijacking of the Lufthansa airliner to Mogadishu in October 1977, which was carried out by the PLO and organized by Wadi'Haddad, who was at that time in East Germany, as a service to the Red Army Faction of West Germany. The latter group had abducted Hanns Martin Schleyer five weeks earlier (his body was found in the trunk of a car on 17 October 1977) and the Mogadishu hijacking was meant to exert added pressure on the West German government.[191] That kidnapping of Schleyer is said to have been initiated in East Berlin.[192] In fact, the Soviet Union seized on the Lufthansa skyjacking to urge the West to stop giving political asylum to 'criminals' who fled the Communist bloc, an allusion to the

* They fell out subsequently (*Jerusalem Post Weekly*, 20 January 1976).

hijackings committed in the Soviet Union which have been discussed earlier.[193] Only very limited coverage was given to the Mogadishu event itself. In any event, pressure could have been exerted on Wadia Haddad at the time by the Soviets or the East Germans to stop the action.* The fact that it was not would suggest acquiescence in the deed, if not collusion.

In 1979 evidence was surfacing of third-generation RAF activity in Central America.[194] Every year additional facts have emerged, and are still emerging, which unmistakably point to collusion if not co-ordination of the different international terrorist groups.

Those links have been confirmed by Western governments and the media for some years now.[195] It is, however, of importance to look at the data which have been emerging, and fill in the *pointilliste* picture. Where has direct involvement by the Soviet Union been evident, where has there been involvement of any Soviet surrogate - such as the Cuban DGI, or the East German, Bulgarian and Czechoslovakian secret services - in extending help in any way to any of the groups? And also, how have the groups been connected with the PLO which, as has already been discussed, was singled out by the Soviet Union for special attention? It is essential to add, however, that it is not within the scope of this study to attempt any new proof of Soviet complicity in the deeds of various terrorist groups in the contemporary context. To pursue the goal of finding the 'smoking gun' - actually to catch the KGB *in flagrante delicto* - is best left to the security services. However, where such proof of complicity has been found and already established, as in the historical perspective of this study, it is important to present it to complete the analysis of Soviet policy in this context. It stands to reason that if there is evidence of direct or indirect Soviet involvement it must ultimately be part of a Kremlin policy and must fulfil some specific goal.

The Soviet unofficial position on international terrorism in the last two decades, as discussed above (pp. 136-42) has, at any event, shown no hypocrisy *vis-à-vis* its official statements on the subject. These official statements have explicitly approved of international terrorism as part of the revolutionary process, and the unofficial policy has provided evidence of that approval. Equally, the ideology and the official position on the question have supported each other faithfully. As has been seen, the unofficial position until the 1950s has shown the Kremlin to have matched words on terrorism with terroristic deeds. The USSR has consistently been involved in a variety of geographic locations and with a heterogeneous and amorphous selection of groups and individuals

---

* Haddad was in an East German hospital at the time.

who have perpetrated terrorist activities. This interest and participation by the Soviet Union has either been direct, as was seen earlier, with Soviet consuls in remote places organizing violence or KGB agents participating directly in terrorist activities, particularly in the early years following the Bolshevik *coup;* or it has been indirect, by exploiting local conditions and by encouraging various factions to use violence, either on KGB instigation or by the use of surrogates. What emerges from the evidence which has been surfacing lately is that the Kremlin has continued to be involved in the fostering of international terrorism, but on a much more sophisticated and intense level - so much so that the connections which lead back to the Kremlin are multiple ones, as if to ensure that at least one link should effectively fulfil the goals pursued. In the event that one should be uncovered or destroyed, its interests would always be served by another. Apart from actual KGB or GRU involvement, there have been mainly five additional vehicles which it is now known have operated for the Kremlin: 'Carlos', Henri Curiel, Giangiacomo Feltrinelli, other communist parties such as the PCF and the PCI and, of course, the PLO. The assistance given by Eastern bloc countries is also a matter of record.

In an attempt to present a complicated pattern in a relatively simple fashion; the individuals and their links with Moscow will be discussed first. Then some of the more important individual groups which have had close relations with the East, such as the IRA, RAF, BR and ETA, will be discussed. As will be seen, there is much interlinking with the KGB, GRU and Eastern bloc countries, as well as local communist parties, 'Carlos', the PLO, Curiel, Feltrinelli and Boudia. In fact, one finds the PLO connection with most European groups as having been established as early as the 1960s, with training of their own personnel having taken place earlier.

Henri Curiel Henri Curiel has been the subject of much speculation and controversy and many court cases. Various intelligence services in the West have kept bulging files on his activities. There was speculation at the time when Curiel was identified as a logistic supporter of international terrorism that the leak had come from the French DST which, together with the police, had been the target of criticism for its incapacity or unwillingness to control terrorist operations in France.

The first vivid exposé on him was published by Georges Suffert in *Le Point* on 21 June 1976, and the first revelations of his activities were apparently provided as a result of the arrest of Breyten Breytenbach, the South African poet who spent nine years in a

South African prison for terrorist activities. He had gone to South Africa after having lived in Paris for many years[196]

Born on 13 September 1914 in Cairo, Egypt, to a Jewish family, Curiel was one of the original founders of the Communist Party of Egypt and had an instrumental role in the founding of the Sudanese Communist Party as well. In the early 1930s, he became involved in politics, mainly stimulated by the rise of nazism and by the Civil War in Spain. He became very active in anti-fascist groups and in groups opposing ant-semitism. During this same period he established close friendship ties with the Trotskyite Loftallah Soliman who was later found to be connected with the Palestinians in France.[197] Also during this period his first cousin, Georges Behar, who was later to be better known as George Blake, the MI6 mole, moved in with the Curiel family after his father's death and finished his studies in Cairo. George Blake was of course arrested in England, later to make his escape from Wormwood Scrubs prison in 1966, assisted by Sean Bourke of the IRA who died in 1982.[198]

In 1941, Curiel purchased the bookstore Rondpoint in Cairo and edited the communist newspaper *Murriet El Shaab* (Democratic Solidarity). His bookstore was also the sole distributor in Cairo for Soviet books, journals, brochures and newspapers published by Mezhdunarodnaya Kniga.

As soon as diplomatic relations between Egypt and the USSR were established in 1943, Curiel became the assiduous host of the Soviet representatives there, particularly Abdel Rahman Sultanov, the Middle East GPU operative.

The distribution of literary and propaganda materials from the Soviet Union was not limited to the intellectual milieu of Cairo but spread to the French Communist Party in Algeria. In connection with Algeria Henri Curiel acted as host to André Marty, member of the PCF and a member of the ECCI of the Comintern since 1932. Given the importance of André Marty, who was appointed by Stalin to head the Algerian Communist Party, the hosting of this man during his stopover from Moscow to Algiers was no doubt a sign of confidence from the Soviet Union in Curiel and a mark of his standing.

Curiel's political activities in Egypt ultimately caused his arrest by King Farouk, but he was later released and banished from Egypt in August of 1950, at which time he and his wife went into exile in Italy. There he lived at 41 via Piave in Rome, and was closely associated with and assisted by Velio Spano, alias Paolo Tedeschi, one of the original leaders of the PCI, and by a relative, Raymondo Isaac Aghion. Paolo Tedeschi established a school for terrorist training in 1950 and Aghion had been a member of the Comintern and later of the Cominform.[199] Both these men provided Curiel with the necessary liaisons with the French Communist Party and the Italian Communist Party.

In 1953 Curiel was listed as a foreign agent by the French security services (DST), having entered France clandestinely in 1951. He became actively involved with the FLN in Algeria, providing the group with weapons and false documents. For that role he was imprisoned in France until his release in the general amnesty of 1962.

In 1965 he worked with the national liberation movements in Angola, Mozambique, Haiti, Santo Domingo and Kurdistan. He also had direct contacts with the Montoneros, the Chilean MIR and the American Black Panthers.

Henri Curiel was by his own admission an 'orthodox communist' and effected the rhetoric of Soviet ideology. He presented himself as a 'peace-loving militant' and as early as 1963 set up an organization called Solidarité which, also by his own admission operated on an official level as well as an unofficial one.

The official level of Solidarité was a humanitarian one, helping refugees, exiles, persecuted individuals and activities which were concentrated mainly in the Third World, and both Curiel and his wife were members of the World Peace movement.

The second level of activity proves to be the more interesting one for present purposes. Solidarité provided logistical support to subversive, terrorist and insurgent groups in France. This logistic support included the provision of false documents, ('safe'-houses) and weapons, all of which, it is now known, were provided to the PLO, ETA the Latin American groups, as well as the Italian groups and others. For example, the links between Solidarité and 'Carlos' came to light only after the murders of the rue Toullier. The DST discovered incriminating papers in the apartments of some of the 'Carlos' accomplices which listed names and addresses of members of Solidarité. The contact with 'Carlos' was through an antique dealer, Pereira Carvalho, rue de Verneuil, alias Fereira, alias Acheme. In reality Carvalho was in charge of weapons procurement to terrorist groups. This link was discovered by the DST on 26 July 1974, when a Japanese arriving from Beirut was arrested at Orly and tried to swallow a piece of paper with the contact name Acheme inscribed on it.[200] He turned out to be a member of the JRA which placed itself at the service of the PLO, as was seen by their Lod massacre action. Another contact who also was in touch with 'Carlos' was Mohammed Boudia and a few words need to be said about him, for he also connected with Curiel.

Mohammed Boudia, well known to Curiel since his Algerian days as the publisher of *Alger Ce Soir* was the administrative director of the Théâtre de l'Ouest in Boulogne-Billancourt, France.

He also was the head of the PLO branch operating out of Paris, organized by Wadia Haddad. This revelation was given to the Israeli security services by Evelyn Barge, cashier at the Théâtre de l'Ouest, arrested while entering Israel with explosives. Boudia was responsible for a number of terrorist operations which included the execution in West Germany of five Jordanians suspected of working for Israel, the destructism by fire of Dutch petrol reserves, and the blowing up of a motor factory in Hamburg which exported to Israel. He was also wanted in Italy for demolishing a pipeline in Trieste in 1972.

Boudia lived in Paris in a *pension* called Maydieu which was run by a priest named Barth who had very close links to Curiel, who was in fact on the board of directors of Solidarité.

As early as 1969 Boudia established contacts with Raoul Ernesto Zamora, a representative of the Cuban DGI, and with the FAR (Fuerzas Armadas Revolucionarias), an offshoot of the ELN which had originally been set up by Cuba to activate unrest in Bolivia. During the same period he was to co-ordinate PLO activities with the ERP (Ejercito Revolucionario del Pueblo) and the Secretariat of the Fourth International, the Trotskyites, as indeed did Curiel. During the years 1970–2 he was also in contact with 'Carlos'. The latter in fact was to take over the command of the Boudia group after Mohammed Boudia himself died in a car explosion.

Boudia thus appeared to be the co-ordinator of terrorist activities carried out with the logistic support of Henri Curiel and his Solidarité. Solidarité, moreover, had links with the Baader-Meinhof gang, (particularly Klaus Croissant), the Turkish terrorists, a Bulgarian who often met Boudia, the FLQ, the Black Panthers and the Red Brigades.

Le Point, which openly accused Henri Curiel of heading an international terrorist organization, was never sued by Curiel for defamation of character. On the contrary, three months after that exposé Solidarité was officially disbanded. It was replaced by an organization called Aide et Amitié. A year later Curiel was accused by *Der Spiegel* in their 24 October 1977 edition of co-ordinating various terrorist activities including those of the RAF. Perhaps because the trial would not take place on French territory so there could be no recourse to the DST files, Curiel decided to sue *Der Spiegel*. The trial was set to begin on 31 May 1978. On 4 May 1978 Henri Curiel was shot dead by unknown assassins on the staircase of the building where he lived, 4 rue Rollin in Paris.

His organization, however, did not die with him. Several arrests by the French police, notably at Ivry on 5 May 1980, brought to light arsenals of weapons and false documents. One of the culprits has been identified as a member of 'Les Amis d'Henri Curiel', a group formed after his death. Maria Amaral, whose domicile was raided, was a director of Solidarité. During the raid, 1,000 false passports were confiscated. Among them were 600 blank Turkish passports, 200 falsified Turkish passports, 20 Argentinian passports, French, Belgian, Dutch, Zairian, and so on, together with the necessary chemical products for falsification and, in addition, instructions for the manufacture of explosives.

Evidence of Curiel's direct links with the NKVD was uncovered very early in 1952 in Casablanca, and it has been suggested that he also worked for British intelligence for some time, providing them with identification checks of pro-Nazi elements in Egypt, and for the French by vetting prospective recruits for the Free French.[201] This would, of course, explain why this bulging files at the DST brought no prosecution. His worst punishment after the general amnesty was to be sent into 'exile' in Digne. It would also explain his remaining in France though he was stateless, with all the hardships that entails, for so many years. When asked by a *Foreign Report* correspondent why he did not choose to move to Moscow, which he admired so much, and acquire a Soviet passport, he answered that he felt he could be 'more useful abroad'.[202]

For twenty-seven years he lived with only one known source of income: an import-export company which banked at the Banque Commerciale de l'Europe du Nord (BCEN), the Soviet-owned Bank in Paris. Two members of the board of directors of Solidarité, Raymond Biriotti and Bernard Riguet, also banked at the BCEN. They founded a company called the Société d'Echanges et de Représentation, which provided Solidarité with funds.[203]

The massive Curiel dossier has never been refuted, although Georges Suffert was sued by Madame Curiel after the assassination of her husband. The suit was for 'defamation of character'. The court found in favour of Georges Suffert. It is of interest that, in spite of all these facts which established Curiel as a KGB operative and a co-ordinator of logistic support for international terrorism, one of the first acts of the Mitterrand Socialist Government was to exonerate him through a court order.[204]

'Carlos'   Much has been written and said about 'Carlos'[205] which has surrounded him with a nebulous aura of 'superman'. He has been portrayed as a freelance killer out for hire by the highest bidder. It appears, however, that he was and probably still is in the service of the KGB.

He was born in Venezuela to a communist father who named him llych Ramirez Sanchez, in honour of Vladimir Ilych Lenin.

He was recruited by the KGB in Venezuela and sent to Cuba in the middle part of the 1960s, where he was trained at Camp Mantanzas in terrorist tactics under KGB Colonel Simenov, who was overseeing the Cuban DGI.[206] One of his instructors in Cuba was Antonio Dages Bouvier, an Ecuadorian, who was later to share a flat with Carlos in London.[207]

From Cuba, Ilych Ramirez Sanchez was sent to Moscow for further training. He attended the Patrice Lumumba University and was given intensive Soviet indoctrination as well as more advanced training in violence. His noisy expulsion in 1969 from the university and from the Soviet Union appears now to have been a cover-up.[208]

Upon leaving the USSR, Ilych apparently travelled to East Berlin where, in 1970, he received information on the leaders of the Baader-Meinhof gang (RAF) which had initiated the terror campaign that was to plague West Germany into the late 1970s.[209]

It was with the shooting of Michael Moukharbel, the Palestinian terrorist whom 'Carlos' killed along with two DST agents in the rue Toullier in Paris, that his subversive connections began to emerge. The Cuban DGI collaboration was made public by the French government and as a consequence three Cuban diplomats were expelled.[210] The Minister of Interior, Michel Poniatowski, named the three as Raoul Rodriguez Sainz, first secretary; Ernesto Reyes Herrera, second secretary; and Pedro Larra Zamora. In London, one of the 'Carlos' women accomplices had regular contacts with Angel Dalaman at the Cuban embassy there.[211] Links reportedly existed between 'Carlos' and the BR of Italy, the RAF of West Germany, and the Central and South American groups, as well as the JRA. In 1975 the PFLP claimed him as having been one of their members as well since 1970, and admitted that he now headed the Boudia group operating in Paris.[212]

Radio Moscow, in the only comment on the 'Carlos' rue Toullier affair, stated on 16 July 1975 in their French language broadcast that the murders were a 'simple case of gangsterism' which 'is being presented by Poniatowski as an international conspiracy'. The broadcast went on to quote the French Communist group in the National Assembly as 'stressing that the twist given to it . . . was to worsen relations with the socialist countries and to present the French Communists as secret accomplices of this terrorist group'. It was a return to the cold war period, the broadcast accused.

Notwithstanding these classical denials, the facts which emerged showed the Cubans funnelling money and instructions to 'Carlos', who had by then masterminded and carried out several terrorist attacks. Also involved was the staunchly pro-Soviet Colombian Communist Party, through Nydia Tobon, member of the secretariat of that party and a close colleague of 'Carlos'.[213]

'Carlos' took over the command of the Boudia group of the PLO in Paris, organized at the time by Wadia Haddad as has already been mentioned. The fact suggests at least two possibilities. (1) With Boudia's death, the KGB was able to install 'Carlos' in the Palestinian group to exercise better control. There are indications that Mohammed Boudia had himself been a KGB operative, or at least in close contact with that organization, which would indicate even earlier infiltration by the Soviets,(2) Why would a Palestinian group accept a Venezuelan with a playboy image as its leader, unless he was imposed on the group? In either case, it would be justifiable to assume that the Kremlin was able to exercise a certain degree of control over the activities of 'Carlos' and, thereby, over the group's activities. This is not necessarily intended to say that the KGB or the International Department decided which specific targets 'Carlos' would hit, but by providing him with the necessary logistics and telling him to 'run with it', the ultimate goal of disruption would be achieved all the same.

According to the MOSSAD, Boudia was in fact a KGB operative who worked to unite various terrorist groups into an international network; and his KGB boss was Yuri Kotov, who had served in Israel listed as a foreign ministry attaché. With the 1967 break in diplomatic relations, Kotov was transferred to Beirut. He later went to Paris where he became the KGB's chief of the Western European Division. This activity pre-dated the semi-official interest shown by the USSR in the PLO (1968) and would point to a much earlier interest in the idea of implementing the paramilitary dimension of its military philosophy in the West European and African theatres. For example, as will be seen, there were links as early as 1964 with ETA and Henri Curiel's personnel; also early links with Mozambique and South America.

Both 'Carlos' and Moukharbel had been in close contact with Wilfried Böse,[214] a member of the RAF whom 'Carlos' recruited.[215] The OPEC raid which captured the oil ministers in Vienna was carried out by 'Carlos' together with Hans-Joachim Klein who was an associate of Klaus Croissant and a member of the RAF, and Gabriele Kröcher-Tiedemann, a member of M2J who surfaced from asylum in South Yemen to carry out that raid. The link with Wilfried Böse also suggested that 'Carlos' was a co-ordinator of the various terrorist groups operating in Europe. He delegated Böse to do some information-gathering for the Basque separatist group ETA, which Böse agreed to do.[216] He was arrested before leaving for Spain. 'Carlos' also had a Basque girl friend in London who was arrested after a cache of arms was found in her apartment.

In September 1973, 'Carlos' organized an operation which from both the Palestinian and Soviet points of view was extremely successful. It also indicated the high degree of collusion between the Eastern bloc countries, 'Carlos' and the Palestinians. The Czechoslovak authorities assisted the boarding of the terrorists from the Sai'qa faction of the PLO on the train carrying Jewish emigrants from the Soviet Union which they were subsequently to hijack. The Soviet Union provided the exact train schedule. Neither the Austrian government nor the Jewish Agency knew on which train the emigrants were due to arrive in Austria. The terrorists boarded the train in Czechoslovakia with machine guns. As a consequence of that hijacking, the Schonau transit camp which received Jewish emigrants coming out of the Soviet Union was closed.[217] Thus the interests of the USSR and of the PLO were both served satisfactorily by the closure of the camp.

After the OPEC raid 'Carlos' disappeared from the active scene of terrorism in Europe. Libya, which in the person of Colonel Qaddafi was a patron of his activities and those of the groups connected with him, afforded him a temporary haven when his face became too easily recognizable. But his links and contacts continued there as well. Among his guests was another partner of Klaus Croissant, Jorg Lang, who was formely in the Stuttgart Socialist Lawyers' Collective, and closely linked to the RAF.

Giangiacomo Feltrinelli On the evening of 14 May 1972 Giangiacomo Feltrinelli exploded himself into notoriety. In Segrate, near Milan, his mutilated body was found as a result of an apparent blunder in setting up explosives on a power line on one of his own properties. The investigations which followed his death revealed an intricate pattern of logistic and financial support for international terrorism, including that which aimed at subverting his own country, Italy.

An eccentric millionaire, Giangiacomo Feltrinelli, or Giangi as his friends called him, had been a member of the Communist Party of Italy since the 1940s. He had grown up in the lap of luxury in Villa Feltrinelli near Milan.

The years 1962 to 1965 were identified as his years of hesitation.[218] It would appear from the evidence which has surfaced so far that those were in fact the years of preparation for what was to follow.

With his vast fortune and through profits from his publishing house-the first to publish Boris Pasternak's *Doctor Zhivago* in the West - he financed to a large extent not only the Marxist-Leninist Communist Party[219] but also the international terrorist network in Western Europe.

The facts which have emerged have presented a picture of a man who, whether as a 'useful idiot' or by conviction as an agent of the Soviet secret services, led a life of violence and intrigue in an attempt to destabilize the Western European democracies.

During the early 1960's Giangi appeared to lead a *dolce vita*. He purchased a beautiful white property, the Villa Deati, where he was to entertain among others Ulrike Meinhof and her husband. He also appeared to be infatuated with Castro. In 1964 he travelled to Cuba to meet his idol and he was eventually to publish the review *Tricontinental* for Castro in Europe. In 1967 the military intelligence services of Italy (SID) began a watch on this millionaire who also had contacts with the bandits in Sardinia.

Ideologically, Feltrinelli considered himself a 'militant communist' and by 1969 he had become convinced that 'armed resistance' was the only way to prevent an authoritarian *coup* which he fully anticipated. With megalomaniac single-mindedness he dedicated himself to setting up terrorist cells, which he liked to visualize as partisans in the glorious tradition of the fight against the fascists. He even took to wearing a Cuban-type military uniform and practised throwing hand grenades in a friend's garden.[220] His *nom de guerre* was 'Osvaldo, as a couple of *pentiti* told the Italian police.

The Gruppi di Azione Partigiana (GAP) were the result, the targets of their tactics being mostly economic, such as arson attacks on oil refineries and shipyards, but also including the United States consulate in Genova and the offices of the Unified Socialist Party. The technique of using different names for the perpetration of terrorist attacks was heavily used by the GAP, not in this case as a technique for dissociating itself from the deed as the PLO has done, but as a technique for mythically aggrandizing the extent of dissatisfaction and proletarian support for the 'cause'. With Feltrinelli's death the GAP ceased its activities and the Red Brigades (BR) absorbed the members and finances of the group.

In 1967, shortly before organized terrorism started in Western Europe, Feltrinelli returned to Cuba and then went on to Bolivia to assist at the trial of Regis Debray (now a member of the Mitterrand government) who had been involved in the Che Guevara debacle. Some have suggested that Feltrinelli facilitated the destruction of Che Guevara as a service to the Soviet Union which became annoyed with his independent anti-Soviet posture.[221] The Bolivian Minister of Interior fled to Cuba in 1968 shortly after the death of Guevara, suggesting that Cuba might have also been instrumental in bringing about his demise. The police chief Quintanilla, who had pursued Guevara and detained Feltrinelli for still unknown reasons during one of his trips to Bolivia, was himself shot in Hamburg while representing Bolivia as Consul in West Germany. Quintanilla's killer turned out to be a young German terrorist, Monkia Ertl, who used a pistol which had been bought by Feltrinelli.

Feltrinelli had numerous and close links with members of the German terrorist groups and these go back to at least 1966, when he seems to have first met Ulrike Meinhof. This date precedes the first terrorist act perpetrated by Gudrin Ensslin and Andreas Baader by three years. His best-known contribution to the West German terrorist scene was financial in nature - large cash payments which he generously and unquestioningly donated.[222] He participated in a May Day demonstration, along with Ulrike Meinhof and Andreas Baader, in West Berlin in 1968.*

In 1967 he travelled to Beirut to visit George Habash, leader of the PFLP group of the PLO, and suggested that he take his terrorism to the 'international scene'[223]† Shortly afterwards the first gruesome operations by the PLO on Western European soil took place. It could, naturally, be pure coincidence that the PFLP went international shortly after Feltrinelli's suggestion.

In 1968 Feltrinelli published a paper called 'Italy 1968: Political Guerrilla Warfare', gave a speech in Berlin supporting armed violence, joined the French students in their rioting and was expelled from France for that activity.

Evidence which the Italian police have since discovered shows that Feltrinelli provided over twenty 'safe' apartments in Milan and large payments of cash through a *centrale* he set up in Switzerland, to various groups including the Red Brigades, Prima Linei, Nuclea Armati Proletarii and foreign groups.

In 1969, following a long visit to Cuba, he finally went underground. That was the beginning of terrorist activity in Italy. In fact, that same year simultaneous bombing attacks in Rome and Milan and on trains marked the beginning of the gradual erosive process which has resulted in a multitude of governments succeeding each other in an attempt to deal with the problem. Using various pseudonyms from 1969 onwards, he organized the GAP, and in 1971 he organized an international terrorists' conference in Florence which took place in a Jesuit college and which was attended by the IRA, ETA, ERP Trotskyites and the PLO.[224]

---

* There is no evidence that he saw Meinhof on this occasion, and he did not know Baader. Meinhof and Baader had not yet met each other.

† The PFLP was formed only in December 1967. Habash had been founder leader of the Arab National Movement before that, which had been international in the sense that it had branches in many Arab countries. That Feltrinelli gave him the idea of hijacking planes on international flights does not seem very plausible. Wadia Haddad was in charge of 'foreign operations' for the group, organized the first hijacking of an Israeli plane, and the September 1970 hijackings which precipitated King Hussein's forceful expulsion of the PLO from Jordan. Later, Haddad insisted on continuing such activities when the rest of the PFLP leadership wanted them to stop.

Feltrinelli's links with the Soviet Union and the Eastern bloc became publicly evident only after his death, if one is to discount his Castro link as purely an eccentric one. *Portere Operaio,* an ultra-communist newspaper, stated on 26 March that Feltrinelli had been a member of the Communist Party before joining the Socialists, and that he actually joined as an agent of the Communist Party's secret service. He was already involved in financing Pietro Nenni in the PCI in the early 1940s.[225]* Among his close friends was Pietro Secchia, one of the old communist partisans, second in command to Luigi Longo.

In 1978, in a testimony in the Camera dei Deputati, Vito Miceli, director of the Italian security services, demanded the expulsion of twenty Soviet bloc agents for 'their collusion with Feltrinelli and the subversive movements gravitating around him'.[226] Prime Minister Guilio Andreotti, for unknown reasons, did not agree to bring the problem to a confrontational level with the USSR. Proof of direct KGB involvement from the Rome embassy was presented during the testimony. The Czechoslovak connection was ever-present. Feltrinelli's passport, found in a police dragnet in one of his 'safe' apartments, reportedly had twenty-two entry visas into Czechoslovakia.[227] Other 'safe' houses were stocked with arsenals of Soviet bloc weapons, terrorist hit maps and various other incriminating documents. In Czechoslovakia Giangi met 'comrades' from other terrorist groups of various countries. He was, in fact, allowed to stay for months on end lavishly entertaining all types of terrorists in a bourgeois villa. In a courtroom in Italy, several years later, Augusto Viel who had stayed with him at that villa and is now in jail as a member of the BR, was to eulogize Feltrinelli as a 'revolutionary who had fallen in battle . . . [whose greatest contribution was to have] developed a Continental Strategy of long-lasting and decisive importance'.[228]

While it is still not clear whether Feltrinelli was himself a KGB operative, there is still not clear whether Feltrinelli was himself a KGB operative, there is no question but that he was a terrorist, and that he provided immeasurable services for the KGB and the PCI, both in terms of propaganda outlets through his well-known publishing house and through his vast fortune with which he financed not only his own subversive activities but also those of the West German terrorists and numerous Italian groups, and provided logistic support to Palestinian terrorists operating in Europe. His suggestion to Habash to 'go international' could have been his own idea, but it could have also been an instruction passed on. Whether

---

* This seems unlikely. He was born in 1926 and was between 14 and 19 years old in the first five years of the 1940s.

he encouraged the German terrorists to start their campaign of murder or whether he just assured them of the logistic support necessary for a sustained activity of that nature is not of great importance. The result was the same whichever he did.

The confessions at the formal indictment in the Aldo Moro case presented by Carlo Fioroni, *pentito* of the Red Brigades, revealed that not only did Feltrinelli have frequent and close contacts with Renato Curcio, the original founder of the Brigate Rosse, and with Carlo Piperno and Toni Negri, of the Potere Operaio group which would become the Autonomia Operaia, but that there were actual lateral membership shifts from one group to another and frequent co-ordinated activities.[229] Thus, Feltrinelli's influence spread within Italy itself. This also reveals a blurring of distinctions between various degrees of 'extremism of the Left' and 'of the Right'.

Italian Terrorism   The most recent revelations by Antonio Savasta and other members of the Red Brigades at the so-called 'Aldo Moro trial' have confirmed once again the strong links which have existed between the PLO, Eastern bloc countries and the Italian terrorists.[230]

The *super-pentito*, guilty of seventeen murders himself, testified at length on the General Dozier kidnapping, on Aldo Moro's incarceration and murder, and on dealings with the PLO, a French logistic support centre and Bulgaria.

The PLO had provided at least two large shipments of arms to the Red Brigades since 1979, one of which was to be held on Italian soil for future use by the PLO itself. The other was for use by the Red Brigades. These arsenals have been found by the police since the confessions. In exchange for keeping the weapons, the Red Brigades were to perpetrate some terrorist acts as a favour to the PLO against Israeli personnel employed at the Rome embassy, or what Savasta called 'Zionist' employees. Savasta went out of his way to clarify that the group of the PLO with which the Red Brigades made the deals was *not* the 'extremist' PFLP of George Habash but Arafat himself, who recognized the necessity of 'armed struggle against imperialism', thus confirming that the PLO is a terrorist group.

The Bulgarian connection is an important revelation, which only confirms previous involvement, the more so because the secret services of Bulgaria announced their interest in supporting the Red Brigades during the General Dozier kidnapping. Bulgaria offered logistic support and weapons and stated that its main interest was that the 'guerrilla action' should continue in Italy. Th liaison man with the KGB was Maurizio Follini who was allowed passage through Bulgaria with weapons after the KGB had cleared his credentials. This fact was testified to by Follini's girl friend who was travelling with him.

During Savasta's lengthy interrogation, the Aldo Moro kidnapping was extensively discussed by the court. The BR's purpose in picking on Aldo Moro was 'to disarticulate the State'.[231] The Red Brigades, he said, were not interested in attaining political recognition from the government.

Although Savasta suffered numerous memory lapses in giving his testimony, he was nevertheless able to confirm that meetings had taken place between Mario Moretti, Anna Laura Braghetti and the PLO in Paris, arranged by what he called an 'agency', friends who had contacts with national liberation movements as well as ETA and the IRA.[232] And he once again confirmed the other links of the BR with ETA, the IRA, and the RAF. For the Moro affair, he admitted receiving logistic support from the French 'agency'. This agency, although not named by Savasta, was named by Patrizio Peci in an earlier confession and identified as Henri Curiel's organization.[233]

Arafat's PLO emerges from the evidence presented at this recent trial as the overall co-ordinator of the links and weapons procurement within the Italian context. During the Moro kidnapping, which lasted nearly two months, Arafat was apparently requested to intercede with the Red Brigades for Moro's release. This he refused to do saying that 'he had nothing to do with the Red Brigades, he did not know them'. During those anguished days, however his organization was filling the holds of the ship *Papago* for the Red Brigades who had travelled to Cyprus to pick up weapons and sailed the ship to Venice. Also during that time, Mario Moretti was making bi-monthly trips to Paris to deal with PLO representatives there.[234] This policy on two levels conducted by the PLO was in reality duplicitous only in the sense that the group's 'political' image had been accepted by these same Western liberal democracies in which the PLO has consistently helped to accelerate and increase terrorist activity. It was not, however, contradictory to the PLO's Charter and terrorist activities world-wide.

It is interesting that in an article by Giuseppe Rosselli in *Paese della Sera* -a newspaper which is informally affiliated with the Italian Communist Party - on 4 May 1982, the veracity of Savasta's statements were questioned for the mere fact that the PLO had declared itself to be completely 'dissociated from any terrorist group and especially the Red Brigades', a position very much in accord with the Soviet Union's official statements on the PLO, which have also been echoed by the Western media in general.

Although Savasta's testimony has not yet been completed at the time of writing and the indications are that, at any event, the infrastructure of the terrorist cells did not permit one person to know everything there is to know,[235] the extended confirmation of the foreign involvements places Italian terrorism in a very different category from a strictly 'indigenous' one, and in fact if it was ever to be regarded as a symptom of a 'national disease', its internationalism is now admitted to be complete. From the point of view of the terrorist group, it may consider itself as strictly indigenous if it uses outside help just to further its own purposes. However, when one adds to the picture Feltrinelli with his *centrale* in Zurich and KGB connections, the PLO with its USSR sponsorship, and Curiel's logistic agency (another KGB link), together with the Czechoslovakian and Bulgarian secret services and the KGB itself - all directly involved in training the terrorists, harbouring them when pursued, and providing them with the necessary weapons - then the dimensions become international from the point of view of these sponsoring entities and must be regarded as such by the target state as well if the problem is ultimately to be dealt with.

The Red Brigades identify themselves with 'proletarian internationalism' and with the 'war for world liberation against imperialism', both of which coincide with the Soviet position on the 'class struggle' and its 'international character'. Furthermore, the Red Brigades defined the terrorist actions they perpetrated as 'the organizational form of proletarian internationalism in the metropolitan centres', [236] an identical rhetoric and position to the one consistently repeated by the USSR, and one that parallels the notion of the conflict from *within* which was identified by Khrushchev as the conflict typology of this area.

The Italian terrorist plague in fact provides an example perhaps more than any other Western European target state, of the continuity of the paramilitary structure which somehow was not dissolved after the end of the Second World War. It appears to have remained a 'sleeper' structure which was reactivated when the socio-economic and political atmosphere permitted the renewal of unconventional activities.

It has been suggested that after 1945 the Soviet Red Army actually took over a part of the PCI's partisan organization and apparently restructured it in the early 1960s for paramilitary terrorist action. The accuracy of this information was confirmed by General Vito Miceli (SID).[237] It confirms the Soviet politico-military emphasis on unconventional warfare which gained in tactical importance at that time.

The history of the Italian paramilitary entities should therefore

not be overlooked in the context of Italian terrorism. Both the PCI
and Czechoslovakia are the leading contributory protagonists to
this chapter of Italian history.

The roots to the East go back to the Second World War, and
possibly earlier when the PCI kept its files in Prague,
Czechoslovakia. The communist partisans who had hoped for a
'liberation' of Italy from fascism and the setting up of the 'Soviet
Republic of Italy' formed paramilitary groupings such as the Stella
Rossa (Red Star) and the Volante Rossa (Red Strike Force) in the
mid 1940s and carried out numerous terrorist acts well into 1949,
mostly in the northern part of Italy. One of the leaders of the
communist partisans was Pietro Secchia who, it will be recalled,
was Giangiacomo Feltrinelli's life-long friend. There is evidence to
indicate that Feltrinelli himself took military information to the
Prague base in 1950.[238] (There was also a regular courier service
between Italy's Communist Party members and the headquarters
in Prague.)

The Volante Rossa was paralleled by the PCI's own secret militia
which Secchia was in charge of and which was to be put into action
only when deemed necessary. A 'sleeper' network, very much
reminiscent of the Rote Kapelle set up by Moscow in Western
Europe in the 1930s[239] and possibly an extension of it, was therefore
in existence. The actual operations of the partisan movement were
controlled by NKVD Major General Pavel Sudolplatov, who after
the war ended set up an underground infrastructure 'to establish
combast operations for weakening the network of military bases of
the American Command in Europe'.[240]

Similar to the Volante Rossa concept of the praetorian guard,
used for both internal protection of the Party apparatus and for
external sensitive missions, was its precursor, the so-called
Dzerzhinsky Division which was formed by the Soviet Union as
early as 1924 by the fusion of two CHEKA units.[241]

The PCI used the Volante Rossa to keep order and to protect and
escort foreign visiting communist leaders, as for example the PCF
leader Maurice Thorez at the Sixth Party Congress.[242] In an attempt
to dissociate itself from the members of the Volante Rossa when
captured and exposed by the police, the PCI would call them
provocateurs, Trotskyites and reactionaries[243] - a practice very
similar to that used by the USSR throughout. The paramilitary
units were never officially disbanded, however.

Pietro Secchia went into exile in Czechoslovakia in 1953, and as
has already been mentioned, was paid frequent visits there by
Feltrinelli. Feltrinelli went through three terrorist training courses
in Czechoslovakia, one at Karlovy Vary which is run by the KGB,
and two at a special school run by the GRU thirty miles south of
Karlovy Vary, at Doupov.

Renato Curcio, the first leader of the Red Brigades, similarly commuted back and forth between Italy and Prague, and continued the links with the ex-partisan communists there. Arrested with him was Giovanbattista Lazagna, a member of Secchia's original group. Lazagna in turn conspired with Feltrinelli.

How much control over the Red Brigades and associated terrorist groups was actually imposed by Czechoslovakia and the old guard is not known, but certainly advice and encouragement, together with the necessary logistics and training, were freely forthcoming. The KGB association with Feltrinelli would attest to the fact that the activities of the Italian terrorists were of great interest to the USSR.

How much control the PCI has had on Italian terrorism is still a matter of contention and liable to various interpretations. A few years ago several parliamentary members were convinced that the terrorist phenomenon is 'neither fully spontaneous, nor totally autonomous'.[244] The Soviet Union's complicity in it has now been established and it is a multiple-sided complicity projected through various agents: the PLO, the KGB, the Czech services, the Bulgarian services, and its own GRU and KGB training camps.

President Pertini of Italy made repeated reference to this complicity in an interview for French television on 22 January 1981 and earlier in 1980. He stated that he believed that the terrorists operating in Italy did so from foreign bases. 'I don't think the bases are in France. They are in other countries. Do not ask me which, because that could create international complications and I do not want to create complications'.[245] Although the Soviet Union was not specifically named, the Soviet Foreign Ministry called in Italy's ambassador a few days later, denouncing as 'absurd' hints by Pertini that the Red Brigades and the Soviet Union had contacts with each other. Calling the remarks 'insulting'. TASS quoted the Soviet Foreign Ministry as follows: 'The leadership of Italy cannot but be aware of the principled position of the Soviet state, which has always denounced and is denouncing terrorism.'

Following a statement to Parliament by Sig. Forlani, that Italian intelligence services had uncovered arms and documents providing evidence of links and connections between the various European terrorist groups and East European countries, Czechoslovakia similarly denied helping the terrorists in Italy.[246] The vast and intricate connections are, however, a matter of record.

The initial reaction in Italy and the West generally to the evidence of Soviet involvement in the support of terrorist activity on Italian territory was one of general disbelief, if only because the PCI appeared to be losing some of its appeal at the polls precisely because of the connections between it and so many of the terrorists. It had therefore been generally assumed that the Kremlin would not jeopardize the image of the PCI which has the largest popular vote of any Communist party in a Western democratic country. However, there are not two schools of thought concerning this question. First, the Soviet Union may in fact have decided to apply the terrorist option not only for its larger and longer-term objectives, but also in order to create problems for Enrico Berlinguer, the current leader of the PCI.[247] Berlinguer, a strong exponent of 'Eurocommunism' since 1968, was seen to take an increasingly moderate line to maintain the popularity of the party with the electorate, a line which culminated in the 'historic compromise' with Aldo Moro, leader of the Christian Democrats. His claim to independence from Moscow was asserted again with his condemnation of the USSR's invasion of Afghanistan. Secondly, if it was not the intention to create problems for Berlinguer, then the support which is on record as extended by the USSR to Italian groups would allow the PCI to maintain the moderate image it has so carefully cultivated *vis-à-vis* the 'extreme left' which was said to be out of the control of the PCI - a similar position to Lenin's arguments against 'Left'-wing individual terrorism, and similar to the Kremlin's position which has consistently placed itself as a more moderate actor in relation to PLO extremism.

There is evidence to satisfy both theses. The first has been reinforced mainly by the terrorist's behaviour and Czechoslovak actions against Italian Communist Party members. BR member Piancone implied a direct connection between the Red Brigades and the PCI when he stated that 'in the event of a violent governmental repression against terrorism, the PCI will guarantee our physical survival'.[248] In 1978 a Red Brigades banner was found locked in a storeroom within the PCI headquarters, thus demonstrating to the public a link between the two.[249] Attention was drawn also to the fact that BR leaflets which criticized the PCI referred to it as 'Berlinguer's Party,', thus emphasizing the discontent with the leadership and not the PCI *per se*. Czechoslovakia took some steps which also appeared to express discontent with the leadership. Although host to many Italians who work for Radio Prague to broadcast propaganda in Italian, the Czechoslovakian government took the unusual step of expelling several of them, and furthermore a less favoured treatment for Italian Communists in business dealings was announced by the Czech Co-operative League.[250]

On the other hand, Czechoslovakia granted asylum between 1970 and 1974 to Red Brigadists Alberto Franceschini, Fabrizio Pelli and Augusto Viel, all wanted by the Italian police for terrorist activities. There is also some evidence to indicate that the PCI has, or some of its members have consciously been involved in the terrorist violence in Italy and elsewhere. Besides the obvious fact that the PCI has seldom been the target of physical violence by the Red Brigades or associated groups, the most incriminating link is that the most of the BR membership was made up of PCI members who 'broke ranks' to join the extra-parliamentary left. The PCI was at any event ideologically responsible for its youth organization (FGCI). Remarkably, between 1968 and 1970 membership of the FGCI dropped very dramatically from over 135,000 to less than half that number. The drop-outs apparently streamed to the violent extra-parliamentary left groups which started to proliferate at the time.[251]

During those same years the PCI was directly involved with the PLO, which was in turn involved with Italian terrorist groups. In 1969 PCI delegations visited terrorist training camps run by al-Fatah in Jordan. In March 1970 the Italian Communist Party sponsored a press conference in Rome for Abu Basam of al-Fatah.[252] And in August 1970 a Fatah delegation visited Italy and met various political leaders including the PCI.[253]

Until 1977 the PCI refused to concede that any of the terrorism which has plagued Italy was in any way connected with the 'Left', and maintained that the 'forces of reaction' were mainly responsible for what has been called Black Terror (as opposed to Red Terror). However, even after the concession that left terrorism did in fact exist was reluctantly made in 1977-78 by Ugo Pecchioli, PCI expert on police matters, the guilt was still attributed to these 'forces of reaction'. In fact, the PCI position on this question has coincided with the Soviet position. During a 1978 visit to Moscow, the PCI and the CPSU jointly condemned terrorist activity as 'absolutely contrary to the workers' movement and to the democratic movement', and attributed its existence to the assistance given by the 'forces of reaction' to criminals in perpetrating terrorist acts.[254] These 'forces of reaction', which were not further defined, aimed at 'blocking the development of the democratic achievements of the workers and of the Italian people'. So the position taken, at any event in the Italian context, is that the democratic achievements of the workers are to be protected and that the terrorism which does in fact exist is working against these achievements, and since the USSR is always looking after the interest of the workers, it can only be explained that the support comes from 'the dark forces of reaction'. This reiterates the constant theme in all Soviet military and ideological writings that the USSR gloriously and single-handed crushed fascism. When the evidence presented has made it impossible to deny that a terrorist act was perpetrated by the 'left', then these acts have been labelled as 'extremist', thus positioning both the PCI and the USSR in a moderate position *vis-à-vis* this extremism. But this was really not a new development, reflecting back once again on Lenin's condemnation of the 'individual' terrorist. Although Lenin argued that point in the light of his concept and obsession with centralized power, wanting to keep all actions within his personal control, that argument has over the years been exploited by the USSR as a 'moderating weapon' which has been readily accepted in the Western media and in academic circles, and has allowed the CPSU, and the PCI, to present itself *as centre of 'Left'.*

The PCI has tried consistently to present itself in that mould, and has gone to a great deal of trouble to appear as a trustworthy member of the Italian political community. There has therefore been consistent denial of any links between itself and Italian terrorism and between Italian terrorism and Eastern European states. To demonstrate to what extend the PCI is a moderate party, or in an attempt to dissociate itself from the terrorist activity, or as a symptom of its growing tension over the evidence which has been surfacing, the PCI's Department Dealing with Problems of State published in 1981 a lengthy and elaborate statistical study on Italian terrorism from its inception in 1969 to 1980. There are several salient points in the study which deserve mention, not least of which is the declared intent of the work in the introductory preface by Ugo Pecchioli: 'It is opportune to emphasize that this research is part of the unrelenting dedication of the PCI in the fight against terrorism to safeguard the republican legality . . . '[25]

The main points which the study makes and which indicate the PCI's perceptions of Italian terrorism are as follows.

(1)   Terrorism finds its roots in the crisis of Italian society. This crisis is not in itself the cause of terrorism but it facilitates it.

(2)   At least partially, the terrorism is anit-communist in nature and aimed at destroying the 'compromesso storico' which saw the PCI for the first time as part of the government.

(3)   The attacks of the BR and other groups have always had it as a goal to undermine the PCI, hence the verbal attacks on 'Berlinguer's Party'.

(4)   The terrorist violence in Italy has as its ultimate goal the creation of conditions which will allow an anti-democratic, authoritarian solution (for Black Terror) and the necessary conditions for a civil war (for Red Terror).

(5)   What is described as Red Terror in Italy, as well as in other Western European countries, is essentially attributable to small clandestine groups mainly composed of intellectuals with desperate utopian ideals far removed from the realities of the day.

(6)   Although Italian terrorism has its roots in Italy and nowhere else, one cannot discount the hypothesis which claims foreign centres of support for terrorism.

(7)   The whole controversy over foreign involvement in Italian terrorism has ultimately only achieved the reduction of Italian authority and credibility and can only have had an anti-communist aim since to intimate that Moscow is behind it is to assert that the PCI, not having broken relations with the CPSU, is not entitled to govern in any way.

(8)   The testimonies of the *pentiti* are not to be trusted.

These arguments, which run through the various contributions to the study by Ugo Pecchioli, Giulio Andreotti, Franco Ferrarotti and Nicola Tranfaglia, all tend to dissociate the PCI from the terrorist activities and, in fact, make it the target of the BR, for example. This position inevitably falls back on the 'forces of reaction' being the source of the terrorism and TASS's accusation that the CIA was behind Moro's kidnapping is cited as an example. There is, however, never an outright condemnation of the BR terrorism and Nicola Tranfaglia, for instance, presents an apologia in which he claims that the BR activity is understandable since the history of the PCI, which has gone through its disappointments in the aftermath of the Second World War, and through clandestine activities in its heroic fight against fascism and the German occupation, was bound to produce what he calls 'deviationist behaviour.'[256]

Moreover, the statistics presented throughout the study attribute the largest majority of terrorist acts to what it calls right-wing groups, a small percentage to extremists of the left, and a lesser proportion to 'left' groups - and the last are the only ones in quotation marks, thus implying that they are not of the left

The consistent attribution of most of the terrorism to the neo-fascists in a country which was not long ago suffering the totalitarianism of Mussolini has induced an indulgence of the left-wing 'deviationists' which are benevolently seen as the *enfants terribles*. This view has even been taken by many non-communists.

Of course, whether the PCI itself, with the approval of Berlinguer, is involved in the support of Italian terrorism, or whether it has in fact been infiltrated by KGB agents acting to discredit Berlinguer, or even the whole party - either to replace the leadership or return the PCI to an opposition role where it is more likely to remain closer to Moscow - is not central to the question of the USSR's position and policy on the use of terrorism. In either case, the fact of USSR and Eastern bloc and PLO surrogates remains, and must be perceived as serving both the politico-military strategic aims of the Politburo to destabilize NATO and the Western alliance as a long-term objective, and an attempt to control the problem of 'Eurocommunism' in the short term. The PCI may have suffered some loss of popularity at the polls as a result of its identification in the public view with terrorist activities, but for the Kremlin it would not be the first time a communist party was sacrificed to larger considerations. The polarization of Italian politics has been a success until now and has made Italy practically ungovernable.[257] Its membership of NATO has weakened that organization's power to react.

West German Terrorism The Baader-Meinhof group[258] emerged, as did all the other terrorist groups in Western Europe, out of the student revolts of 1967-8. Although mostly referred to by the media as an anarchist group, it was in fact communist, both in leadership and ideology, although the latter was often unfocused.

Both Ulrike Meinhof and her husband Klaus Rainer Röhl were card-carrying members of the Communist Party of East Germany. Röhl, since about 1955, had been working with an East German SED agency, had joined the KPD,[259] and had received funding from the East Germand SED to finance his magazine *Konkret*, which was a leading periodical of the left. He appears to have singled out Ulrike Meinhof for conversion from a blurred leftism to orthodox communism, mainly because he was interested in her talents as a writer. The indoctrination was successful and Ulrike went to East Berlin with Röhl and joined the Party. Until 1964 Röhl remained a Party member at which time he said he quit. No reasons were given. Whether Ulrike continued her membership is not known and Röhl slurred over that point when the inquiry was made.[260] The contact with East Germany and with East Berlin in particular continued throughout, however. Röhl and Meinhof received over $250,000 to finance their writing activities from the German Democratic Republic.[261]

The story of how Meinhof's behaviour and thinking evolved from nuclear disarmament activism to terrorist activities has been told elsewhere, but what is of interest here is the early connection with the Eastern bloc which most certainly started out as a simple subversion enterprise into the Western liberal institutions, through propaganda, and was an exploitation of the growing unrest amoung the leftist intellectuals and the student circles.

There were, moreover, other connections which were established a good two or three years before the Baader-Meinhof gang started its terrorist activities. For example, Giangiacomo Feltrinelli made his first contacts with Ulrike Meinhof in 1966,[262] at a time when the Röhls entered the fashionable society of Hamburg - the 'erotische Schickeria' as it was generally called - and bought a house in the expensive suburb of Hamburg, Blankenese. Her role, as she saw it herself, was to be a subversive element in the Establishment. This was her job as a journalist and as a socialist, she said. By 1968 she was defending what she called 'counter-violence' and began to adopt the language of the USSR, protesting against militarism and United States imperialism. Vietnam was a major focus of attention then. When Soviet forces marched into Prague together with other Warsaw Pact forces, she sympathized with the USSR and chastized the European left which condemned it. In an article in *Konkret* in September of 1968, she wrote:'On 21 August the European left gave up its solidarity, its sympathy, its gratitude towards the Soviet Union as the first Socialist country, as that state which defeated German fascism at Stalingrad.[263]

On 14 May 1970 Ulrike Meinhof helped free Andreas Baader who had been arrested by the German police while on his way to recover weapons from a cemetery, and from then on went underground. Out of that first action the idea to form the Rote Armee Fraktion (RAF) was developed and the life of terrorism began and continued until she committed suicide in her prison cell in 1972.

Whatever the motivations which led the RAF to terrorism, there is no question but that the group received support from East Germany, 'Carlos' and, particularly, the PLO.

East Germany allowed various members of the Baader-Meinhof group wanted by West German police for terrorist activities to use East Berlin as a departure point for world travels. In 1970, shortly after Baader's springing, Horst Mahler and Hans Jürgen Bäcker flew from East Berlin to Beirut on false passports.[264] The trip was arranged by the PDFLP run by Hawatmeh. In Beirut, they were joined by Ulrike Meinhof, Gudrun Ensslin and Andreas Baader who had travelled the surface route through Bulgaria down to Syria. They all were there to receive training at a PFLP training camp in Jordan. In October 1970 Ulrike Meinhof met al-Fatah members at a café in Frankfurt to buy twenty-three Firebird pistols. This was the same year when 'Carlos' was given a briefing session on the Baader-Meinhof gang in East Berlin. From then on there was to be co-operative action with the PLO and the other groups. The Munich massacre of Israeli athletes in 1972 was organized by the PLO together with the RAF which provided the Palestinian terrorists with 'safe' houses and logistic support in general.* An attack on a Jewish old people's home had been a first joint action.

The members of the RAF and M2J, which was subsidized by Feltrinelli, were trained for terrorist work in South Yemen, Jordan and Libya in PFLP-run camps. South Yemen and Libya have very close links with the Kremlin.

The connection with the PLO started earlier than 1970. The German branch of the Fatah-controlled Palestinian Students' General Union maintained close ties with German radical leftist students and a number of these were recruited for training in Fatah camps.[265] As many as 150 left-wing students from Europe and the United States arrived in Amman for a special one-month training course at a camp called the 'European Camp' run by Arafat's Fatah.[266] And Gabriele Krocher-Tiedemann, granted asylum in South Yemen after being exchanged for the kidnapped Peter Lorenz, reappeared on the terrorist scene with 'Carlos' to carry out the OPEC raid in Vienna in 1976, together with Hans-Joachim Klein. Earlier, in the Stockholm raid on the German embassy in 1975, the weapons used by the RAF were traced back to the *centrale* in Switzerland run by Petra Krause, who had worked for Feltrinelli. At Entebbe, Wilfred Böse and Brigit Kuhlmann, along with five PLO terrorists, were killed by Israeli commandos freeing the hostages. Antonio Dages Bouvier, the KGB instructor who had taught 'Carlos' and had shared a flat with him in London, was seen co-ordinating the ground activity with the Palestinian terrorists after the hijacked Air France airplane landed in Uganda. Libya and Somalia, besides Idi Amin himself, were also implicated in the planning.[267] Among the demands of the Palestinian-led terrorist group was the release of Petra Krause.

Although German terrorism went into a sharp decline after the suicide of its main leaders - Meinhof first, then Baader and Ensslin in 1977 following the failure of the Mogadishu hijacking - there lately has been a notable redrudescence of terrorist activity aimed chiefly at United States and NATO personnel and property. Similar targeting can be seen in Italy where the kidnapping of General Dozier in December 1981 was the first to aim at a NATO target.

The PLO's role in Germany has been all-inclusive. In addition to training the RAF and M2J at the Shatila camp in Beirut, there is now hard evidence of collusion between the PLO and neo-nazi groups. In March 1981 the biggest crackdown in West German history took place and the revelations seemed to astound the authorities. A network of connections was revealed which stretched from Western Europe to the United States, to the PLO and to Iran. Manfred Roeder, a leading neo-nazi, and Karl-Heinz Hoffman, leader of a group which was banned in 1980, had close contacts with the PLO in Lebanon and at least thirty of their members went there for training.[268] The Christian Phalangists exhibited two

---

* There is a lack of evidence for this, though it is not unlikely.

captured neo-nazis of the Hoffman group three months later in Beirut.[269] The official spokesman presented Walter-Ulrich Behle and Uwe Johannes Mainka, at a press conference. Hoffman, who founded the neo-nazi Military Sports Group, and who advocated the overthrow of the German government, had a business relationship with the PLO, selling them trucks. The camp where the training took place was the Bir Hassan camp near Beirut, run by the PLO.

The full circle of extremism was demonstrated when Hoffman was implicated in the Oktoberfest bombing in Munich on 28 September 1980, as well as the Bologna railway station bombing on 2 August 1980, both of which were planned with the help of Abu Iyad of the PLO and Italian terrorists,[270] thus underlining the inaccuracy of applying political labels of 'left' or 'right' to any of the terrorist groups operating in the liberal democracies. Labels tempt judgements of 'good' and 'bad' terrorism which cannot be acceptable in the Western European and American context, and, at any event, the co-operation exhibited by these groups to one another in itself blurs any distinctions. Manfred Roeder and three of his cohorts were given life sentences in Stuttgart in June 1982.[271]

Thus, in the West German context, familiar links exist and have existed for a long time, some since before the terrorist campaign itself. The KGB and Eastern bloc interest has been at the base, with PLO co-ordination at the fore.

The terrorism which the West Germans ruthlessly practised was, from the point of view of the individuals of the groups, and in light of their personality traits, an expression of bored frustration of middle-class individuals with the necessity for relief of inner weaknesses and instabilities. Their exploitive value was not, however, diminished because of that. On the contrary, the incredulity displayed in the West, that the Soviet Union should back such a group of 'crazies', was an added advantage. From the Soviet perception of its power projection techniques, neither the group itself, nor any of its leaders were ever meant* to form a power base for a potential takeover of governmental authority. For the sponsors of their activities the goal was to destabilize, to soften the morale and to erode any sense of logic and security in the population itself.

The IRA The history of the IRA (Irish Republican Army) is a long and bloody one.[272] After a long dormant period, the movement

---

* The implication that the USSR had formulated plans for the RAF is unfounded. That the young terrorists' activities were regarded with approval in the Soviet Union is indubitable.

began a gradual rebuilding starting in 1964. Under the influence of a young Marxist computer scientist, Roy Johnson, appointed by the IRA to its Army Council, a noticeable shift to the left occurred.[273] By 1966 the reorganization was complete and culminated in the expulsion of some two hundred and fifty old-timers and their replacement by young Marxists who joined both the IRA and Sinn Fein, the political arm of the movement. Two years later the terrorist revival was a reality. This new recrudescence had a novel twist to it for the Irish scene: the civilian target became a predominant feature of IRA tactics.[274] A two-pronged policy was actually proposed in 1969 which would involve a recognition of the 'partition parliaments' as well as armed action. The March 1969 document 'Ireland Today' included the following directive: ... 'that the undermining of confidence in existing parliaments and eventual abstention from them in order to establish an alternative form of government must be a major objective of the movement.'[275] It is of interest that in 1969 the possibility of a link-up with the Southern Communist Party was suggested. There followed, in fact, a merger between the Northern Communist Party and the Southern Communist Party, which took place at a meeting which was attended by numerous Soviet representatives of the press, and the idea of the 'National Liberation Front' was introduced in the policy document of March 1969.[276]

The Provisional IRA's international links have been of long standing. In the 1950's there was some contact with Nicos Sampson, the EOKA terrorist operating in Cyprus against the British government, and steadily the links spread to a multitude of terrorist groups, especially Trotskyite and Marxist groups.[277] After the murder of a young teacher, Peter Graham, revelations of gun-running on behalf of various Trotskyites from the continent began to emerge.[278]

The intricacies of some of the gun delivery patterns were revealed by British intelligence sources in 1975. What Special Branch called 'the French Connection' was in fact close contact between the IRA and the Breton Separatist Catholics. A recent shipment of weapons was dispatched by the PLO via Syria and Libya to Canada, where the FLQ (Front de Liberation Quebequois) transferred it back through Le Havre for delivery to the IRA. The weapons were East German and Czechoslovakian.[279] Other routes have been confirmed by British intelligence sources and have included the delivery of Soviet Strela SA-7 missiles to the IRA which were initially smuggled via Belgium in Libyan diplomatic pouches.

A few of these shipments have been intercepted. On 17 October 1971, for example, a very large consignment of arms (166 crates) shipped directly by Omnipol, the security service controlled arms factory in Czechoslovakia, to the Provisional IRA, was seized at Schiphol Airport in Amsterdam. On 28 March 1973 the *Claudia*, a Cyprus-registered vessel, was intercepted off the coast of Waterford. Its cargo contained 250 rifles, 240 small arms, anti-tank mines and explosives, also of Czechoslovakian origin.[280]

The Israeli intelligence services sent information to the British government of an Arab shipment of weapons destined for Dublin and dispatched by al-Fatah. On 21 December 1977 the cargo of the *Tower Stream* ship was seized and revealed 2 Bren guns, 29 Kalashnikov rifles, 29 submachine guns, over 100 hand grenades, rocket launchers with rockets and a large amount of explosives.[281]

The relationship with the PLO began early, just after the reorganization of the IRA in 1966 when several members went to Jordan for training in PFLP-run camps. Such training was particularly noticed in 1968 and 1969.[282] In 1971 the IRA attended Feltrinelli's terrorist conference in Florence.

On 27 and 28 May 1972 the IRA organized a conference of their own in Dublin for international terrorists which was attended, among others, by the JRA and nine members of the PFLP. The PLO subsequently established contacts with both the Official Marxist wing which ostensibly does not take part in terrorist activity, and the Provisional wing which does.[283] The bombing campaign in London in December 1973 marked the beginning of co-operative action between the PLO and the IRA. This was admitted to in an announcement of solidarity with the IRA made in Beirut by spokesmen for the PLO, announcing 'joint military operations on British territory against Zionist organizations'.[284]

Both a KGB connection to the IRA and a Cuban DGI link have now been established, as have the firm links with ETA, the RAF, the PLO, Tupamaros and others. Mr Victor Louis, the KGB public relations operative, has had frequent meetings with the IRA, for example. The British and Irish Communist Parties provided the conduit for this and other meetings. KGB officer Yuri Ustimenko, under the cover of being the TASS correspondent in Dublin, has had regular and frequent meetings with Irish Communist Party Secretary-General Michael O'Riordan. Meetings with IRA members have also been held by N. V. Glavatsky, a KGB officer posing as an Intourist representative. And there have been official meetings with members of the Central Committee of the CPSU, both in Great Britain and in Ireland.[285]

The bomb which killed Airey Neave in the drive of the car park of the Houses of Parliament in London was a sophisticated 'dual-trigger' device used for the first time in England (by the INLA), but known to be widely used by the PLO and the BR.[286]

Thomas MacMahon, the convicted murderer of Lord Mountbatten and members of his family in 1979, was trained in a PFLP camp and was a member of both the Official Sinn Fein and the Provisional IRA, which demonstrates that the two wings are not entirely distinct.[287] TASS reported the death of Lord Mountbatten in an explosion, avoiding the mention, however, that the IRA terrorists had killed him.[288] And no mention was made of the massacre of eighteen British soldiers which occurred on the same day. The Kremlin's official attitude to the terrorism in Ireland has been that it is regrettable, but an inevitable result of British policy. The news media are in fact normally restricted to reporting the casualties caused by the Protestant violence or by British troops and tend to ignore altogether the terrorist activity of the IRA. In an article in *New Times*, for example, the idea that a repressive government exists in Northern Ireland which would therefore justify armed action against it is clearly presented. V. Pavlov wrote: 'The country's peaceful landscape is deceptive. Northern Ireland is dotted with prisons and concentration camps where freedom fighters are tortured.'[289] The author then footnotes a mention of the Provisionals as the Irish Republican movement advocating armed action and terrorism.

The day after the Mountbatten murders, and in the wake of the world shock and uproar which followed the gruesome event, *Pravda* did call the killers of Mountbatten 'terrorists' and identified them as belonging to the Provisionals, which is call 'the Right Wing of the IRA', thus attempting once again to blame the existing violence on 'the forces of reaction' and by implication distancing the USSR from the act, at least ideologically.[290]

Soviet interest in and connection with the IRA is not a new development and dates back to the early 1920s. The interest which had been expressed by Lenin in the Irish 'just cause even though not Marxist'[291] was followed by a near-continuous contact between the IRA and Moscow. The meetings were mainly with David Fitzgerald and Peadar O'Donnell who made frequent visits to Moscow during the 1920's, and through O'Donnell and Frank Ryan who officially represented the IRA at the World Congress of the Anti-Imperialist League in Brussels in 1927. In 1929 at Frankfurt, Sean Macbride and Donal O'Donoghue were assured of the backing of the Congress for the 'next attempt' by the IRA to set up its desired state.[292]

The time for the Soviet Union to be interested in extending active support was not yet ripe, however. In spite of an offshoot of the Third International being introduced into Ireland by Peadar O'Donnell and Sean Hayes (the European Peasants Committee),[293] there was practically no positive reception to the idea of the IRA being 'the armed members of the toiling and working classes', and diplomatic relations with Great Britain carried a heavier weight in the scale of policy options available to the Kremlin at the time. So when Stalin met 'Pa' Murray in 1925, Stalin's overriding concern was not to be 'seen' supporting the Irish lest it should anger the British.[294] And nothing much came of any hopes for support.

The change which occurred in the quality of the attention given to the IRA in the 1960s, however, coincides with the 'armed proletariat' idea which the Kremlin began to emphasize, and with all the overt declarations by both the CPSU leaders and the military strategists. It is true that most of the financial aid to the IRA has come from Irish-Americans sympathetic to the cause. But that has only facilitated the Kremlin's role, and made it more cost-effective. (This is also true in regard to the PLO which is financed mostly by Saudi Arabia and other Arab oil states.) Other groups are encouraged to 'expropriate funds' so that capitalism can finance its own destruction.

The erosive effect on the British government, in both economic and morale terms, has always been an aim of Soviet subversion. In financial terms, between 1969 and 1980 the terror in Ulster had cost British taxpayers £380 million in compensation awards alone. The annual 'running costs' of Northern Ireland are over £2,000 million including the security services and the necessary governmental bureaucracy.[295]

In a report by A. Maslennikov, London correspondent for *Pravda*, on 29 October 1980, the IRA prisoners who went on hunger strike were described as 'freedom fighters' indicating an official approval of IRA terrorist activities and placing the group officially in a paramilitary context.

The success achieved by the terrorism in Northern Ireland has been considerable. It has polarized Protestant and Catholic opinion in Ulster, precipitated the fall of the Prime Minister of Northern Ireland in 1971, and has changed the role of the British army from a peacekeeping force to an aggressive force *vis-à-vis* the IRA.

ETA (Euzkadi ta Azkatasuna)   The first Basque terrorists to be trained in the Eastern bloc were sent to Cuba in 1964 - a date which once again precedes by several years the renewed outbreak of violence in Spain and suggests the application of a plan, rather than a spontaneous occurrence. This is not meant to imply that the cause which the Basque separatists fight for was in any way created by the sponsors who organized the training. It is only to suggest that the sponsors made a decision at that time in order to exploit the existing sentiments and to encourage them to develop on a violent path. In 1964 there were also contacts with Henri Curiel's Solidarité, which in retrospect reinforces the view that this was a strategic preparation.[296]

More recently the training of the ETA terrorists has been provided by the PLO and Czechoslovakia. The Czechoslovak connection was confirmed in 1981 by the Spanish police. The official newspaper of the police, *Policia española*, published proof that Basque terrorists had in recent years undergone military training in Czechoslovakia. TASS responded with 'An absurd lie' in *Rude pravo*.[297] On 9 March 1981 Spain expelled Vladimir I. Efremenkov 'for carrying out activities incompatible with his diplomatic status and contrary to the security of the State'.[298] This evidence of Soviet involvement in contemporary Spanish terrorism is now a matter of record. In addition to official police evidence, it was also confirmed by the Spanish intelligence services which had corroborated the existence of contacts between ETA and the KGB in 1977,[299] and sources close to the then Prime Minister, Adolfo Suarez, insisted that the general feeling in the Cabinet was that GRAPO, another terrorist group operating in Spain, was a KGB creation, posing ideologically as right-wing rather than left-wing, and handled by the Cuban DGI.[300] At the end of 1978 the Spanish intelligence services witnessed a meeting in St Jean de Luz in France between the KGB and ETA's representative Eugenio Echeveste Arizgura, *nom de guerre* 'Anchon'.[301]

The links with all the other international terrorist groups are tight. 'Carlos', the RAF, Feltrinelli, the IRA, the BR and particularly the PLO are all parts of the intricate web of co-operation. ETA attended the Feltrinelli terrorist conference in Florence, and the Dublin Conference 'For a Revolutionary Western Europe'. In 1978 terrorists from all parts of the 'international network' attended a West German 'anti-fascist' conference.[302] The PLO provided weapons and special explosive devices, as well as training in their camps in Lebanon and elsewhere.[303]

The history of Soviet interest in the Basque nationalists dates back to the Civil War years, as we have already seen.[304] Thus here again one finds consistency and continuity in Soviet behaviour.

Whereas while Franco still ruled Spain the classic attack on a fascist military government could draw the necessary sympathy from liberals, and somewhat 'justify' the cause, after his death in 1975 ETA terrorism multiplied at a frightening rate although the excuse for extremism no longer existed.

The Soviet reaction when confronted with the published evidence of their own complicity in Basque terror is of interest to note, for it is predictable and represents a consistent strategic response which aims at two ends and which is present in all Soviet responses to terrorism which have taken place on Western European soil in the liberal democracies. First, an immediate denial of involvement is indignantly pronounced. Secondly, terrorism is admitted as existing, thus creating over the long run an image of growing discontent in capitalist societies. This position has also been taken by the Soviet Union when it publishes the denial of PLO responsibility in PLO-perpetrated acts of terrorism on West European soil. The PLO denial of involvement is not usually followed by a Soviet denial of the act being of a terrorist nature; thus the political labelling which the USSR attributes to the act propagandizes the idea that there is political discontent and therefore a 'cause', usually justified by the existence of the 'forces of reaction'.

In response to the *Policia española* accusation of evidence of Czechoslovakian training, the following TASS statement represents that consistent type of response:[305]

> Why are such lies going up again? The answer can only be this. The Spanish bourgeois society is unable to cope with the wave of terrorism. Therefore, the right-wing forces are trying to cover up by invented slander the real culprits. The fabrications of the Spanish newspaper, which were picked up by Western news agencies, cannot conceal the fact that the roots of Basque terrorism should be sought in Spain itself, in the 40-year long history of the Francoist dictatorship . . . To smear others will not help bring out the truth, will not be able to put an end to the dramatic showing of social contradictions in Spain which manifests itself in political terrorism . . .

Of course there had been no accusations by the Spanish authorities to state that the roots of Basque terrorism were elsewhere, only that ETA had received logistic and material support from the Eastern bloc. ETA has, in fact, also had very close links with the Spanish Communist Party and the illegal Workers' Commissions,[306] and one of the factions of ETA (split like the IRA into Marxist and non-Marxist sections) merged with the Liga Communista Revolucionaria of the Spanish section of the Trotskyite Fourth International.[307]

The new democracy of Spain was of considerable importance to the USSR, particularly in the context of NATO which it was considering joining. The immediate short-term strategic interest was to create an unstable situation which would make Spain a potential liability to NATO and would thus perhaps exclude her. This goal received a high priority in the Kremlin's decision-making process as a right-wing coup was anticipated and encouraged by the terrorism which rendered Spain unstable. In 1979 Andrei

Gromyko, Foreign Minister, even went so far as to indicate to the Spanish Foreign Minister, Marcelino Oreja, that it was in his power to control the level of terrorism in Spain by suggesting a bargain: If Spain desisted in its attempts to join NATO, it would be rewarded by the USSR's assistance in curbing the terrorism which had been so erosive of domestic stability. A contrary decision by Spain would, on the other hand, leave Spain very vunerable indeed to terrorist ravages.[308]

The invasion of the Cortes by the Fascist military elements in the foil *coup* of February 1981, and the more recent attempted reactionary *coup* of June 1981, show the young democracy teetering on the brink of disastrous right-wing repression in the wake of the recently heightened level of terrorism. The only beneficiary, in the global strategic context, of the possible demise of the fledgeling Spanish democracy would be the USSR, for it would create a further instability in NATO, which it has now joined.

REVOLUTIONARY TERRORISM

This section presents a brief discussion of the Soviet position on revolutionary terrorism, as defined within the framework of this study in Chapter 1. As stated earlier, this type of terrorism is at present mostly to be found in Third World countries and usually precedes a civil war which is normally labelled as a 'national liberation' war. The close identification the USSR has always maintained with national liberation movements has allowed it openly to incite to armed violence for the overthrow of the existing regime. In the contemporary context, the PLO emerges as one of the special co-ordinators of that activity, along with the KGB itself and surrogate actors such as Cuba, as the main protagonists for implementing Politburo policy, in the same way as they appear in the support and organizing of sub-revolutionary terrorism, as discussed in the previous section. That the two typologies of terrorism have the same patrons is another indication that both serve to advance the paramilitary policy of the Soviet government.

The PLO, singled out for special attention by the USSR, has provided an invaluable paramilitary service to the Kremlin and its links have extended worldwide. The PLO had long been involved in Latin American terrorism and has not limited itself to a regional aspect in the Middle East. Its deep involvement in the El Salvadoran insurgency and in Nicaragua[309] has already been mentioned and must be placed in the perspective of Soviet needs. The PLO has had an ambassadorial status in Nicaragua where it keeps an embassy. In a speech printed in *Tricontinental* in 1969, Arafat had clearly enunciated his position in this respect: 'The Palestinian movement considers itself a part of the people's struggle against international imperialism. We are fighting the same enemy, whether it is in Latin America, Vietnam or Palestine.'

It is probable that in the Latin American scene the PLO has acted as a proxy for the USSR which has repeatedly suffered major setbacks when attempting direct KGB manipulations in Central and South America. In 1971, for instance, an epic counter-intelligence *coup* took place with the uncovering of a Soviet plan to take over Mexico.[310] After the students rioted in Mexico City in 1968 - riots which had been heavily exploited if not instigated by the KGB and which in fact did not escalate into general violence as the Soviet Union had hoped - Mexican security forces stumbled on a takeover plan by the KGB which was to be implemented with terrorist tactics. Earlier, the testimony given by Raya Kiselnikova, who had defected to Mexico in 1970 and had been working at the Soviet embassy there, had provided details of the KGB's use of Mexico City as a base for espionage and subversion in the Western hemisphere. There is, of course, nothing new in the fact of Soviet involvement in that geographic area, and there is the precedent of Central and South American activity by the Soviet Union which caused the severing of diplomatic relations with Uruguay during the 1930s.[311] There was also continued activity in the Latin American continent with Cominform arms trafficking in the 1950s. In a telegram of particular secrecy sent from the Admiralty in Rio de Janeiro to Sir N. Butler at the British Foreign Office, there were reports of shipments of arms to Brazil from Polish ports,[312] and incitement to activism in the trade unions of Nicaragua.[313]

The KGB in 1971 was directly implicated in the organization and tasking of the mission. Oleg Maksimovich Nechiporenko was the planner who had been posted to Mexico City ten years earlier, in 1961. He was joined there in 1966 by Boris Pavlovich Kolomyakov, a top Latin American specialist in the KGB. The Movimiento de Acción Revolucionaria (MAR), which was briefly catapulted to fame and was to carry out the plan, was founded in Moscow by Fabricio Gomez Souza who had been sent to Patrice Lumumba University in 1963. By 1968, thirty other Mexicans had joined him there. They were all sent for training to Pyongyang, North Korea, where the best-equipped guerrilla and terrorist centre existed at the time. Five days after the discovery of MAR, the Mexican government of Luis Echeverria Portillo expelled the Russian ambassador as well as Oleg Nechiporenko and three other members of the Russian embassy. For pragmatic reasons, the USSR did not protest against those expulsions. The following year, in 1972, ninety-four diplomats from the Soviet embassy were expelled from Bolivia because of outright collusion with the ELN

(Ejercito de Liberación Nacional), the group which had been founded by Che Guevara.[314] Argentina, Colombia, Ecuador and Uruguay also expelled Soviet diplomats.

More recently the Sandinistas, who successfully overthrew the military government of Somoza in Nicaragua had been trained in Cuba and by the PLO. In August 1979 the European representative of the Sandinistas, Jorge Mundi, spoke of those ties:[315]

> We have long had close relations with the Palestinians. Many of the units belonging to the Sandinista movement were at Palestinian revolution bases in Jordan. In the early 1970's, Nicaraguan and Palestinian blood was spilled together in Amman and in other places during the Black September battles ... It is natural, therefore, that during our war against Somoza we received Palestinian support for our revolution in various forms.

Cuba has in fact been supplying insurgents in El Salvador, Guatemala and the Caribbean region, as well as the FALN, the terrorist group claiming the liberation of Puerto Rico.[316] Cuba, as pointed out earlier, has been a general surrogate for the Soviet Union and has also been very instrumental in training and supplying the PLO, and with the absence of any significant reaction to these surrogate role players by the Western democracies, the USSR has increasingly relied on their services. Cuba, for example, whose economy is faltering badly, is subsidized by the Soviet Union at over $8 million a day,[317] an amount which not only allows it its own foreign policy adventures, but forces upon it many of the Soviet adventures in power projection. The presence on Cuban soil of a Soviet combat brigade which numbers about 3,000 men, and the provision to Cuba of the most modern military equipment the USSR produces and for which Cuba, unlike other clients, does not pay, are the other sides of the strategic projection by the Soviet Union into the Central American geographical area which seeks to exploit targets of opportunity.[318] The close association with local insurgent groups which the USSR has established has at times been revealed in somewhat naïve circumstances. For example, in the January 1981 'final offensive' which was launched by the rebels in El Salvador and was, from all accounts, a military mistake, the Soviet Union indicated prior knowledge by announcing that offensive on Radio Moscow a good six hours before it was actually launched.[319]

The groups which operate in Latin America are regarded by the Soviet Union as having the same strategic value as the groups operating in Western Europe and the Middle East, though the revolutionary gains expected of them are different. Training has been offered by the Eastern bloc to Nicaraguans as well as the PLO, Italians and Germans; that is, to some who are sub-revolutionary terrorists and some who are revolutionary by the Soviet definition. Moreover, there has been no distinction in the quality of the training offered, which has concentrated on urban-type terrorist tactics. In the Central American context, terrorist tactics have often preceded civil wars by several years and have served to prepare the ground for the escalation of violence by 'softening' the morale of the population. These terror tactics increased repressions and counter-terror by already repressive regimes. But this approach was not limited in its application and has been employed against democratic regimes as well, such as Uruguay which turned military and repressive in the process of destroying the Tupamaros who had so debilitated the democratic institutions and damaged the fabric of that society. The terrorism applied by these groups is perceived by the Kremlin as having a different goal from that of the groups operating in Western democracies: that is, a revolutionary takeover by the insurgents.[320]

The countries chosen as targets for the revolutionary process in the Latin American context, as in the African context, have mostly been those run by military juntas which have been extremely unpopular and have allowed a facile application of the 'justifiable war' concept by the Soviet Union. But it must be emphasized that the USSR has displayed a pragmatic selectivity in this context as well. Not all junta regimes have suffered Cuban and Soviet-supported rebellions. Only those which Soviet perception has identified as likely to produce a revolutionary situation have been targeted. And even after a successful military *coup* has replaced a regime which was perceived as 'progressive' by the Soviet Union, the Kremlin has not hesitated to deal with the successor regime if it was deemed to meet its pragmatic needs in the short-term. Should democratic regimes replace the juntas, there is no reason to expect an abandonment of this policy by the USSR as long as it can maintain an aggressive confrontational position to the 'anti-imperialist' forces. In such a case, the doctrinal rhetoric would revert to the same language used in the Western European context where the workers are identified as the potential revolutionaries.

The standard doctrinal position which had always seen the military as the servant of the ruling oligarchies and the bourgeoisie was granted the necessary elasticity to extend a 'progressive' nature to those military regimes which the Soviet Union perceived as increasingly prone to adopt an anti-imperialist and anti-United States position - this being the policy goal which remains predominant in Soviet strategic thinking. Thus the Soviet commentary on certain military regimes in Latin America describes them as 'progressive', and explains that where the communist parties are weak and the working class has not been roused to action, the 'progressive' military regimes are the best vehicle for 'the further development of the revolutionary process'.[321] In essence, the Kremlin perpetually shapes the doctrine to catch up with reality. Thus Brazil in the early 1970's was viewed in this way, as was Peru.[322]

The relative strength of the local communist parties in particular countries may determine whether or not the terrorist option is applied. Where those parties are electorally strong, as in Western Europe, the application of terrorism has been sub-revolutionary in nature. Dealings on a state-to-state level have always been an essential part of Soviet strategic applications and regarded as a necessary compromise for the ultimate success of the revolution. But incitement to revolutionary violence would be carried on at the same time as state-to-state activities. In the early 1970's, for example, it was repeatedly called for by various Soviet leaders for such countries as Guatemala and Nicaragua, among others,[323] both of which subsequently suffered several years of terrorist activity before the conditions escalated into a civil war. The lessons learned by the USSR in the light of the failure of Che Guevara were to be applied with more emphasis on urban, rather than rural, terror which had proved to have a far greater impact.[324] This type of terrorism has characterized the conflicts in both Latin America and Western Europe. And this method of combat has been re-emphasized by the Soviet Union since the 1960s.

For example, in South Africa, the fight for equality of the Blacks did not interest the USSR until the 1960s. In fact, the Communist Party of South Africa's slogan in the early years was 'Workers of the World Unite for a White South Africa'.[325] By 1924 the utility of espousing the Black cause was recognized by the Communist International. Manuilsky, the chairman of the Colonial Commission of the Comintern, submitted a programme which suggested that a special section for Negro affairs should be set up to establish close contact with Negro organizations in America, South America and the colonies. This question even then was considered in terms of how it would affect the relationship with the United States, where Manuilsky stated 'the Negro movement in America was growing rapidly forward'. On 12 July 1924 an extended plenary session of the ECCI decided to create this permanent commission of the Black question.[326] The Communist Party of South Africa subsequently changed its slogan.

It was not until the 1960s, however, that the 'cause' of 'liberating' South Africa for the Blacks was adopted, as part of the USSR's opportunistic foreign policy which shifted to the sponsorship of surrogates. Support was then extended to the ANC (African National Congress) since it was identified as the most likely vehicle for Soviet power projection (see Appendix C).[327]

According to the history of this association between the Communist Party and the ANC as described by the Party itself, 'leaders of the African National Congress and the Communist Party set themselves to recruit the fighting cadres which entered the field of action on December 16, 1961, with the opening of the campaign of planned sabotage throughout the country'.[328] The outcome was the organization of terrorist cells which were not to be identified or directly associated with the Communist Party even though their membership was a mixture of Communist Party members and the ANC.[329]

The centre for the logistic support extended to the ANC is the Soviet embassy in Zambia, which is believed to be co-ordinated by the KGB, headed by Dr Vasily Solodnikov, the Ambassador of Lusaka.[330] In 1980 a high-ranking KGB officer, Alexei Kozlov, was arrested in South Africa and confirmed that his job was to monitor the performance of the ANC terrorists.[331] In 1981, after more than two weeks of silence on the question, the Soviet Union reluctantly admitted that two of its advisers had been killed and one officer captured by South African forces in a raid on Angolan guerrilla bases, from which terrorist activity was carried out in south-west Africa. The President of the ANC, Oliver Reginald Tambo, stated that the ANC was not a communist group, and it might well not be, but what must be understood is that the utility of any particular terrorist group is not assessed according to whether it is or not. Often support is extended to fascist groups in order to create a left swing in the electorate, for example. The Soviet Union may not even believe that by supporting the ANC it would ultimately control and 'Sovietize' South Africa. But should the ANC manage to overthrow the government of South Africa, the 'correlation of forces' would be seen as having shifted once more in favour of the USSR.

There is no guarantee that the Kremlin would not attempt to undermine the ANC in turn, should it come to power. The support for the creation of the State of Israel in 1947-8 which very rapidly deteriorated to a totally antagonistic position is another example of this opportunistic feature of Soviet foreign policy.

The paramilitary grid which has been formed is equally not impaired by considerations of ideological 'purity' from the Soviet point of view, just a state-to-state relations are not hindered by that factor.

As has already been mentioned, in the case of terrorist groups, this ideological 'purity' of the group has *not* been a prerequisite for interest, support, enticement, training, arming and financing by the Soviet Union. The PLO and the KGB have been involved with disparate groups all over the Western world as previously indicated, but the examples discussed in this section are by no means exhaustive. The PLO has had close contacts and co-operation with Turkish terrorists since the late 1960's.[332] On 17 May 1971 the TPLA kidnapped the Israeli Consul General in Istanbul as a favour to the PLO. He was found murdered on 23 May 1971. Other close contacts have been with the Trotskyite Fourth International - an organization which always supports the USSR in all its foreign policy decisions, and with which, for example, Bob and Bertha Langston were the contacts for the PLO in the United States from 1967.[333] Moreover, the Trotskyite International supported the Baader-Meinhof gang even though the latter was not Trotskyite,[334] and has always been explicit in favour of using terrorist tactics when they were perceived as necessary. In this connection, there has been evidence that the Abu Nidal group of the PLO,* which calls itself the 'Corrective Movement of al-Fatah' and is usually considered to be against Arafat, has had the same connections as Arafat with the Italian Red Brigades, the RAF and 'Carlos'.[335]

The PLO trained the hijackers of the Pakistani airliner which landed at Kabul Airport in March 1981, an airport controlled by Soviet troops since the invasion of Afghanistan in December 1979, and where the hijackers were provided with better weapons by the ground authorities.[336]

The Armenian terrorists have also received co-operation and training from the PLO. This group, which has been very active in the last five years and has murdered eighteen Turkish diplomats all over the Western world and committed bomb outrages in city centres, is the most difficult one to dissociate from outright Soviet control. It is a Marxist-led group mostly made up of young middle-class members. The group has a pro-Soviet ideology which considers Soviet Armenia, which was taken by the USSR in 1920 when Turkey and the Soviet Union divided the territory of Armenia between them, as the legitimate homeland of the Armenian peole and favours enlarging the Soviet province of Armenia with land 'liberated' from Turkey.[337] PLO leaders have often made stops in the capital of the Armenian province which is in the Soviet Union, and until recently the Armenians published a propaganda sheet in Beirut.

---

* See ed. note on page 197.

To conclude, the Soviet position on international terrorism has been consistent and favourable to its use, as revealed by the statements made by government officials and by the evidence of material support extended to the groups which perpetrate it in the West. In the regional context of the Middle East, the Soviet embrace of the PLO on both official and unofficial levels has been part of the overall strategy of encouraging anti-Western trends in that area, but it is obvious that the same strategy appears to have been served in the larger geopolitical extensions of Soviet foreign policy. The PLO, in fact, received this support in return for advocating the Soviet line and co-ordinating Western European and Third World terrorism. Arafat was apparently singled out to lead this part of the Soviet Union's 'struggle for peace' perceived by the Kremlin as the best possible means of projecting Soviet power, not only in the Middle East but generally in its attempts at shifting the 'correlation of forces' in favour of the USSR and having predominantly a geopolitical aspect rather than a pro-Palestinian aspect. The early involvement of Cuba and the Eastern bloc in training the PLO, as well as the early links with Western European terrorist groups, might lead one to speculate that international terrorism aimed in an 'anti-imperialist' direction was planned to be the predominant thrust of Soviet power projection from the 1960s onwards, and would thus be consistent with the military statements of policy.

In the West European theatre, the USSR's official position on terrorism has been that the Kremlin itself is not associated with it, and neither is the PLO. A duplicitous position was an obvious one for the Soviet Union to take, given the 'peace offensive' which was offically announced as the foreign policy for this era in the New Communist Programme of the CPSU in 1961, known as the Khrushchev doctrine. Terrorism in the European context was not condemned, but reported in order to promote the idea that political terrorism exists and indicates the 'sickness of capitalist societies'. This is of course consistent with the Soviet perception that 'class societies' must be destroyed, and the constant allusion to terrorism may foment dissatisfaction among the proletariat in general. In addition, for home consumption, it serves the purpose of pointing out that the Soviet society is the only good one, for it does not and cannot suffer any terrorist attack. The statement made by Yuri Zhukov, a member of the Supreme Soviet, after his visit to Rome in 1980, puts it very clearly:[338]

All these terrorist actions are supposed to be Red, but according to me they are only Black . . . Behind them are all the forces of reaction trying to destroy law and order . . . It's odd that all the armed violence is happening in the West. Fortunately for the

East, the terrorist phenomenon does not exist there, inasmuch as our political situation is more healthy.

This statement is a natural extension of the Marxist-Leninist concept of aggression which is that it can only exist in capitalist societies, and is therefore not in contradiction to the Soviet official position on this question. Yet statements such as this one by TASS: 'Italy's leadership may not be aware of the principled position of the Soviet State, which has always denounced and always will denounce terrorism',[339] have been interpreted in the West, where selective perceptions of the Soviet Union so often distort value judgements, to mean that the USSR would not support the development of terroristic activities in the Western world!

Notes

1. *Pravda*, 29 Sept. 1964. The stage of the theatre decorated with a red banner bearing the portraits of Marx, Engels, Lenin, and the dates 1864-1964. This fact alone would serve to emphasize the sense of continuity which the Soviets have themselves. Present were: L. I. Brezhnev, G. I. Voronov, A. N. Kosygin, A. I. Mikoyan, N. V. Podgorny, D. S. Polyansky, M. A. Suslov, N. S. Khrushchev, V. V. Grishin, L. N. Yefremov, V. P. Mzhavanadze, V. I. Polyakov, B. N. Ponomarev, A. P. Rudakov, and V. N. Titov. Together with these CPSU leaders were old communists F. N. Petrov, P. I. Voyevodin and M. A. Komin-Alexandrovsky and representatives of fraternal Communist Parties: Dolores Ibarruri (CP Spain), Jose Gonzales (CP Chile), Edgardo Gallegas Mansera (CP Venezuela), Mohammed Harmel (CP Tunis), Mario Monje (CP Bolivia), Begum Hajra (CP India), Shmuel Mikunis (CP Israel), Mortimer Daniel Rubin (CP USA), and Pardede Paris (CP Indonesia).
2. Interview with Michael Ledeen of Georgetown Center for Strategic Studies, recently published in *Il Giornale Nuovo* (Milan), 1 Jan., 22 May, 18 Sept. 1980. Also confirmed by Dr Ledeen, as Special Consultant to Secretary of State Haig, in a personal interview with this author, US State Department, Washington DC, Nov. 1981. See General Jan Sejna's book describing the Soviet subversion plan of the West which he first talked about in 1968 (Sejna 1982).
3. US Congress, Judiciary Committee. US Senate, Hearings, *Terroristic Activity*, Part 4, 94th Congress, 14 May, 1975.
4. *Kommunist*, No. 2, Jan. 1962, pp. 15-20. In the same editorial, the Soviet position on general and complete disarmament is also made clear: 'By general and complete disarmament we do not mean the disarmament of the liberating armed forces of the oppressed nations but chiefly the dismantling of the giant war machines of the highly developed states'.
5. *Pravda*, 6 Feb. 1965.
6. *Pravda*, 6 June 1972.
7. Mochanov (1972) p. 5.
8. A. Bovin, *Izvestiya*, 11 Sept. 1973.
9. Penkovsky pp. 88 and 102. Colonel Penkovsky, a GRU officer, was sentenced

to death and shot in Moscow in 1963 as an agent of British and American intelligence services.

10. *Ibid.* p. 89.
11. *Soviet Military Power*, U.S. Department of Defense, Washington D.C., 1981, p. 38.
12. A.A. Grecho, *The Armed Forces of the Soviet State*, Moscow, translated under the auspices of the US Air Force, *Soviet Military Thought*, No. 12, Washington DC, 1975, p. 129.
13. *Ibid.* p. 272.
14. *Ibid.* p. 276.
15. General-Major S. N. Kozlov (ed.) *The Officer's Handbook*, Moscow 1971, translated under the auspices of the US Air Force, *Soviet Military Thought*, No. 13, p. 62. For a discussion of Soviet military doctrine and its application, see John J. Dziak (1981a).
16. *The Philosophical Heritage of V. I. Lenin and Problems of Contemporary War*, Moscow, Voenizdat, 1972, translated under the auspices of the US Air Force, *Soviet Military Thought*, No. 5, US Government Publications, p. 9.
17. *Ibid.* p. 13.
18. *Ibid.* p. 30.
19. *Ibid.* p. 31.
20. *Ibid.* pp. 31-32.
21. Marshall M. V. Zakharov, 'Leninism and Soviet Military Science' (*Leninism i sovetskaya voyennaya mauka*), *Krasnaya Zvezda* (Red Star), Moscow, 5 April 1970.
22. See Collins (1980).
23. Since 1975, six such ventures have succeeded: Vietnam, Laos, Angola, Ethiopia, South Yemen, and Cambodia.
24. See Barron (1975) pp. 20-90; Collins (1980) pp. 77-80.
25. See US House of Representatives, *Soviet Covert Action: The Forgery Offensive*, Hearings, Subcommittee on Oversight, Permanent Select Committee on Intelligence, Ninety-sixth congress, second session, Washington DC 6, 19 Feb. 1980.
26. Myagkov (1976) p. 131.
27. Collins (1980) pp. 77-80; see also Bittman (1972).
28. *Soviet Military Power*, U.S. Department of Defense, 1981, especially p. 90; also Collins and Dziak (1981a).
29. See Schapiro (1976-7) (1980).
30. See Sakharov with Tosi (1981). Also confirmed by the United States Defense Intelligence Agency (DIA). Leonard Schapiro elaborates on the International Department's control of international front organizations in an unpublished manuscript of a forthcoming book on the subject, kindly lent to this author.
31. See Barro (1972) for full details on the KGB structure.
32. Collins (1980) p. 180.
33. See Barron pp. 39-84. Information based on the testimony of Vladimir Nikolaevich Sakharov, a KGB operative and subsequently a CIA agent as well. Sakharov, in 1972, confirmed for example that Soviet pilots flew Egyptian planes in combat against Israel. See Sakharov with Tosi (1981).
34. *Ibid.* p. 72. Information based on testimony given by Ladislav Bittman, former deputy director of the Disinformation and Action Department of Czechoslovak intelligence. He defected to the United States in 1968. See Bittman (1972).
35. *Ibid.* p. 76. Information based on Sakharov testimony and corroborated by Turkish Embassy officials in Washington DC.
36. Laqueur (1972) p. 95.
37. *Izvestiya*, 6 May 1966.

38. MER. v. 3, 1967, p. 319.
39. *Ibid.* p. 315.
40. *Radio Moscow*, 28 Aug. 1967, *BBC/SU*, 30 Aug. 1967; in *MER*, v. 3, 1967, p. 3.
41. Georgi Mirskii, 'Army and Politics of the Third World' *Literaturnaya Gazeta*, 9 Aug. 1967.
42. *Aziia i Afrika Segodnia*, Feb. 1967; also in *MER*; v. 3, 1967, p. 7
43. *MER*, v. 3, 1967, p. 3.
44. *Pravda*, 29 July and 3 Aug. 1967.
45. *Radio Moscow* in Chinese, 15 Jan. 1968, *BBC/SU*, 20 Jan. 1968; in *MER*, v. 3, 1967, p. 20.
46. *Pravda*, 16 Jan. 1968; *Radio Moscow*, 4 and 5 Jan. 1968.
47. Reported in *Jum Hurriyya*, 26 April, 1968, quoted in *MER*, v. 4, 1968, p. 26.
48. *MER*, v. 3, 1967.
49. Reported by Mohamed Heikal in 1970, see *MER*, v. 4, 1968, p. 26; also mentioned in his book (1978) p. 211.
50. *Le Monde*, 7 Dec. 1968.
51. *New Times*, 20 Oct. 1968; see also *New Times*, 26 June 1968.
52. *Radio Moscow*, 6 Jan. 1968.
53. *Pravda*, 20 July 1968.
54. *Hurriyya*, 11 Nov. 1968, cited in *MER*, v. 4 1968, p. 410.
55. *Hurriyya*, 4 Nov. 1968, cited in *MER*, *ibid.*
56. *Hurriyya*, 28 Oct. 1968, cited in *MER*, *ibid.*
57. *Akhir Sa'a*, 17 April 1968, cited in *MER*, *ibid.*
58. *Radio Cairo*, 1 May 1968; *BBC*, 6 May 1968; also in *MER*, v. 4, 1968, p. 422.
59. *Akhbar*, 15 Jan. 1968, cited in *MER*, v. 4, 1968, p. 424.
60. Yassir Arafat *(nom de guerre Abu Ammar)* is a relative of Haj Amin al-Husayni, the Grand Mufti of Jerusalem during the British mandate. While studying at the University of Cairo, Arafat became the first Chairman of the General Union of Palestinian Students in Egypt. He moved to Kuwait in 1956 where he and some friends formed the Movement for the Liberation of Palestine, later to become known as al-Fatah.
61. *BBC*, 10 June 1968; *Radio Algiers*, 5 June 1968; also in *MER*, v. 4, 1968, p. 422
62. See *MER*, v. 4, 1968, pp. 432-6, for full text of the 1968 Covenant.
63. *Trud*, 21 Oct. 1969.
64. *Radio Moscow* in Arabic, 20 Jan. 1969; in *MER*, v. 5, 1969-70, p. 415.
65. *Trud*, 26 Jan. 1969; *Pravda*, 30 Jan. 1969.
66. *Observer* (London), 20 April 1969; also in *MER*, v. 5, 1969-70, p. 415.
67. *Sovetskaya Rossiya*, 15 April 1969.
68. *New Times*, 24 Sept. 1969.
69. *MER*, v. 5, 1969-70, p. 416; also *New York Times*, 17 Jan. 1970 and 7 Feb. 1970; and admission by Bulgarian Ambassador to Beirut of those supplies in *Daily Star* (Beirut), 26 April 1970.
70. *TASS* in English, 20 Feb. 1970; *BBC/SU*, 22 Feb. 1970.
71. Interview on *Radio Moscow*, in Arabic, 5 June 1970; *BBC/SU*, 9 June 1970.
72. *Radio Peace and Progress*, in Hebrew, 19 Feb. 1970, cited in *MER*, v. 5, 1969-70, p. 418.
73. *TASS* in English, 23 Feb. 1970; *BBC/SU*, 25 Feb. 1970
74. *New York Times*, 7 Sept. 1970; *The Times* (London), 7 Sept. 1970.
75. *Reuter*, 12 Sept. 1970, in *MER*, v. 5, 1969-70, p. 839.
76. *FBIS*, 8 Sept. 1970.
77. *Pravda*, 17 Sept. 1970.
78. *New Times*, 23 and 30 Sept. 1970.
79. William P. Rogers, Secretary of State, Press Conference, 9 Oct. 1970, *Department of State Bulletin*, 26 Oct. 1970; also reported in *New York Times*, 10 Oct. 1970.

80. *BBC*, 19 Dec. 1970.
81. *International Herald Tribune*, 16 Oct. 1970; *Radio Ankara*, 15 Oct. 1970; also in *MER*, v. 5, 1969-70, p.457.
82. *International Herald Tribune*, 17 Oct. 1970.
83. *Radio Ankara*, 24 Oct. 1970; also in *MER*, v. 5, 1969-70, p. 457.
84. *International Herald Tribune*, 28 Oct. 1970
85. See Freedman (1978) p. 114 where he states that the years 1970-72, a period of relative calm in the Middle East, were the years in which the USSR lost influence in the area.
86. *MER*, v. 5, 1969.-70, p. 285.
87. *Ibid.*
88. Freedman (1978) p. 114.
89. *Izvestiya*, 8 Sept. 1972.
90. *Pravda*, 11 Sept. 1972; *Sovetskaya Rossiya*, 16 Sept, 1972.
91. *Izvestiya*, 16 Sept. 1972; *Trud*, 16 Sept. 1972; *Sovetskaya Rossiya*, 16 Sept. 1972.
92. Schapiro (1977-78), p. 193.
93. *Radio Moscow*, in Arabic, 3 March 1973; *FBIS*, 5 March 1973; also *Pravda*, 5 March 1973.
94. *Pravda*, 9 March 1973.
95. *Radio Moscow* in Arabic, 14 April 1973, *BBC/SU*, 16 April 1973.
96. *Pravda*, 14 April 1973.
97. *FBIS*, 10 Aug. 1973.
98. *TASS*, 15 April 1974; see also Norton (1974) p. 13.
99. *Pravda, Trud, Krasnaya, Zvezda, Sovetskaya Rossiya*, all of 19 Dec. 1973. Earlier TASS announced that a 'group of terrorists' had perpetrated the attack in Rome on the Pan American plane, see *Radio Moscow* in English, 17 Dec. 1973. The following day a denial of involvement by the PLO was broadcast, *Radio Moscow*, 18 Dec. 1973, *FBIS*, 18 Dec. 1973.
100. See Kohler *et al.* (1974); Freedman (1978); Golan (1977). In 1971-2 the SALT negotiations were on between the superpowers and that may account for the apparent Soviet refusal to provide Egypt with weapons at that time. What may have helped to influence the Kremlin to support the idea of a war was the overthrow of the Allende regime in Chile only a few weeks before the start of the Yom Kippur War. See Kohler *et al* (1974) p. 91. See also Heikal (1978) pp. 254-7 for the Egyptian view of Soviet behaviour leading up to the October War. Heikal maintains that the USSR needed a limited war in order to involve themselves in the Middle East after being ousted from Egypt. If such was the case, the strategy proved successful.
101. *New Times*, no. 36, 1973, for the Arafat invitation; *New York Times*, 19 Aug. 1973, for the opening of the PLO office. Also cited in Freedman (1978) p. 130.
102. *Pravda*, 19 Dec. 1973.
103. See Schapiro (1977-8) p. 193.
104. *New Times*, May 1974; also Vladimir Ermakov in *Pravda*, 19 May 1974.
105. *Radio Moscow* in English to North America, 20 May 1974. See Golan (1980) pp. 221-2. for her view that the Soviet Union indicated its sensitivity to terrorist acts.
106. See Schapiro (1977-8) p. 201.
107. See *MER*, v. 2, 1961.
108. See Romaniecki (1973) p. 1.
109. *Izvestiya*, 30 July 1974. This same issue carried a very long article about the PLO and Arafat.
110. *New Times*, Aug. 1974.
111. *Voice of Palestine Radio* (Clandestine), 29 March 1974, *FBIS*, 1 April 1974.
112. *Novoye Vremya*, 15 March 1974; also *FBIS*, 28 March 1974.

113. See Freedman (1978) p. 170.
114. *New York Times*, 14 Nov. 1974.
115. Robert O. Freedman writes that the USSR was reported to have sent a memo to Arafat, Hawatmeh and Habash after the October War of 1973 asking them for their positions on a possible West Bank-Gaza State (1978) p. 186.
116. *Radio Moscow* in English, 13 Nov. 1974; *FBIS*, 14 Nov. 1974.
117. Podgorny speech in Bulgaria, *Pravda*, 9 Sept 1974. See Golan (1980) Chapter 2, for a full account of the Soviet Union's gradual shift of interest towards Palestinian statehood.
118. See Golan (1980) p. 58.
119. *Ibid.*
120. *Radio Moscow* in Arabic to the Arab World, 16 Aug 1975; *FBIS*, 19 Aug. 1975.
121. See Freedman (1978) p. 208. For a study of the Lebanese civil war, see Koury (1976).
122. Soviet behaviour during the crisis might even suggest a 'play at both ends', so to speak, for the Kremlin even commended PLO's Sai'qa leader Zuhair Mohsen for his role in Lebanese events. Syria had been trying to take over control of the PLO through Sai'qa. See Landa (1976). The conflict in Angola was raging at the time and the Lebanese Civil War could have also served to divert Western policy away from Africa.
123. *Radio Moscow*, 2 July 1976; *FBIS*, 6 July 1976; also *Pravda*, 5 July 1976; *Krasnaya Zvezda*, 10 July 1976.
124. *TASS*, 2 July 1976; *Radio Moscow* in English, 2 July 1976; *FBIS*, 6 July 1976.
125. *Radio Moscow* in English, 24 June 1976; *FBIS*, 28 June 1976.
126. *Radio Moscow* in Arabic, 5 July 1976; *FBIS*, 6 July 1976.
127. Valentin Lapin commentary, *Radio Moscow* in English to Africa, 5 July 1976; *FBIS*, 6 July 1976. Also *Radio Peace and Progress*, in English to Africa, 5 July 1976, cited in *USSR and The Third World*, v. 1 (2-3), 1 April-31 July, 1976.
128. *Radio Moscow* in English, 9 July 1976; *FBIS*, 12 July 1976.
129. See Chapter 3: Legal Aspects of this study. See William Stevenson (1976) for complete background on Entebbe.
130. *International Herald Tribune*, 28 Oct. 1976.
131. See Brezhnev's Trade Union speech, foreign policy portion, *New Times*, no. 13, 1977
132. *Pravda*, 8 April 1977.
133. For full text, see *Pravda*, 2 Oct. 1977.
134. *Radio Moscow* in Arabic, 3 Oct. 1977.
135. *Radio Moscow* in English to North America, 17 Oct. 1977; also in *FBIS*, 20 Oct. 1977.
136. *TASS*, 28 Oct. 1977. This official position was reiterated by Pavel Demchenko in a *Pravda* article, 29 Oct. 1977.
137. *Pravda*, 19 Feb. 1978.
138. *Radio Moscow* in English, 21 and 23 Feb. 1978; also in *FBIS*, for those dates.
139. 29 April 1978, interview by Arafat on Moscow television; see Schapiro (1977-8) p. 203.
140. *Pravda*, 13 March 1978.
141. Deputy Chairman of the Soviet Afro-Asian Solidarity Committee which is alleged to be a KGB front organisation, controlled by the International Department.
142. *Izvestiya*, 22 March 1978; also in *USSR and The Third World*, v. 8 (no. 2-3), 1978.
143. See Schapiro (1977-8) p. 205.
144. *Pravda*, 10 March 1978.
145. Le *Monde*, 27 April 1978; *Daily Telegraph*, 20 April 1978.

146.   See Freedman (1978).
147.   See Appendix D for a list of political meetings between Soviet leaders and PLO members 1977-81 and Appendix B for a list of political meetings between PLO members and other Eastern bloc countries.
148.   *Pravda*, 8 June 1978.
149.   Interview with *Al-Dastur*, London, 30 April 1979; cited in *IDF Spokesman*, Sept. 1981.
150.   Abu Iyad quoted by Associated Press, Qatar, 15 May 1979; cited in *IDF Spokesman*, Sept. 1981.
151.   *Pravda*, 9 March 1973.
152.   *Izvestiya*, 13 Jan. 1977.
153.   *Newsweek*, 23 July 1979; *Jerusalem Post*, 16 and 24 July 1979.
154.   *Daily Telegraph* (London), 1 March 1979; *Newsweek*, 5 March 1979. Arafat's association with Khomeini began in 1970 during the latter's exile in Iraq, followed by training and equipping of Iranian dissidents, followers of Khomeini, by the PLO. Even bodyguard protection of Khomeini was provided in Paris.
155.   *Daily Telegraph* (London), 1 June 1979.
156.   *Daily Telegraph* (London), 4 Dec. 1979.
157.   *Daily Telegraph* (London), 18 July 1980.
158.   *International Herald Tribune*, 23 July 1980.
159.   *Daily Telegraph* (London), 4 July 1981.
160.   *International Herald Tribune*, 27 April 1981.
161.   *International Herald Tribune*, 6 March 1980.
162.   *Daily Telegraph* (London), 18 March 1980; also letter dated 18 June 1981, on the subject sent by Lord Carrington's office to Geoffrey Finsberg, MP, signed by Douglas Hurd, MP, in reply to queries on the British position regarding the PLO by this author.
163.   *International Herald Tribune*, 13 April 1981.
164.   *Daily Telegraph* (London), *The Times* (London), both 21 Oct. 1981.
165.   *International Herald Tribune*, 14 Oct. 1981.
166.   *International Herald Tribune*, 21 Oct. 1981.
167.   For statistical information of terrorist incidents perpetrated by the PLO until 1970, see *MER*, v. 5, 1969-70, p. 223.
168.   *Voice of Palestine Radio* (Clandestine), 21 Oct. 1981, *SWB*, 23 OCt. 1981.
169.   See Golan (1980); CIA Reports on Terrorism since 1967; Schapiro (1977-8); Wilkinson (1979); US Committee on Internal Security, Hearings on Terroroism, Parts 1-5; US House Committee on internal Security, (HCIS), *Terrorism, A Staff Study*, 1 Aug. 1974; Kupperman and Trent (1979); Possony and Bouchey (1978); Romerstein (1981). The unofficial contacts have also been confirmed to this author by reliable sources in Israel.
170.   *MER*, v. 3, 1967.
171.   *Radio Cairo*, 16 May 1967; *MER, ibid*.
172.   *International Herald Tribune, New York Times*, both 9 Aug. 1968.
173.   24 March 1969; in *MER*, v. 5, 1969-70, p. 258.
174.   *Ha'aretz*, 11 May and 12 June 1969; *MER, ibid*.
175.   *MER, ibid*.
176.   See Milbank (1976) p. 21.
177.   *MER, Ibid*.
178.   *Annual of Power and Conflict, 1973-74*, London: Institute for the Study of Conflict.
179.   Western intelligence sources have now confirmed the existence of all these training camps; see also *Foreign Report (The Economist)*, 11 July 1979.
180.   For official Israel Defence Forces letter confirming this information to this author, see Appendix G of this study. (Not reprinted in this book: Ed.)

181. *Kuwaiti News Agency*, 3 May 1980.
182. *Life*, 12 June 1970.
183. Heikal (1978) pp. 210-11. Abu Daoud was shot on 5 Aug. 1981 in Warsaw by an unknown attacker but survived.
184. US Congress, HCIS, *Terrorism*, 1 Aug. 1974, p. 35; this fact was also confirmed to this author by highly placed Israel intelligence sources.
185. *Washington Post*, 8 April 1973.
186. *New York Times*, 25 and 26 June 1974; *Washington Post*, 25 June 1974.
187. US Congress, HCIS, *Terrorism*, 1 Aug. 1974, p. 39; *New York Times*, 23 Dec. 1973.
188. Robert Moss, in address to the Jerusalem Conference on International Terrorism, July 1979.
189. *Hayat*, 2 Feb. 1970, in *MER*, v. 5, 1969-70, p. 259.
190. Merari (1980).
191. CIA, *International Terrorism*, 1977. The German Government issued a White Paper on the hijacking which also showed that the same typewriter was used for the demand notes of both the abductors of Schleyer and the hijackers of the Lufthansa jet. See *International Herald Tribune*, 17 Oct. 1977.
192. *Foreign Report (The Economist)*, no. 1508, 19 Oct. 1977. This was confirmed to this author in a personal interview by Dr Hans Joseph Horchem, head of the West German Office for the Protection of the Constitution.
193. *Daily Telegraph* (London), 21 Oct. 1977.
194. Kupperman and Friedlander (1979) p. 53.
195. Milbank (1976) pp. 20-1; also *Proceedings*, Conference on International Terrorism, Jonathan Institute, Jerusalem, 1979.
196. *The Guardian* (London), 22 June 1976; *International Herald Tribune*, 29 June 1976.
197. Gaucher (1981) pp. 18-19.
198. See *Le Point*, 28 June 1977 for Sultanov and Ponomarev connections.
199. Gaucher (1981) pp. 52-3. The role played by Aghion is described in Hervé (1956) p. 59
200. See Dobson and Payne (1977) for the complete story.
201. *Foreign Report (The Economist)*, no. 1539, 21 June 1978.
202. *Foreign Report (The Economist)*, ibid.
203. *Daily Telegraph* (London), 5 May 1978; *Le Point*, 21 June 1976; see also Jean Montaldo, (1979) pp. 221-82.
204. *Le Monde*, 2 June 1981.
205. See Dobson and Payne (1977); and Smith (1976) for the complete story.
206. *Proceedings*, Conference on International Terrorism, Jonathan Institute, Jerusalem, 1979; also Demaris (1977) p. 23.
207. Demaris (1977) p. 23; also *The Times* (London), 11 July 1975; *Daily Telegraph* (London), 11 July 1975.
208. Smith (1976) pp. 14-15.
209. Demaris (1977) p. 25.
210. *The Times* (London), 11 July 1975.
211. *The Guardian* (London), 12 July 1975.
212. *The Sunday Telegraph* (London), 13 July 1975; *Le Monde*, 16 July 1975.
213. Dobson and Payne (1977) pp. 43-4.
214. Becker (1977) p. 17. See also *Le Monde* 4 July 1975.
215. Possony and Bouchey, (1978) p. 27.
216. Becker (1977) p. 17.
217. A member of the Austrian diplomatic personnel in Israel informed this author that the USSR had instructed the PLO not to carry out terrorist activities on Austrian territory. This was possibly a concession extended to Austria in return for the closure of the Schonau camp and for the official

meeting which Bruno Kreisky organized with the PLO in 1979. It also most definitely suggests Soviet control on PLO behaviour. There has been a virtual absence of terrorist activities on Austrian territory from that date until the Vienna Synagogue bombing of 30 August 1981, which was carried out by the PLO.

218. Bocca (1981) p. 27
219. *Ibid.*
220. *Ibid.* p. 31.
221. Ghirinelli (1977) pp. 243-6. See also *Feltrinelli, Il Guerrigliero Impotente*, Roma: Edizioni 'Documenti', p. 81.
222. Becker (1977) p. 294.
223. Lojacono (1974).
224. *Corriere della Sera*, 29 Dec. 1979; *La Stampa* (Turin), 29 Dec. 1979.
225. Michael Ledeen, Special Assistant to Secretary of State Haig, in an interview with this author at the State Department, Washington DC, Nov. 1981. The background of the Red Brigades will be discussed *infra*.
226. Atti Parlamentari, Camera dei Deputati, VII Legislatura, *Discussioni*, Seduta del 19 maggio 1978, edizione non definitiva, pp. 6-9. See also Pisano (1979), (1980).
227. *New York Times*, 28 April 1978.
228. *Il Giornale Nuovo*, 1 April 1979.
229. *Le Figaro*, 3 Jan. 1980.
230. *Il Messaggero*, 30 April 1982; *Corriere della Sera*, 4 May 1982; *La Stampa*, 4 May 1982; *Il Tempo*, 1 May 1982; *Avanti*, 30 April 1982; *Paese Sera*, 4 May 1982.
231. *Avanti* (Socialist Party newspaper), 30 April 1982.
232. *Paese Sera*, 30 April 1982.
233. Confession of Patrizio Peci, BR member, *Il Giornale Nuovo*, 16 April 1980.
234. *Il Tempo*, 1 May 1982.
235. See Pisano (1979).
236. Strategic Resolution of the Red Brigades issued in February of 1978, cited in Pisano (1980) p. 15.
237. This account was given by Renzo Rossellini on 3 Oct. 1978 in an interview with the French daily *Le Matin*. Rossellini is a journalist of the extra-parliamentary left associated with a radio station called *Città Futura*. See *Il Settimanale* (Rome), no. 42, 18 Oct. 1978.
238. Ufficio Affari Riservati, classified telegram, coded, numbered 41199, dated 15 Oct. 1950; cited in Sterling (1981) p. 32.
239. 'The Red Orchestra', cryptonym coined by the German central security office, the Reichssicherheitshauptampt (RSHA), describing the vast Soviet networks of espionage and subversion discovered in Western Europe after the outbreak of the Russo-German war in 1941. Leopold Trepper was the leader and overall coordinator. *The Rote Kapelle* was started up as early as 1935 in Western European countries. By 1942-43 it had expanded to such proportions that it had become the principal component of the Soviet Military Intelligence Services. See CIA (1979) for complete details.
240. Khokhlov (1959) p. 31. See also Dziak (1981b). Khokhlov was one of Sudolplatov's partisans and later was moved to 'wet activities', i.e. assassinations.
241. Deriabin (1972) p. 258.
242. See Michael Ledeen, testimony to US Senate, Hearing before the Subcommittee on Security and Terrorism of the Committee of the Judiciary, 97th Congress, 24 April 1981, p. 64.
243. Pisano (1980) p. 14.

244. Christian Democratic members Piccoli, Mastella, Borruso, de Carolis, and Rossi di Monteleva. Cited in Pisano (1979) p. 205.
245. *The Times* (London), 2 Jan. 1980. President Pertini's remarks were later 'clarified' by the Italian Foreign Ministry when the Soviet Ambassador was called in to be told that no particular country was responsible for the wave of terrorism in Italy and Turkey. *International Herald Tribune*, 12 Feb. 1981.
246. *Rude Pravo*, 3 Feb. 1981.
247. See *Foreign Report (The Economist)*, no. 1513, 23 Nov. 1977. This was also suggested in the Marxist-Leninist daily newspaper *Lotta Continua* in Sept. 1978 and was reported in *The Guardian* (London) 26 Sept. 1978.
248. Cited in Pisano (1979) p. 204.
249. Ledeen (1978) p. 38.
250. *Ibid*.
251. Pisano (1980) p. 14.
252. *Ma'ariv*, 1 April 1970; *MER*, v. 5, 1969-70, p. 259.
253. *Fath*, 10 Aug. 1970, in *MER*, v. 5, *ibid*.
254. Cited in Pisano (1980) p. 15.
255. See Galleni, ed. (1981). See also, 'Phenomenological and Dynamic Aspects of Terrorism in Italy', in *Terrorism*, the journal, v. 2, nos. 3 and 4, 1979, pp. 159-170.
256. Galleni, ed. (1981) p. 536.
257. See Arrigo Levi article in *The Times* (London), 3 Jan. 1980.
258. For the most complete study of this terrorist group see Becker (1977).
259. Possony and Bouchey (1978) p. 136. See also McClure Testimony, US Congress, SIAIS, *Terroristic Activity*, Part 5, p. 271.
260. Told to this author by Jillian Becker who interviewed Röhl at length during the preparation of her book *Hitler's Children* (1977).
261. The full story was told by Klaus Rainer Röhl in his book (1974). Although there has not been any evidence of direct financial assistance by the Soviet Union to the Baader-Meinhof gang, it is confirmed that the assistance came to it indirectly through agents. This was confirmed to this author, in a personal interview, by Dr Hans Horchem, head of the Office for the Protection of the Constitution, West German Government. It is also known that Giangiacomo Feltrinelli generously contributed money through his *centrale* to the *June 2 Movement*. See Becker (1977) p. 294.
262. Becker (1977) pp. 180-9.
263. Cited in Becker (1977) p. 198.
264. *Ibid*. p. 219.
265. *MER*, v. 5, 1969-70, p. 260.
266. *Sunday Telegraph* (London), 13 Aug. 1969; *Ma'ariv*, 15 Aug. 1969; *Radio Kuwait*, 28 July 1969; *BBC*, 30 July 1969, in *MER*, *ibid*., p. 252.
267. See Stevenson (1976); Smith (1976); Dobson and Payne (1977).
268. *Welt am Sonntag*, 29 March 1981; *Jerusalem Post*, 30 March 1981. For the Shatila training camp in Beirut, see *The Times* (London), 21 Aug. 1982.
269. *Associated Press* article by Kate Dorian, 25 June 1981.
270. *Voice of Lebanon Radio*, 25 June 1981; *SWB*, 27 June 1981.
271. *The Times* (London), 29 June 1982.
272. For background history, see Bell (1970); also Coogan 1980.
273. Coogan (1980) p. 419.
274. Ovid Demaris states that during the years 1919-21, there were only two civilian targets, (1977) p. 316.
275. *Sunday Press*, 28 Dec. 1969.
276. Coogan (1980) p. 429
277. Demaris (1977) p. 352.

278. *Ibid.*
279. *Ibid.*
280. Coogan (1980) pp. 538-9. This was also confirmed to this author by sources close to the Special Branch, and others close to the Home Office.
281. *Ibid.*
282. US Congress, HCIS, *Terrorism*, 1 Aug. 1974, p. 67.
283. *Baltimore Sun*, 4 Jan. 1974.
284. *Washington Post*, 4 Jan. 1974.
285. See Barron (1975) pp. 331-2. For the Victor Louis information see *Daily Telegraph* (London), 7 June 1984.
286. *The Observer*, 1 April 1979.
287. *Daily Telegraph* (London), 24 Nov. 1979.
288. *TASS*, 29 Aug. 1979.
289. *New Times*, no. 15, April 1977.
290. *Pravda*, 29 Aug. 1979.
291. FO 371/8170, File 123, 1922.
292. Coogan (1980) pp. 124-5.
293. O'Donnell represented that committee at the Comintern Congress in Berlin in 1930. *Ibid.*
294. *Ibid.*, p. 126.
295. *Daily Telegraph* (London), 3 July 1980.
296. See Gaucher (1981) pp. 52-3.
297. *Radio Moscow, TASS* in English, 7 Jan. 1981; *FBIS*, 8 Jan. 1981.
298. *International Herald Tribune*, 9 March 1981.
299. *Foreign Report (The Economist)*, no. 1476, 23 Feb. 1977. This was also confirmed to this author at the Ditchley Conference on International Terrorism, No. 1979, by Señor D. Rodolfo Martin Villa, who was Interior Minister of Spain at the time. See also *l'Espresso* (Rome), 10 April 1980.
300. *Foreign Report (The Economist)*, no. 1471, 19 Jan. 1977.
301. *Cambio 16*, 24 Nov. 1978.
302. Dr Hans Horchem in an interview with this author in London.
303. Evidence presented to the Spanish authorities by General Aharon Yariv, former intelligence officer of Israel and an authority on international terrorism. *Foreign Report (The Economist)*, no. 1730, 10 June 1982.
304. See Chapter IV *supra.*
305. *TASS* in Rude Pravo, 7 Jan. 1981; *Radio Moscow* in English, 7 Jan. 1981; in *FBIS*, 8 Jan. 1981.
306. US Congress, HCIS, *Terrorism*, p. 68.
307. *Ibid.* p. 69.
308. *El Pais*, 23 Feb. 1979. It was not until November of 1979 that the report appeared in the Western press. See *Daily Telegraph* (London), 21 Nov. 1979.
309. *Near East Report*, v. XXV, n. 9, 27 Feb. 1981.
310. For details of Nechiporenko's activities which involved the organisation of several tactical applications including strike planning as well as terrorist attacks on the civilian population of Mexico, see Barron (1975) pp. 301-5. See also Gouré and Rothenberg (1975) p. 132.
311. See Chapter 4: Historical Perspective of this study.
312. FO 371/90589, 1951.
313. FO 371/90843, 1951.
314. US Congress, HCIS, *Terrorism*, Aug. 1974, p. 7. Also cited in Gouré and Rothenberg (1975) p. 132.
315. *Al Watan* (Kuwait), 7 Aug. 1979, in Arabic; in *FBIS*, 10 Aug. 1979.
316. *Der Spiegel*, 28 Sept. 1981 Vice President Rodriguez of Cuba admitted to this policy of support for insurgent and terrorist groups. Also see *Strategic Survey*, 1979, London: International Institute of Strategic Studies, p. 112.

317. US Department of State, *Cuba's Renewed Support for Violence in the Hemisphere*, Research paper presented to the Subcommittee on Western Hemisphere Affairs, Senate Foreign Relations Committee, Washington DC Dec. 14 1981.

318. US Department of State, 'Cuban-Soviet Impact on the Western Hemisphere', *Current Policy*, no. 167, Washington DC, April 17, 1980.

319. Interview with Mr John Bushnell, US Department of State, Nov. 1981.

320. See Cline (1980) p. 161; Gouré and Rothenberg (1975) pp. 17-18; US Senate Select Committee to Study Governmental Actions, *Covert Action in Chile 1963-1973*, Dec. 18, 1975; 'Central America and Mexico: A Forecast of Strategic Trends 1980-1983', *International Strategic Issues*, v. 1, n. 1, April 1980; US Department of State, *Communist Interference in El Salvador: Documents*, 23 Feb. 1981.

321. See Tkachenko (1972) p. 100.

322. Gouré and Rothenberg (1975) p. 17.

323. *Ibid.*

324. 'Central America and Mexico: A Forecast of Strategic Trends 1980-1983', *International Strategic Issues*, v. 1, n. 1, April 1980.

325. See Eric Walker, *History of South Africa*, for information on early trade union and Communist Party opposition to blacks competing equally in the labour market; see also W. H. Hutt (1964).

326. Purport List for the Department of State 1910-1944, Sub. no. 216, Latvia, Tel. 120, 1 Aug. 1924, National Archives, Washington DC.

327. BBC/TV, *Panorama*, 'South Africa: to the last drop of our Blood', Report by Peter Taylor, 15 June 1981.

328. Lerumo (1971) p. 108. This writer using an African name was identified after his death as Michael Harmel, a white communist working out of Prague, Czechoslovakia. See Romerstein (1981) p. 39.

329. Admission in court by Bram Fischer who was one of those arrested in 1963 at the Rivonia headquarters of the terrorist organisation. He subsequently wrote a book about it; see Fischer (1966) esp. p. 28.

330. South African Military intelligence sources. Also reported on BBC/TV, *Panorama, ibid.*

331. Prime Minister Botha of South Africa, in *International Herald Tribune*, 21 Sept. 1981.

332. See *MER*, v. 5, 1969-70, p. 252; *Le Monde*, 4 July 1975; US Congress, HCIS, *Terrorism*, Aug. 1974, p. 47; Brian Crozier testimony, US Congress, SIAIS, *Terroristic Activity*, Part 4, pp. 187-8.

333. US Congress, SIAIS, *Trotskyite International*, p. 99.

334. *Ibid.*

335. Wilkinson (1976) p. 8.

336. *International Herald Tribune*, 17 March 1981; see also *Washington Post* editorial in the *International Herald Tribune*, 18 March 1981.

337. *International Herald Tribune*, 24-25 Jan. 1981.

338. In an interview with Giulio Andreotti, *Il Giornale Nuovo*, 30 May 1980.

339. *TASS*, 27 Jan. 1981.

6

Conclusions and Observations

This study establishes that the active support of international terrorism in countries outside the Soviet bloc has been part of Soviet government policy since 1917 and is consistent with Soviet ideology.

Soviet policy, both internal and external, is totally reliant on Leninist dogma as justification for any decision-making, and Communist doctrine can consequently not be discounted as mere rhetoric. The ideology, whether 'believed in' or merely invoked by pragmatic necessities of power control by the Soviet policy-makers, needs to be supported by behavioural actions which would ensure continued belief in the system. The theoretical objective of world communism remains by necessity, therefore, a tangible goal which needs to be satisfied. The analysis of Soviet official statements of policy on the question of the use of terrorism has shown the ideology to be a reliable guide to future acts.

In the specific context of international terrorism, Marxist-Leninist dogma on the question has been explicit. At no time did the doctrine object to the use of terrorism on principle. On the contrary, its application was specifically encouraged when deemed expedient. It was to be carried out by a professional revolutionary élite under centralized control, as opposed to what Lenin called 'individual terrorists' acting on their own. The terrorist option formed part of Lenin's approach to war, peace and aggression, and was regarded as an essential instrument for the achievement of revolution.

The record shows that in the early years, crude applications - reflecting Soviet weakness - of the tactic were evident in a broad world spectrum, implemented not only by Soviet official representatives abroad, but also by agents of the Comintern and foreign communist party members. The terrorist tactic remained a part of a multiple-level foreign policy which was characteristically pragmatic and flexible. In fact, at no time until the end of the Second World War did the Soviet Union desist in the use of international terrorist tactics; only gradations in emphasis on the paramilitary approach, depending on circumstances, can be observed. This practice continued in times of peace (as understood in the West) between the two World Wars, as well as in times of war, thus 'proving' the Soviet definition of 'perpetual class struggle' and exemplifying its forward-moving foreign policy. Within that definition, civil wars are encouraged to develop and the USSR is in a perpetual state of war, with peace being one tactic of the overall strategy.

Marxist-Leninist ideological foundations have predetermined the Soviet legal conceptualization of aggression and indirect aggression. As defined by the Soviet Union, aggression can only exist when an action is taken by a non-revolutionary Western state. It therefore *never* finds aggression committed by itself or any Socialist bloc state. Indirect aggression, of which one facet is the exercise of coercion through the medium of rebel groups in the target state, falls within this same Soviet definition.

The Soviet official position on international terrorism, as presented at the United Nations deliberations, for example, has been consistently true to the Leninist position on the question. In Soviet perception, 'terrorism' is only possible in capitalist societies. Any act perpetrated against the Soviet Union is defined as 'criminal', no political motivation being applicable against Soviet communism which, once established, is irreversible. On the other hand, the Soviet Union has consistently applied the word 'terrorist' to Western state behaviour and frequently to attacks taking place on Western soil against Western targets. This has allowed for the long-term infiltration of the idea that terrorism (having a political motive and therefore a 'just cause') can and does exist in the 'sick' societies of capitalism'. This position is consistent with its ideological doctrine and shows no ambivalence *from its point of view.* The Soviet legal argumentation has at no time rejected or condemned terrorist activities as a tactic in the larger geopolitical conflict, as long as that conflict could be regarded by the Kremlin as 'revolutionary' and therefore perpetrated by 'freedom fighters' or by 'workers' against the 'exploiters'. The only public caution to national liberation movements has been that terrorism should not be used as the principal method of combat. It is obvious that this policy position affects only the Western alliance.

The monolithic elitism which Lenin established as the basis for the governing apparatus of the USSR, has continued to be reinforced since 1917 with the CPSU being the only policy-maker. This control by the CPSU extends over all branches of the Soviet government, including the military machinery which implements political policy.

A change of emphasis in Soviet perceptions of the future typology of wars emerged in the aftermath of the Second World

War and the explosion of the atomic weapon. This reappraisal of military strategy became apparent in Soviet policy statements, both political and military, in the early 1960s, when a larger emphasis was placed on the idea of the growth of conflict *within* the capitalist societies, and of an 'armed proletariat' rather than conflict between capitalist and socialist countries: that is to say, civil wars and agitational activity rather than superpower confrontational wars. This focus on civil disorders within the Western alliance was explicitly set out in the New Communist Programme in 1961 (known as the Khrushchev doctrine) and was reflected in official statements on *détente*, peaceful coexistence, national liberation and international terrorism.

Reinforcing the notion that this shift of emphasis was a specific policy decision, there was a concomitant dramatic enlargement of KGB, GRU and satellite intelligence services to implement this direction. In this context, the KGB emerges as the principal instrument. Its role has been generally underestimated in the West. The KGB, preferring as it does paramilitary techniques rather than large-scale military invasions, has largely been regarded by Western analysts as a 'moderating' factor in Soviet foreign policy when measures of 'hard'- or 'soft'-line policy applications are considered. The preoccupation with large-scale military confrontations between the superpowers has allowed the paramilitary role played by the KGB to be largely ignored as a major factor in Soviet foreign policy and military doctrine.

In the contemporary context, the Soviet Union has been a major sponsoring state in support of international terrorist groups. This is in no way an aberration from its principled position on the question, as has been seen. To effect this paramilitary power projection, the USSR has systematically supported terrorist groups, whether of the 'right', 'left', or 'extreme left', to achieve its politico-military ends.

The 'political' image which the USSR set about creating for the PLO appears to be a policy decision taken in the wake of Soviet inability to maintain reliable state-to-state relations in the regional context of the Middle East. The evidence argues in favour of the thesis that the PLO was initially approached, and subsequently emerged, as a paramilitary surrogate for a larger geopolitical application. There is in fact nothing which would indicate that the Soviet Union would have stopped supporting the PLO covertly had state-to-state relations been such as not to require an alternative ally in the Middle East which could maintain the Soviet anti-imperialist position.

Documents captured by the Israel Defence Forces (IDF) in Tyre, Sidon and Beirut in 1982 confirm this. Not only is the PLO revealed by them as being the major *factotum* terrorist organizer of international groups worldwide, but in addition it appears to have had a special relationship with the KGB. The documents also show that none of the 'splinter' groups is in fact renegade, but that they divide the responsibility for linking with the various terrorist groups and all come under the control of the PLO.* Abu Nidal's position is still somewhat ambiguous. The documents show that his group is part of Fatah, Arafat's mainstream group, but is controlled by the East German secret service.†

The question arises as to the extent to which the Soviet government is able to exercise control over terrorist organizations or activities. It must be reiterated that the presence or absence of total control by a sponsor state over a terrorist group is an elusive factor which is difficult to ascertain. However, the degree of sponsorship might be an indicator of the level of control. In the case of the PLO this sponsorship was complete. To define control as actual participation in targeting decisions is unsatisfactory, and in the light of the Soviet record on the question of terrorism, somewhat unnecessary. To create chaos in a target state and slowly to erode the economy and morale of that state, it is not necessary for the group to be told where to hit. Any killing, bomb, or hijack will do. A sponsor state makes a policy decision when it initiates the sponsorship of any such group.

Since 1917 the Soviet view of its own level of development has influenced its choice of policy applications. The avoidance of direct confrontation on the battlefield was a necessity in the early years because of the overall Soviet weaknesses and inferior military strength *vis-à-vis* the Western powers. Thus the extensive and continuous use of manipulating devices such as deceit, sabotage, terrorism and political manoeuvring were all promoted, and a large network of agents was developed to destroy the enemy from the rear.

In the immediate aftermath of the first atomic weapon explosion in 1945, the growing emphasis on this paramilitary dimension reflected the Soviet inability to match the United States in this force

---

*See ed. note p. 139. Some of the constituent factions had terrorist arms e.g. Black September, which was the terrorist arm of al-Fatah. Such sub-groups came under the control of the faction which formed them.

†Abu Nidal was expelled from al-Fatah, and condemned to death *in absentia* in 1974. He set up a rival 'al-Fatah' in Baghdad, financed by the government of Iraq. In September 1980 he moved his headquarters to Damascus. and was supported by the government of Syria. His group killed a number of PLO representatives loyal to Arafat, including Sa'id Hammami in London in 1978. In 1978 he allied himself with another break-away section of al-Fatah led by Abu Daoud.

development and the necessity of avoiding a direct confrontation became more important than ever.

The main struggle for power in the postwar era between the Soviet Union and the United States has been constrained by fear of an escalation to nuclear war of any confrontational issues. This has encouraged the Soviet perception of the dynamic 'class struggle' to find its expression at sub-state levels of violence which have included surrogate wars as well as surrogate international terrorism.

With the recent unprecedented growth of Soviet military might, the paramilitary factor takes on added importance in the 1980s. The military acquisitions by the Soviet Union in quantitative terms appear to have served mainly as an intimidating device which has concentrated the attention of Western analysts, and thus allowed the USSR a greater latitude in paramilitary adventures. But the danger of nuclear devastation has not receded, and with the development of more sophisticated weapons has in fact increased. Although the massive military build-up cannot be ignored as a major factor influencing relations between the superpowers, it is unlikely that the Soviet Union would initiate action which would by necessity incur major devastating losses on both sides with no concomitant political gain to be discerned. It is therefore equally unlikely that any successor leadership to Brezhnev would initiate a policy change on the question of the use of international terrorism as a major factor in Soviet power projection. Several critical variables tend to reinforce the concept that there will most likely be an increased reliance on this method of warfare.

(a) The ailing Soviet economy, additionally drained by massive military expenditures and poor harvests, will emphasize the cost-effectiveness of the paramilitary dimension,

(b) The very sudden obsolescence of its newest weapons* in the Lebanese War of 1982 will accentuate further the need to avoid confrontational military engagements with the West, thus once again making the terrorist option the most attractive one,

(c) The monolithic structure of the Soviet Union allows for little deviation from the fold and all indications from the past point to the fact that the future will bring little discernible change in direction,

(d) The unrest in Poland and the military quagmire in Afghanistan are added factors which would make the paramilitary option seem preferable.

Since 1917, the Soviet Union has consistently, although not always successfully, attempted to change the 'correlation of forces' by implementing the terrorist option since 1917. This remains very

*In Syrian, not PLO, possession. The USSR sold off old stock to the PLO.

much part of the doctrinal focus of the Soviet government. The measure of its success in the last fifteen years is the fact that so far the West has refused to face the implications of this aspect of Soviet policy.

Appendix A

Political Meetings between PLO Leaders and Soviet Officials 1977-1981

1977

19 June	Naif Hawatmeh, head of the DFLP wing of the PLO, arrives in Moscow for a week-long visit.
10 July	Arafat meets with Soviet Ambassador Soldatov in Beirut.
11 July	Zuheir Munsin, head of the PLO 'Military Department', meets with Soviet Ambassador in Damascus.
25 Aug.	Arafat's deputy Abu Iyad meets with Soviet Ambassador Soldatov.
27 Aug.	Arafat visits Moscow.
29 Oct.	Abu-Saleh, PLO Executive member, visits Moscow.
10 Nov.	PLO spokesman Abd-el Muhsin abu Maizer visits Moscow.

1978

10 Mar.	Arafat and Brezhnev meet in Moscow.
24 May	First delegation of Fatah leaders visits Moscow.
8 June	Naif Hawatmeh meets with Ponomarev, Secretary General of the CPSU in Moscow.
17 July	32 Palestinian pilots, 60 mechanics, return from advanced training in USSR, East Germany and Czechoslovakia.
25 July	Arafat visits Moscow.
31 July	3 meetings between Arafat and Soviet Ambassador Soldatov.
4 Aug.	Abu Iyad in Moscow.
6 Aug.	Farouq Qadoumi, head of the PLO 'Political Department', visits Moscow.
9 Aug.	Abu Iyad, Khaled Al-Hassan, Abu Mazen in Moscow.
23 Oct.	Arafat in Moscow.
2 Nov.	Arafat visits Moscow.
14 Nov.	George Habash, head of the PFLP wing of the PLO, visits Moscow.
21 Dec.	Soviet committee for friendship with the Palestinians is formed.

1979

13 Feb.	Fatah leaders Arafat, Abu Iyad and Abu Jihad meet with Soviet Ambassador Soldatov.
25 Feb.	Arafat meets with Soldatov.
25 Mar.	Arafat meets with Soviet Foreign Minister Gromyko.
25 May	Arafat meets with the East German Ambassador to Beirut and with the Director of the Middle East Section of the Soviet Foreign Ministry.
13 July	Arafat meets with Soldatov.
19 Aug.	Farouq Qadoumi meets with Soldatov.
27 Aug.	Abd-el Muhsin abu Maizer visits Moscow.

6 Sept.	Arafat meets with Soldatov.
6 Sept.	PLO delegation visits the Soviet Union.
12 Oct.	The Commander-in-Chief of the PLA meets Soldatov.
24 Oct.	Soviet missile experts visit PLO positions in Lebanon.
17 Nov.	Arafat meets with Gromyko in Moscow.
27 Nov.	Yasser Abd Rabhi, head of the PLO 'Department of Information and Culture', visits Moscow.
28 Dec.	Arafat meets with Soldatov.

1980

28 Jan.	Arafat meets with Gromyko in Damascus.
6 Feb.	George Habash visits Moscow.
24 Feb.	George Habash invited to Afghanistan.
3 Mar.	Naif Hawatmeh visits Moscow.
28 Mar.	Soldatov hands Arafat two messages from Brezhnev.
2 April	Soviet Komsomol delegation meets with Abu Iyad in Beirut.
9 April	Arafat meets with Soldatov.
6 July	George Habash visits Moscow.
20 July	Arafat holds talks in Moscow on supply of anti-aircraft guns, tanks, katyushas.
24 Aug.	Farouq Qadoumi and Abd-el Muhsin abu Maizer meet with Soldatov.
2 Sept.	Fatah leader Abu Mazen visits Moscow.
25 Nov.	Abu Mazen visits Moscow.
26 Nov.	Soviet Ambassador in Damascus hands Arafat message.
28 Nov.	Abd-el Muhsin abu Maizer meets with the Soviet Ambassador to Washington.
28 Nov.	Increase in number of Palestinian students in Moscow.
3 Dec.	Arafat meets with Soviet Ambassador to Damascus.
3 Dec.	Abu Mazen meets with Deputy President of the Supreme Soviet in Moscow.
5 Dec.	Arafat meets with a member of the Presidium of the Supreme Soviet in Beirut.
7 Dec.	PLO delegation visits Moscow.
10 Dec.	Arafat meets with Soldatov and with the deputy president of the Afro-Asian Solidarity Committee in Damascus.

1981

7 Jan.	Arafat meets with Soldatov.
22 Feb.	PLO delegation headed by Farouq Qadoumi participates in 26th Congress of the CPSU.
23 Feb.	Arafat meets with Soldatov.
14 Mar.	Arafat meets with Soldatov.
16 Mar.	Hassan Ba al'Uni, PLO representative in Tunis, meets with the Soviet Ambassador to Tunisia.
14 April	Abd-el Muhsin abu Maizer meets with the Soviet Chargé d'Affaires in Damascus.
15 April	Mahmud Abbas, member of the Fatah Central Committee, visits Moscow.

25 April	Arafat meets with Soldatov.
29 April	Arafat meets with the Soviet Chargé d'Affaires in Beirut.
3 May	Arafat meets with the Soviet Chargé d'Affaires in Beirut.
11 May	Abd-el Muhsin abu Maizer meets with the Soviet Chargé d'Affaires in Damascus.
13 May	PLO leaders Mahmud Abbas, Khaled al-Fahum and Abd-el Muhsin abu Maizer meet with a friendship delegation from the USSR.
17 May	Arafat meets with Soldatov.
20 May	Naif Hawatmeh visits Moscow.
27 May	Farouq Qadoumi meets with Soldatov.
1 June	Arafat meets with Soldatov.
9 June	Arafat meets with Soldatov.
12 June	PLO representative in London Ramlawi meets with the Soviet Ambassador to Great Britain.
25 June	Arafat meets with Soldatov.
26 June	Farouq Qadoumi heads a PLO friendship delegation to Moscow.
25 July	Arafat meets with Soldatov.

Appendix B

Political Meetings PLO-Eastern Bloc 1978-1981

1978

15 Jan. Naif Hawatmeh, head of the DFLP wing of the PLO, meets with the President of the East German Solidarity Commission in East Berlin.

5 June Arafat meets with East German leader Erich Honecker in E. Berlin.

10 June Shafiq al-Hut, head of the PLO office in Lebanon, meets with Cuban leader Fidel Castro during a convention of the non-aligned countries in Cuba.

24 July Naif Hawatmeh visits Cuba.

15 Sept. Arafat meets with a member of the Hungarian Communist Party's Section for Foreign Affairs, in Damascus.

11 Oct. Fatah's military chief Abu Jihad meets with the Cuban Ambassador to Lebanon.

23 Nov. Arafat meets with Yugoslavian President Tito.

4 Dec. Khaled al-Fahum, Chairman of the Palestinian National Council, meets in Damascus with the Chairman of the Bulgarian Parliament.

31 Dec. PLO delegation meets with the Cuban Ambassador to Lebanon.

1979

2 Feb. Farouq Qadoumi, head of the PLO 'Political Department', meets in Beirut with an East German delegation.

24 Mar. Khaled al-Fahum visits Budapest.

24 Mar. Farouq Qadoumi visits the Cuban Ambassador in Beirut.

24 April Naif Hawatmeh meets with the Cuban Transport Minister.

24 April Fatah Central Committee member Abu Mazzan visits Prague.

25 May Arafat meets with the East German Ambassador in Beirut.

30 May Farouq Qadoumi meets with the East German Ambassador in Beirut.

26 June Arafat meets with the Cuban Ambassador in Beirut.

9 July PLO spokesman Abd-el Muhsin abu Maizer visits Hungary.

11 July Arafat visits Bulgaria.

12 July Arafat meets with the Bulgarian Ambassador in Beirut.

18 July Khaled al-Fahum visits Yugoslavia.

16 Aug. PLO delegation visits Bulgaria.

20 Aug. Arafat meets with Romanian President Ceausescu in Bucharest.

20 Aug. Fatah Central Committee member Abu Saleh meets with a Polish delegation in Beirut.

25 Aug. Abd-el Muhsin Abu Maizer visits Bucharest.

19 Sept. Farouq Qadoumi meets with an East German delegation in Beirut.

25 Sept. Naif Hawatmeh visits Bulgaria.

| 7 Nov. | Arafat meets the Cuban Ambassador in Beirut. |
| 22 Nov. | PLO delegation visits Bucharest. |

1980

2 Feb.	Naif Hawatmeh visits East Berlin.
24 Feb.	A delegation of the PDF wing of the PLO returns from a tour of Cuba, Czechoslovakia, Bulgaria and the Soviet Union.
11 April	Arafat meets with the Cuban Foreign Minister in Prague.
29 May	Abd-el Muhsin abu Maizer meets with the Czechoslovakian Ambassador in Damascus.
24 July	Arafat visits Prague.
30 July	Arafat visits Bucharest.
13 Aug.	A delegation of the PFLP wing of the PLO visits Bucharest.
5 Sept.	Arafat visits Bucharest.
11 Sept.	PLO Central Committee member Abu Ali Mustafa visits Hanoi.
16 Sept.	Naif Hawatmeh visits Hungary.
27 Oct.	Isaam al-Kadi, a leader of the As-Saiqa wing of the PLO, meets in Bucharest with Romanian President Ceausescu.
27 Oct.	A Cuban information delegation meets with PLO leaders in Tyre.
Oct.	The Czechoslovakian Military Attache visits the General Command of As-Saiqa in Damascus.
21 Nov.	Abu Jihad, head of the military arm of Fatah, meets with East German delegation in Beirut.
24 Nov.	PLO leaders Arafat, Qadoumi and Abu Saleh meet in Damascus with a member of the Political Office of the East German Communist Party.
21 Dec.	Arafat visits East Berlin in order to receive a medical examination.
30 Dec.	Arafat meets with Honecker in East Berlin.

1981

	A delegation of the DFLP wing of the PLO, led by Tuissir Khaled, participates in the Communist Party Convention in Cuba.
12 Jan.	Czechoslovak and Soviet experts set up plant in southern Lebanon for the manufacture of bombs and chemical weapons for the PLO.
13 Jan.	PLO delegation signs agreement in Prague granting diplomatic privileges.
17 Jan.	Arafat visits East Berlin and obtained agreement on the despatch of 50 military advisers to train PLO men.
26 Jan.	Arafat and Fatah Central Committee member Abu Sharar meet in Beirut with an East German delegation.
6 Feb.	Arafat's deputy Abu Iyad meets with the Yugoslavian Defence Minister in Belgrade.
12 Feb.	Arafat meets with the Vietnamese Ambassador to Damascus.
15 Feb.	The Cuban Deputy Economy Minister meets with PLO leaders in Tyre.
15 Feb.	A PFLP delegation led by George Habash visits Czechoslovakia.

17 Feb.	The Speaker of the Vietnamese Parliament meets with the PLO representative in Hanoi.
19 Feb.	The head of the PPSF wing of the PLO, Dr Samir Ussa, meets with the Hungarian Ambassador in Lebanon.
1 Mar.	The PLO representative in Hanoi meets with the Speaker of the Vietnamese Parliament.
4 Mar.	Farouq Qadoumi meets with the Czechoslovakian Foreign Minister in Prague.
10 Mar.	Abu Iyad visits Prague.
11 Mar.	Arafat meets with the Hungarian Ambassador in Beirut.
11 Mar.	Arafat meets with the Bulgarian Ambassador in Beirut.
11 Mar.	Arafat meets with the Cuban Foreign Minister in Beirut.
10 April	Arafat meets with Honecker in East Berlin.
14 April	Abd-el Muhsin abu Maizer meets with the East German Chargé d'Affaires in Damascus.
29 April	Abu Iyad meets with the Cuban Chargé D'Affaires in Beirut.
30 April	Farouq Qadoumi meets with the Bulgarian Ambassador in Beirut.
3 May	Farouq Qadoumi heads PLO delegation to Bulgaria.
15 May	Abu Iyad meets with the Cuban Chargé d'Affaires in Beirut.
22 May	The PLO representative in Belgrade meets with the Chairman of the Foreign Affairs Committee of the Yugoslavian Parliament.
25 May	Arafat meets with President Ceausescu in Bucharest.
10 June	A PFLP delegation led by George Habash visits East Berlin.
23 June	Arafat meets with the Yugoslavian Ambassador in Beirut.
25 June	Arafat meets with the East German Ambassador in Beirut.
2 July	Arafat meets with the Polish Ambassador in Beirut.
9 July	Arafat meets with the Yugoslavian Prime Minister in Belgrade.
10 July	A PFLP delegation led by George Habash meets with the Secretary General of the Central Committee of the East German Communist Party.
23 July	Arafat meets with the Yugoslavian Ambassador in Lebanon.

Appendix C

How the ANC became a Communist Front

To gain a clear understanding of the role of the tripartite USSR/ANC/SACP (South African Communist Party) alliance it is important to study the record in chronological order. This is how a genuine nationalist movement was transformed into a Soviet surrogate:

1900: Communism emerges in SA in mining/industrial areas. Initially most communists were British or Australian, concentrating on the 'White proletariat'.

1912 The SA Native National Congress (later renamed the ANC) is established in Bloemfontein under moderate, non-communist leadership, to 'protect and promote' Black interests.

1915 International Socialist League of SA (ISLSA) is founded in Johannesburg and launches a weekly called *The International.*

1919 Third International Labour Organization (Comintern) is founded in Moscow on Lenin's intitiative. Object: universal dissemination of communism.

1920 Addressing second Comintern congress, Lenin describes 'national revolutionary' governments as a 'transitional measure' pending the emergence of pro-Soviet communist regimes in Africa and elsewhere.

29 July 1921 SACP officially launched as an orthodox, pro-Moscow movement. SACP is admitted to the Comintern. SACP officials attend several Comintern congresses in USSR, Lenin states the Comintern regards SA 'as one of its frontlines'.

1927-8 Third Comintern International is held in Moscow - a critical landmark in SA history. Concluding that the bourgeoisie of colonial territories have not come up to scratch, Comintern leaders direct that SACP 'must determinedly and consistently put forward the creation of an independent native republic' in SA. The ANC should become 'the sole representative of the oppressed masses of SA'; be converted into a 'militant nationalist revolutionary organization'; should set about undermining the leadership of Black chiefs. This dictate creates almost fatal split in SACP.

1928 SACP reports that 1,600 of its 1,750 members are Whites, centred mainly in Johannesburg, Cape Town and Potchefstroom. Many SACP members are expelled for opposing above directive, which they view as unrealistic. But Moscow, planning far ahead, is adamant. A Black republic it must be.

1931 SACP down to 150 members, mostly White. Fully supporting concept of Black republic, begins saturation programme of indoctrination. Blacks are subjected to an onslaught of CP dogma at night schools and such like.

1931 Professor Ivan Potekhin, the Kremlin's top Africanist, instructs and advises visiting SACP members at Moscow's Lenin Institute.

1946 White-dominated SACP wins complete control of ANC leadership.

1950-5 Era of Third World emerges. Soviet foreign policy strategies increasingly stress importance of the Middle East and Southern Africa to Moscow's plans for world hegemony.

1954 Moscow-published symposium, *The People of Africa*, spells out how Marxism-Leninism can be applied to African conditions.

February 1956 Krushchev's 'secret speech' at 20th Soviet Communist Party Congress not only initiates anti-Stalin campaign, but also blames Stalin for 'not exploiting anti-Western sentiments of Southern Africa's liberation groups'.

1957-9 Preparation for future Soviet conquest of Africa begins in earnest with founding of Africa Institute under Potekhin.

1957 Writing in Soviet periodical, *Strategy and Review*, Major General A. N. Lagovsky describes his 'weak link' principle: growing Western reliance on Southern Africa's strategic minerals. That Lagovsky specialized in economic warfare indicates the geopolitical nature of his studies. Policy advocated: creation of a tier of Southern African Marxist states fully responsible to Moscow's strategic dictates for further struggle against the West; this to be concealed and justified under all-embracing doctrine of 'national liberation' movements.

1959 Pan African Congress formed as a breakaway movement from ANC. PAC censures ANC for its reliance on White leadership, links with Moscow, divorce from African masses.

1960 ANC, PAC and SACP all banned in South Africa.

June 1961 Khrushchev notes that while nuclear war is ruled out under '*détente*', national liberation movements are 'not only permissible but inevitable'. CPSU lays down a long-range programme for eventual Soviet primacy in Africa.

1961 Arms, money and training are provided by Moscow to African insurgents. In his official history of the SACP, Michael Harmel, writing under the pseudonym of A. Lerumo, admits SACP decided in 1961 to lead ANC into campaign of sabotage and violence.

1968 Top Russian defector Dr Igor Glagolev, former senior research officer at Soviet Academy of Science, discloses that the Politburo has given Southern Africa priority attention. Key factor: the Vietnam war is running down, so the CPSU Central Committee decides that, as this happens, Soviet military aid, agents and other resources should be redeployed from Vietnam to support 'wars of liberation' in Southern Africa.

Today, the ANC has been so thoroughly infiltrated and taken over by the SACP that the two are virtually synonymous. Seven of the ANC's 22 National Executive Committee members, including the Deputy Secretary

General, belong to the SACP. While steadfastly refusing to admit he is a communist, ANC president Oliver Tambo is a long-time member of the Presidium of the World Peace Council, the major Soviet international front organization, heavily involved in anti-SA activity.

Joint planning by the USSR, ANC and SACP of the strategy to be used against SA is co-ordinated in Moscow, where there has recently been increasing pressure on the ANC to provide proof that it is capable of 'intensifying the struggle'.

In his 1979 work, *Conflict in the South of Africa,* Anatoly Gromyko, a top Soviet Africanist and son of longtime Foreign Minister Andrei Gromyko, mentions the 'fine work' done through the SACP, ANC and SA Indian Congress. He states quite categorically that the SACP is 'intimately' connected with the ANC; that these organizations will use 'military force' to gain power in SA that when achieved, they will demand a 'monopoly of power' - that is, dictatorship.

Bibliography and References

Acheson, Dean A. (1969), *Present at the Creation*, (New York: Norton).

Alexander, Yonah (ed.) (1976), *International Terrorism* (New York: Praeger).

Alexander, Yonah (1978), 'Terrorism in the Middle East, a new phase', *The Washington Quarterly*, vol. 1, no. 4 (Autumn), pp. 115-117.

Alexander, Yonah, Carlton, David, and Wilkinson, Paul (eds) (1979), *Terrorism, Theory and Practice* (Boulder, Colo.: Westview Press).

Alexander, Yonah, and Finger, Seymour Maxwell (eds) (1977), *Terrorism: Interdisciplinary Perspectives* (New York: John Jay).

Ali, Tariq (1978), *1968 and After: Inside the Revolution* (London: Blond & Briggs).

Al-Shaer, Mohamed (1977), 'Twelve years of struggle', *New Times*, no. 1 (January).

Annales d'Etudes Internationales (1972), *Les Nouvelles formes de conflits*, vol. 3 (Geneva: L'Institut Universitaire des Hautes Etudes Internationales).

Annals of the American Academy of Political and Social Science (1962), *Unconventional Warfare* (AAPSS, May).

Ardatovsky, Vadim (1977), 'Italy: troubled spring', *New Times*, no. 19 (May).

Arendt, Hannah (1970a), *On Violence* (New York: Harcourt Brace Jovanovich).

Arendt, Hannah (1970b), *Men in Dark Times* (London: Jonathan Cape).

Arendt, Hannah (1979), *On Revolution* (New York: Penguin; 1st edn 1965).

Arendt, Hannah (1980), *Between Past and Future* (New York: Penguin).

Arismendi, Rodney (1970), *Lenin, La Revolución y America Latina* (Montevideo: Ediciones Pueblos Unidos).

Asprey, Robert B. (1975), *War in the Shadows: The Guerrilla in History*, 2 vols (Garden City, NY: Doubleday).

Bar-Haim, Sara (1976), 'The Palestine Liberation Army: stooge or actor', unpublished paper presented at the International Conference on the Palestinians and the Arab-Israeli Conflict, Haifa University, Haifa, Israel, April.

Barnet, Richard J. (1972), *Intervention and Revolution* (London: Granada).

Barron, John (1975), *KGB: The Secret Work of Soviet Secret Agents* (Buffalo, NY: Corgi Books).

Bartlett, Sir Frederic Charles (1940), *Political Propaganda* (Cambridge: Cambridge University Press).

Bassiouni, M. Cherif, and Nanda, Ved P. (eds) (1973), *A Treatise on International Criminal Law*, vol. 1 (Springfield: Charles C. Thomas, Publishers).

Becker, Jillian (1977), *Hitler's Children* rev. edn (London: Panther Granada).

Bell, J. Bowyer (1970, *The Secret Army: A History of the IRA 1916-1970* (London: Anthony Blond).

Bell, J. Bowyer (1975), *Transnational Terror* (Washington, DC: American Enterprise Institute for Public Policy Research).

Bell, J. Bowyer (1977), *Terror Out of Zion: Irgun Zvai Leumi and the Palestine Underground 1929-1949* (New York: Avon Books).

Bell, J. Bowyer (1978), *A Time of Terror* (New York: Basic Books).

Beloff, Max (1947), *The Foreign Policy of Soviet Russia, 1929-1941,* 2 vols (London: Oxford University Press).

Bergier, Jacques (1976), *La Troisième Guerre Mondiale est Commencée* (Paris: Albin Michel).

Bittman, Ladislav (1972), *The Deception Game* (New York: Ballantine Books/Espionage Intelligence Library).

Bjelajac, Colonel Slavko N. (1962), 'Unconventional warfare: American and Soviet approaches', *Unconventional Warfare*, Annals of the American Political Science Association (May), pp. 74-81.

Blishchenko, Igor (1978), 'The legal standing of the PLO', *New Times*, no. 4.

Bocca, Giorgio (1981), *Il Terrorismo Italiano 1970/1980* (Milan: Biblioteca Universale Rizzoli).

Brierly, J. L. (1961), *The Law of Nations*, 5th edn (New York and Oxford: Oxford University Press).

Browder, Robert Paul (1953), *The Origins of Soviet-American Diplomacy* (Princeton, NJ: Princeton University Press).

Brown, Archie, and Michael Kaser (eds) (1978), *The Soviet Union Since the Fall of Khrushchev*, 2nd edn (London: Macmillan).

Brown, Anthony Cave, and MacDonald, Charles B. (1981), *On A Field of Red: The Communist International and the Coming of World War II* (New York: Putnam).

Brown, Seyom (1974), *New Forces in World Politics* (Washington, DC: The Brookings Institution).

Brownlie, Ian (1963), *International Law and the Use of Force by States* (Oxford: Clarendon Press).

Bukharov, Victor (1974), 'Palestinian National Council session', *New Times*, no. 25.

Burton, Anthony (1975), *Urban Terrorism* (London: Leo Cooper).

Burton, Anthony (1977), *Revolutionary Violence* (London: Leo Cooper).

Cantore, R. (1978), *Dall' Interno della Guerriglia* (Milan: Mondadori).

Carlton, David, and Schaerf, Carlo (eds) (1975), *International Terrorism and World Security* (London: Croom Helm).

Carr, E.H. (1934), *Karl Marx - a Study in Fanaticism* (London: Dent).

Carr, E.H. (1950-3), *The Bolshevik Revolution*, 3 vols (London: Anchor).

Carr, E.H. (1964), *Studies in Revolution* (New York: Grosset & Dunlap).

Carrere d'Encausse, Helene (1979), *Decline of an Empire* (from the original French title *L'Empire éclaté*) (New York: Newsweek).

Chambers, Frank P. (1962), *This Age of Conflict,* 3rd edn (New York and Burlingame: Harcourt, Brace & World).

CIA (1979), *The Rote Kapelle, The CIA's History of Soviet Intelligence and Espionage Networks in Western Europe, 1936-45* (Washington, DC: University Publications of America).

Claudin, Fernando (1975), *The Communist Movement from Comintern to Cominform* (Harmondsworth: Penguin).

Cline, Ray, S. (1980), *World Power Trends and US Foreign Policy for the 1980s* (Boulder, Colo.: Westview Press).

Clutterbuck, Richard (1975), *Living With Terrorism* (London: Faber).

Clutterbuck, Richard (1977), *Guerrillas and Terrorists* (London: Faber).

Collins, John M. (1980), *US-Soviet Military Balance: Concepts and Capabilities 1960-1980* (New York: McGraw-Hill).

Confino, Michael, and Shamir, Shimon (eds) (1973), *The USSR and the Middle East* (Jerusalem: Israel Universities Press).

Conquest, Robert (1961), *Power and Policy in the USSR: the Study of Soviet Dynasties* (London: Macmillan).

Conquest, Robert (1970), *The Nation Killers: The Deportation of Nationalities* (London: Macmillan).

Conquest, Robert (1972), *Lenin* (Glasgow: Fontana/Collins).

Coogan, Tim Pat (1980), *The IRA* (London: Fontana).

Craig, Gordon Alexander, and Gilbert, Felix (eds) (1953), *The Diplomats 1919-1939* (Princeton, NJ: Princeton University Press).

Crozier, Brian (1965), *South-East Asia in Turmoil* (Harmondsworth: Penguin).

Crozier, Brian (1974), *Transnational Terrorism* (Gaithersburg, Md: International Association of Chiefs of Police).

Crozier, Brian (1978a), *Strategy of Survival* (London: Temple Smith).

Crozier, Brian (1978b), 'The surrogate forces of the Soviet Union', *Conflict Studies*, no. 92 (London: Institute for the Study of Conflict, February).

Dallin, A., and Breslauer, G. (1970), *Political Terrorism in Communist Systems* (Stanford, Calif.: Stanford University Press).

Davies, Joseph E. (1943), *Mission to Moscow* (Garden City, NY: Garden City Publishing Co.).

Dayan, Moshe (1976), *Story of My Life* (Jerusalem: Steimatzky's Agency).

Daycock, Davis William (1980), 'The KPD and the NSDAP: a study of the relationship between political extremes in Weimar Germany 1923-1933', PhD thesis, London School of Economics and Political Science, University of London).

Degras, Jane (ed.) (1956, 1960, 1965), *The Communist International 1919-1943: Documents*, 3 vols (London: Oxford University Press, for the Royal Institute of International Affairs).

Demaris, Ovid (1977), *Brothers in Blood: The International Terrorist Network* (New York: Scribner).

Demchenko, Pavel (1972), 'Arab oil for the Arabs', *New Times*, no. 25.

Deriabin, Peter (1972), *Watchdogs of Terror: Russian Bodyguards from the Tsars to the Commissars* (New Rochell, NY: Arlington House).

Deutsch, Karl W. (1968), *The Analysis of International Relations* (Englewood Cliffs, NJ: Prentice-Hall).

Deutscher, Isaac (1979), *Stalin*, rev. edn (Harmondsworth: Penguin).

Dillon, Dorothy R. (1962), *International Communism and Latin America* (Gainesville, Fla: University of Florida Press).

Dinerstein, Herbert S. (1967), *Castro's Latin American Comintern* (Santa Monica, Calif.: Rand, September), P-3678.

Dinstein, Yoram (1972), 'Criminal jurisdiction over aircraft hijacking', *Israel Law Review*, vol. 7.

Djilas, Milovan (1962), *Conversations with Stalin* (New York: Harcourt, Brace & World).

Dobson, Christopher (1974), *Black September* (London: Robert Hale).

Dobson, Christopher, and Payne, Ronald (1977), *The Carlos Complex*, 1st US edn (New York: Putnam).

Dobson, Christopher, and Payne, Ronald (1979), *The Weapons of Terror* (London: Macmillan).

Donovan, Robert J. (1967), *Israel's Fight For Survival Six Days in June* (New York: Signet Books).

Douglass, Joseph D., Jr (1980), *Soviet Military Strategy in Europe* (New York: Pergamon).

Dugard, John (1973), 'Towards the definition of international terrorism', *American Journal of International Law*, vol. 67, no. 5, November, pp. 94-100.

Dziak, John J. (1981a), *Soviet Perceptions of Military Power: The Interaction of Theory and Practice* (New York: Crane, Russak & Company).

Dziak, John J. (1981b), 'Soviet intelligence and security services in the eighties: the paramilitary dimension', *Orbis*, Winter, pp. 771-86.

Eddowes, Michael (1977), *The Oswald File* (New York: Clarkson N. Potter, distributed by Crown Publishers).

Epstein, Edward Jay (1978), *Legend: The Secret World of Lee Harvey Oswald* (London: Arrow Books).

Evans, Alona E. (1973), 'Aircraft hijacking: what is being done', *American Journal of International Law*, vol. 67, no. 4, October, pp. 641-71.

Evans, Alona E., and Murphy, John F. (eds) (1978), *Legal Aspects of International Terrorism* (Lexington, Mass.: Lexington Books, for the American Society of International Law).

Farer, Tom J. (1971), 'The laws of war 25 years after Nuremberg', *International Conciliation*, no. 583, May.

Fatemi, Faramarz S. (1980), *The USSR in Iran* (South Brunswick, NJ, and New York: Barnes).

Feltrinelli: Il Guerrigiero Impotente (Rome: Edizioni 'Documenti').

Ferencz, Benjamin B. (1972), 'Defining aggression: where it stands and where it's going', *American Journal of International Law*, vol. 66, no. 3, July, pp. 491-508.

Ferencz, Benjamin B. (1973), 'A proposed definition of aggression: by compromise and consensus', *International and Comparative Law Quarterly*, vol. 22, pt 3, July, pp. 407-33.

Fischer, Bram (1966), *What I Did Was Right* (London: Mayabuye Publications).

Francis, Samuel T. (1981), *The Soviet Strategy of Terror* (Washington, DC: The Heritage Foundation).

Franch, Thomas M., and Lockwood, Bert M., Jr (1974), 'Preliminary thoughts towards an international convention on terrorism', *American Journal of International Law*, vol. 68, no. 1, January, pp. 69-90.

Freedman, Robert O. (1972), 'Soviet dilemmas in the Middle East', *Problems of Communism*, vol. 23, no. 3, May-June, pp. 71-3.

Freedman, Robert O. (1978), *Soviet Policy Toward the Middle East since 1970*, rev. edn (New York: Praeger).

Friedlander, Robert A. (1976a), 'The origins of international terrorism: a micro legal-historical perspective', *Israel Yearbook on Human Rights*, vol. 6, pp. 49-61.

Friedlander, Robert A. (1976b), 'Terrorism and political violence: do the ends justify the means?', *Chitty's Law Journal*, vol. 24, no. 7, September, pp. 240-5.

Friedlander, Robert A. (1978), 'Coping with terrorism: what is to be done?', *Ohio Northern University Law Review*, vol. 5, no. 2, pp. 432-43.

Friedlander, Robert A. (1979a), *Terrorism and the Law: What Price Safety?* (International Association of Police, Bureau of Operations and Research).

Friedlander, Robert A. (1979b), 'The terror syndrome: cause and effect', *Ohio Northern University Law Review*, vol. 6, no. 1, pp. 109-19.

Galleni, Mauro (1981), *Rapporto sul Terrorismo: Le Stragi, gli Agguati, i Sequestri, Le Sigle, 1969-1980* (Milan: Rissoli editore).

Garcia Trevino, Rodrigo (1959), *La Ingerencia Rusa en Mexico (y Sudamerica)* (Mexico: Editorial America).

Gaucher, Roland (1965), *Les Terroristes* (Paris: Editions Albin Michel).

Gaucher, Roland (1974), *Histoire secrète du Parti Communiste Français* (Paris: Editions Albin Michel).

Gaucher, Roland (1981), *Le Réseau Curiel ou la subversion humanitaire* (Paris: Editions Jean Picollec).

Ghirinelli, Antonio (1977), 'Der Verleger als Terrorist. Der Fall Feltrinelli', *Criticon*, no. 43, September/October.

Ginsburgs, George (1970), 'The Soviet Union and international cooperation in legal matters: criminal law - the current phase', *International and Comparative Law Quarterly*, vol. 19, pt 4, October, pp. 626-70.

Golan, Galia (1976), *The Soviet Union and the PLO*, Adelphi Paper, No. 131 (London: Institute for International and Strategic Studies).

Golan, Galia (1977), *Yom Kippur and After: The Soviet Union and the Middle East Crisis* (New York: Cambridge University Press).

Golan, Galia (1980), *The Soviet Union and the Palestine Liberation Organization: An Uneasy Alliance* (New York: Praeger).

Goncharov, Vladimir (1980), 'TASS commentary on Afghanistan', 3 January, repr. in *Survival*, vol. 22, no. 2, March/April.

Gouré, Leon (1976), *War Survival in Soviet Strategy* (Coral Gables, Fla: Center for Advanced International Studies, University of Miami).

Gouré, Leon, Kohler, Foy D., and Harvey, Mose L. (1974), *The Role of Nuclear Forces in Current Soviet Strategy* (Coral Gables, Fla: Center for Advanced International Studies, University of Miami).

Gouré, Leon, and Rothenberg, Morris (1975), *Soviet Penetration of Latin America* (Coral Gables, Fla: Center for Advanced International Studies, University of Miami).

Grechko, Marshal A. A. (1971), *Na strazhe mira i stroitel'stva Kommunizma* (On Guard for Peace and the Building of Communism) (Moscow: Voenizdat).

Grechko, Marshal A. A. (1973), 'On guard over peace and socialism' (Na strazhe mira i sotsializma), *Kommunist*, no. 7, May.

Green, L. C. (1962), 'Political offences, war crimes and extradition', *International and Comparative Law Quarterly*, vol. 11.

Greilsammer, Alain (1977-8), 'Communism in Israel: 13 years after the split', *Survey*, vol. 23, no. 3, Summer, pp. 172-92.

Groom, A. J. R. (1978), 'Coming to terms with terrorism', *British Journal of International Studies*, vol. 4, pp. 62-77.

Gross, Leo (1976), 'Voting in the Security Council and the PLO', *American Journal of International Law*, vol. 70, no. 3, July, pp. 470-91.

Gruber, Helmut (1974), *Soviet Russia Masters the Comintern* (New York: Anchor/Doubleday).

Grundy, Kenneth W. (1971), *Guerrilla Struggle in Africa* (New York: Grossman).

Halperin, Ernst (1976a), *Terrorism in Latin America* (Washington, DC: Sage).

Halperin, Ernst (1976b), 'Terrorism in Latin America', *The Washington Papers*, vol. 4, no. 33, (London/Beverly Hills: Sage Publications The Center for Strategic and International Studies, Georgetown University).

Hammond, Thomas T. (ed.) (1975), *The Anatomy of Communist Takeovers* (New Haven, Conn.: Yale University Press).

Harkabi, Y. (1973), 'The problem of the Palestinians', *Israel Economic Committee on the Middle East*.

Hart, Douglas M. (1982), 'Low-intensity conflict in Afghanistan: the Soviet view', *Survival*, vol. 24, no. 2, March/April, pp. 61-9.

Harvard Research in International Law (1935), 'Extradition', *American Journal of International Law*, vol. 29, supp. 15.

Heikal, Mohamed (1978), *Sphinx and Commissar: The Rise and Fall of Soviet Influence in the Middle East* (London: Collins).

Heilbrunn, Otto (1962), *Partisan Warfare* (London: Allen & Unwin).

Heilbrunn, Otto (1963), *Warfare in the Enemy's Rear* (London: Allen & Unwin).

Heilbrunn, Otto (1965), *Conventional Warfare in the Nuclear Age* (London: Allen & Unwin).

Herman, Valentine, and van der Laan Bouma, Rob (1980), 'Nationalists without a nation: South Moluccan terrorism in the Netherlands', *Terrorism* (Journal), vol. 4, no. 1-4.

Hervé, Pierre (1956), *Dieu et César sont-ils Communistes?* (Paris: Editions de la Table Ronde).

Heyman, Edward, and Mickolus, Edward (1978), 'Imitation by terrorists: quantitative approaches to the study of diffusion patterns in transnational terrorism', unpublished paper, presented 1-3 May to the Joint National Meeting of the Operations Research Society of America and the Institute of Management Sciences, New York.

Higgins, Rosalyn (1961), 'The legal limits of the use of force by states: United Nations practice', *British Yearbook of International Law*, vol. 37.

Hobsbawm, E. J. (1973), *Revolutionaries* (New York: New American Library/Meridian).

Hoffman, Erik P., and Fleron, Frederic J., Jr (1981), *The Conduct of Soviet Foreign Policy* (New York: Aldine).

Hoffman, Stanley H. (ed.) (1960), *Contemporary Theory in International Relations* (Englewood Cliffs, NJ: Prentice-Hall).

Horchem, Dr Hans Josef (1979), 'Die Sowjetunion und der internationale Terrorismus', *Frankfurter Allgemeine Zeitung*, vol. 10, no. 245, October.

Horne, Alistair (1979), *A Savage War of Peace: Algeria 1954-1962* (Harmondsworth: Penguin).

Horner, Charles (1980), 'The facts about terrorism', *Commentary*, vol. 69, no. 6, June, pp. 40-5.

Hull, Cordell (1948), *Memoires*, 2 vols (New York: Macmillan).

Hurewitz, J. C. (ed.) (1969), *Soviet-American Rivalry in the Middle East*, Proceedings of the Academy of Political Science, vol. 29, no. 3 (March).

Hutchinson, Martha Crenshaw (1975), 'Transnational terrorism and world politics', *Jerusalem Journal of International Relations*, vol. 1, no. 2, Winter, pp. 109-29.

Hutt, W. H. (1964), *The Economics of the Colour Bar* (London: Andre Deutsch for The Institute of Economic Affairs).

Hyams, Edward (1975), *Terrorists and Terrorism* (London: Dent).

Hyland, William G. (1981), 'Soviet theatre forces and arms control policy', *Survival*, vol. 23, no. 5, September/October, pp. 194-200.

Jenkins, Brian M. (1972), *An Urban Strategy for Guerrillas and Governments* (Santa Monica, Calif.: Rand, August), P-4670/1.

Jenkins, Brian M. (1974), *Soldiers versus Gunmen: the Challenge of Urban Guerrilla Warfare* (Santa Monica, Calif.: Rand, March), P-5182.

Jenkins, Brian M. (1975), *High Technology Terrorism and Surrogate War: The Impact of New Technology on Low-Level Violence* (Santa Monica, Calif.: Rand, January), P-5339.

Jenkins, Brian M. (1977), *Combatting International Terrorism: The Role of Congress* (Santa Monica, Calif.: Rand, January), P-5808.

Jenkins, Brian M., and Johnson, Janera (1975), *International Terrorism: A Chronology 1968-1974*, Report prepared for the Department of State and Defense Advanced Research Projects Agency (Santa Monica, Calif.: Rand, March), R-1597-DOS/ARPA.

Jessup, Philip C. (1948), *A Modern Law of Nations: An Introduction* (New York: Macmillan).

Jones, Juanita, and Miller, Abraham (1979), 'The media and terrorist activity: resolving the first amendment dilemma', *Ohio Northern University Law Review*, vol. 6, no. 1, pp. 70-81.

Kanet, Roger E., and Bahry, Donna (eds) (1975), *Soviet Economic and Political Relations with the Developing World* (New York: Praeger).

Katz, Robert (1980), *Days of Wrath* (Garden City, NY: Doubleday).

Kaznacheev, A. (1962), *Inside a Soviet Embassy: Experiences of a Russian Diplomat in Burma* (Philadelphia, Pa: Lippincott).

Kennan, George F. (1960), *Russia and The West under Lenin and Stalin* (Boston, Mass.: Little, Brown).

Kennan, George F. (1967), *Memoirs 1925-1950* (Boston, Mass.: Little, Brown).

Kerr, Malcolm H. (1971), *The Arab Cold War: Gamal Abd al-Nasir and His Rivals, 1958-1970*, 3rd edn (London: Oxford University Press).

Khokhlov, Nikolai (1959), *In the Name of Conscience* (New York: McKay).

Kielinger, Thomas (1980), 'A Soviet diplomat: we bridle slowly but do some fast riding', *Die Welt*, 14 January.

Kohler, Foy D., Gouré, Leon, and Harvey, Mose L. (1974), *The Soviet Union and the October 1973 Middle East War: The Implications for Detente* (Coral Gables, Fla: Center for Advanced International Studies, University of Miami).

Koury, Enver M. (1976), *The Crisis in the Lebanese System* (Washington, DC: Enterprise Institute).

Kozak, Jan (1975), *Without a Shot Being Fired*, 5th Eng. edn (London: Independent Information Centre). At the time of writing, Mr. Kozak was a Member of the Secretariat of the CP in the Agitprop department.

Krivitsky, Walter (1963), *I Was Stalin's Agent* (London).

Krosney, Herbert (1979), 'The PLO's Moscow connection', *New York Magazine*, 24 September, pp. 64-72.

Kudryavtsev, Viktor (1970), 'The political consolidation in the UAR', *New Times*, no. 43.

Kupperman, Robert H., and Friedlander, Robert A. (1979), 'Terrorism and social control and response', *Ohio Northern University Law Review*, vol. 6, no. 1, pp. 52-9.

Kupperman, Robert, and Trent, Darrell (1979), *Terrorism: Threat, Reality, Response*, Publication No. 204 (Stanford, Calif.: The Hoover Institution).

Kulish, V. M. *et al* (1972), *Voennaya sila i mezhdunarodnye otnosheniya* (Moscow: Mezhdunodnye otnosheniya).

Labedz, Leopold (1979), 'Ideology and Soviet foreign policy', in *Prospects of Soviet Power in the 1980s, Part 1*, Adelphi Paper No. 151 (London: Institute for International and Strategic Studies).

Lador-Lederer, J. (1974), 'A legal approach to international terrorism', *Israel Law Review*, vol. 9.

Landa, R. (1976), 'The Palestinian question: the Socio-political aspect', *Aziia i Afrika Segodnia*, v.3, p.7.

Lapenna, Ivo (1968), *Soviet Penal Policy* (London: The Bodley Head).

Lapierre, Dominique, and Collins, Larry (1971), *Ô Jerusalem* (Paris: Editions Robert Laffont).

Laqueur, Walter (1972), *The Struggle for the Middle East: The Soviet Union and the Middle East 1958-1968* (Harmondsworth: Penguin).

Laqueur, Walter (ed.) (1977a), *The Guerrilla Reader* (New York: New American Library/Meridian).

Laqueur, Walter (1977b), *Guerrilla* (London: Weidenfeld & Nicolson).

Laqueur, Walter (1977c), *Terrorism* (Boston, Mass.: Little, Brown).

Laqueur, Walter (ed.) (1978), *The Terrorism Reader* (New York: New American Library).

Lasswell, Harold D., and Cleveland, Harlan (1962), *The Ethics of Power* (New York).

Lasswell, Harold D., and Lerner, Daniel (eds) (1965), *World Revolutionary Elites: Studies in Coercive Ideological Movements* (Cambridge, Mass.: MIT Press).

Ledeen, Michael (1978), 'Inside the Red Brigades: an exclusive report', *New York Magazine*, 1 May, pp. 36-9.

Leebaert, Derek (ed.) (1981), *Soviet Military Thinking* (London: Allen & Unwin).

Leggett, George (1981), *The CHEKA: Lenin's Political Police* (New York and Oxford: Oxford University Press).

Lenin, V. I. (1935-7), *Sochineniia*, 3rd edn, 30 vols, (Moscow).

Lenin, V. I. (1946-50), *Sochineniia*, 4th edn, 35 vols, (Moscow).

Lenin, V. I. (1958-66), *Polnoe sobranie sochinenii*, 5th edn, 58 vols, (Moscow).

Lerumo, A. (1971), *Fifty Fighting Years* (London: Inkululeko Publications).

Levytsky, Brois (1971), *The Uses of Terror: The Soviet Secret Service 1917-1970* (London: Sidgwick & Jackson).

Lojacono, Vittorio (1974), *I Dossier di Settembre Nero* (Milan: Bietti).

Longo, Luigi (n.d.), *Le Brigate Internazionale in Spagna* (Rome).

Longo, Luigi (1971), *Sulla Via dell'Insurrezione Nazionale* (Rome; 1st edn 1954).

Lowenthal, Gerhard (1979), 'Am Langen Arm des KGB: Terroristen-Boss Arafat', *Deutschland-Magazin*, September, pp. 6-12.

Luttwak, Edward (1969), *Coup d'Etat* (New York: Knopf).

Machiavelli, Niccolo (1982), *The Prince*, translated by George Bull, rev. edn (Harmondsworth: Penguin).

Mallin, Jay (ed.) (1971), *Terror and Urban Guerrillas* (Coral Gables, Fla: University of Miami Press).

Mao-Tse-Tung (1969), *On Revolution and War*, ed. M. Rejai (Garden City, NY: Doubleday).

Mao-Tse-Tung (1978), *On Guerrilla Warfare*, English translation by Brigadier General Samuel B. Griffith II (Garden City, NY: Anchor/ Doubleday).

Ma'oz, Moshe (1974), 'Soviet and Chinese relations with the Palestinian guerrilla organizations', Jerusalem Papers on Peace Problems No. 4, Hebrew University of Jerusalem, March.

Marksizm-Leninizm o Voine i Armii (1958) (Moscow: Voenizdat).

Marx, Karl (1871), *The Civil War in France* (from the German original *Der Buergerkrieg in Frankreich*), address to the General Council of the International Working Men's Associations, 2nd edn (London).

Marx, Karl (1962), *Das Kapital*, 2 vols, repr. (Berlin: Dietz Verlag).

Marx und Engels Werke (MEW) (1956-68), 41 vols (Berlin: Institute für Marxismus-Leninismus).

Matekalo, Ivan (1973), *Les Dessous du Terrorisme International* (Paris: Julliard).

McGwire, Michael (1980), 'Soviet military doctrine: contingency planning and the reality of world war', *Survival*, vol. 22, no. 3, May/June, pp. 107-13.

Medvedenko, Anatoly (1977), 'The Ultras turn to terror', *New Times*, no. 6, February.

Meldal-Johnsen, Trevor, and Young, Vaugh (1979), *The Interpol Connection* (New York: Dial Press).

Merari, Ariel (1980), 'The internationalisation of political terrorism: causes, scope and treatment', Conference on Defence of Democracy against Terrorism in Europe, Tasks and Problems, Council of Europe, Strasbourg, 12-14 November.

Mickolus, Edward (1979), 'Multilateral legal efforts to combat terrorism: diagnosis and prognosis', Ohio Northern University Law Review, vol. 6, no. 1, pp. 13-51.

Middle East Record (MER) (1960-70), 6 vols (Tel Aviv: Shiloah Center for Middle Eastern and African Studies, Tel Aviv University).

Milbank, David L. (1976), International and Transnational Terrorism: Diagnosis and Prognosis (Washington, DC: CIA).

Miller, Abraham H. (1977), 'Negotiations for hostages: implications from the police experience', National Institute of Law Enforcement and Criminal Justice, Terrorism: An International Journal, vol. 1. (Fall).

Miller, Abraham H. (1980), Terrorism and Hostage Negotiations (Boulder, Colo.: Westview Press).

Mironenko, Yuri (1968), 'New Soviet man and the problem of crime', Studies on the Soviet Union, vol. 7, no. 3, pp. 15-26.

Mirsky, Georgi (1967), 'Israeli aggression and Arab unity', New Times, no. 28.

Mirsky, Georgi (1973), 'The Middle East: new factors', New Times, no. 48.

Mochanov, Yu. (1972), 'Soviet foreign policy as a factor promoting the revolutionary transformation of the world', International Affairs (Moscow), no. 12.

Modzhorian, L. A., and Blatova, N. T. (1979), Mezhdunarodnoe Pravo (Moscow: Iuridicheskaya Literatura).

Montaldo, Jean (1979), Les Secrets de la Banque Soviétique en France (Paris: Albin Michel).

Moser, Pierre A. (1980), Arméniens: où est la réalité? (Saint-Aquilin-de-Pacy: Librarie-Editions Mallier).

Moss, Robert (1971), Urban Guerrilla Warfare, Adelphi Paper, No. 79 (London: Institute for International and Strategic Studies).

Moss, Robert (1972), Urban Guerrillas (London: Temple Smith).

Munger, Colonel Murl D. (1977), 'The growing utility of political terrorism', Strategic Studies Institute, US Army War College, Carlisle Barracks, Pennsylvania, 7 March.

Myagkov, Aleksei (1976), Inside the KGB: An Expose by an Officer of the Third Directorate (London: Foreign Affairs).

Nanda, Ved P. (1979), 'Progress report on the United Nations' attempt to draft an "international" convention against the taking of "hostages"', Ohio Northern University Law Review, vol. 6, no. 1, pp. 89-108.

Nasinovsky, E. M. (1968), 'The impact of 50 years of Soviet theory and practice on international law', Proceedings of the American Society of International Law.

Netanyahu, Benjamin (ed.) (1981), International Terrorism: Challenge and Response, Proceedings of the Jerusalem Conference on International Terrorism (Jerusalem: The Jonathan Institute, New Brunswick, NJ: Transaction Books).

Norton, Augustus, R. (1974), 'Moscow and the Palestinians', Occasional

Papers in International Affairs, Center for Advanced International Studies, University of Miami.

Norton, Augustus R., and Greenberg, Martin H. (1980), *International Terrorism: An Annotated Bibliography and Research Guide* (Boulder, Colo.: Westview Press).

Novack, George (1970), *Marxism versus Neo-Anarchist Terrorism* (New York: Pathfinder Press, July).

O'Ballance, Edgar (1974), *Arab Guerrilla Power, 1967-1972* (London: Faber).

Ogarkov, N. V. (1979), 'Strategiya Voyennaya', *Sovetskaya Voyennaya Entsiklopedia*, vol. 7 (Moscow: Voenizdat).

O'Neill, Bard E. (1978), *Armed Struggle in Palestine: A Political-Military Analysis* (Boulder, Colo.: Westview Press).

Page, Bruce, Leitch, David, and Knightley, Phillip (1981), *The Philby Conspiracy* (New York: Ballantine Books/Espionage Intelligence Library).

Paine, Lauran (1975), *The Terrorists* (London: Robert Hale).

Pajak, Roger F. (1981), 'Soviet arms transfers as an instrument of influence', *Survival*, vol. 23, no. 4, July/August, pp. 165-74.

Pansa, Giampaolo (1980), *Storie Italiane di Violenza e Terrorismo* (Rome: Laterza).

Pavlov, V., Mikhalyov, P., Titov, I. (1977), 'The agony of Northern Ireland and London lies', *New Times*, no. 15, April.

Pella, V. (1929), 'Un nouveau délit: la propagande pour la guerre d'aggression', *Revue de droit international*.

Pella, V. (1938), 'La Cour pénale internationale et la répression du terrorisme', *Revue de droit pénal et de criminologie*, vol. 17, April.

Penkovsky, Oleg (1965), *The Penkovsky Papers*, trans. Peter Deriabin (New York: Avon Books).

Petersen, Phillip A. (n.d.), *Soviet Air Power and the Pursuit of New Military Options*, Studies in Communist Affairs No. 3 (United States Air Force).

Petersen, Phillip A. (ed.) (n.d.), *Soviet Policy in the Post-Tito Balkans*, Studies in Communist Affairs No. 4 (United States Air Force).

Pierre, Andrew (1976), 'The politics of international terrorism', *Orbis*, vol. 19, no. 4, Winter, pp. 1251-69.

Pimont, Yves (1972), 'La subversion dans les relations internationales contemporaines', *Revue generale de droit international public*, no. 3, June/September, pp. 766-99.

Pipes, Richard (1979), *Russia under the Old Regime* (Harmondsworth: Penguin).

Pisano, Vittorfranco S. (1979), 'A survey of terrorism of the left in Italy: 1970-1978', *Terrorism: An International Journal*, vol. 2, nos. 3 and 4.

Pisano, Vittorfranco S. (1980), 'The Red Brigades: a challenge to Italian democracy', *Conflict Studies*, no. 120, London Institute for the Study of Conflict, July.

Plascov, Avi (1980), 'The "Palestinian Gap" between Israel and Egypt', *Survival*, vol. 22, no. 2, March/April, pp. 50-58.

Plascov, Avi (1981), *A Palestinian State? Examining the Alternatives,* Adelphi Paper No. 163 (London: Institute for International and Strategic Studies).

Ponchaud, Francois (1977), *Cambodia Year Zero* (Harmondsworth: Penguin).

Ponomarev, Boris (1971), 'Under the banner of Marxism Leninism and Proletarian Internationalism: The 24th Congress of the CPSU', *World Marxist Review,* vol. 14, no. 6, June, pp. 3-19.

Ponomarev, Boris N. (1974), 'The world situation and the revolutionary process', *World Marxist Review,* vol. 17, June.

Ponomarev. B. N. (1980), 'Following an unshakable course of peace', *Pravda,* 5 February.

Possony, Stefan T. (1966), *Lenin: The Compulsive Revolutionary,* rev. edn (London: Allen & Unwin).

Possony, Stefan T., and Bouchey, L. Francis (1978), *International Terrorism — The Communist Connection* (Washington, DC: American Council for World Freedom).

'Prospects of Soviet Power in the 1980's', Part I (1979), Adelphi Paper No. 151 (London: Institute for International and Strategic Studies).

'Prospects of Soviet Power in the 1980's', Part II (1979), Adelphi Paper No. 152 (London: Institute for International and Strategic Studies).

Quainton, Anthony C. E. (1979), 'US prepares for terrorism', *The Shingle,* Philadelphia Bar Association Quarterly Magazine, vol. 42, no. 5, September-November.

Quandt, William B. (1977a), 'Soviet policy in the October Middle East War - I', *International Affairs* (Chatham House), vol. 53, no. 3, July.

Quandt, William B. (1977b), 'Soviet policy in the October Middle East War - II', *International Affairs* (Chatham House), vol. 53, no. 4 October.

Röhl, Klaus Rainer (1974), *Fünf Finger sind keine Faust* (Cologne: Verlag Kiepenheuer & Witsch).

Romaniecki, Leon (1973), 'The Arab terrorists in the Middle East and the Soviet Union', Research Paper No. 4, The Soviet and East European Research Centre, The Hebrew University of Jerusalem, February.

Romaniecki, Leon (1974), 'The Soviet Union and international terrorism', *Soviet Studies,* vol. 26, no. 3, pp. 417-40.

Romerstein, Herbert (1981), *Soviet Support for International Terrorism* (Washington, DC: The Foundation for Democratic Education).

Royal Commission on Espionage (1955), *Report and Transcript of Proceedings,* Sydney, Australia.

Royal Institute of International Affairs, London (1971), *Documents on International Affairs, 1962,* ed. D. C. Watt (London: Oxford University Press).

Rubin, Alfred P. (1972), 'The status of rebels under the Geneva Conventions of 1949', *International and Comparative Law Quarterly,* vol. 21, pt 3, July, pp. 472-96.

Sadat, Anwar el- (1978), *In Search of Identity: An Autobiography* (London: Collins).

Sakharov, Vladimir, with Tosi, Umberto (1980), *High Treason* (New York: Ballantine Books).

Salierno, Giulio (1980), *La Violenza in Italia* (Milan: Mondadori).

Salvadori, M. L. (1978), *Eurocommunismo e socialismo sovietico* (Torino: Einaudi).

Sampson, Anthony (1977), *The Arms Bazaar* (London: Hodder & Stoughton).

Schapiro, Leonard (1955), *The Origin of the Communist Autocracy* (London and Cambridge, Mass).

Schapiro, Leonard (1970), *The Communist Party of The Soviet Union*, 2nd edn (London: Methuen).

Schapiro, Leonard (1973), *The Government and Politics of the Soviet Union*, 5th edn (London: Hutchinson).

Schapiro, Leonard (1976-7), 'The international department of the CPSU: key to Soviet policy', *International Journal*, Winter, pp. 41-55.

Schapiro, Leonard (1977-8), 'The Soviet Union and the PLO', *Survey*, vol. 23, no. 3, Summer, pp. 193-207.

Schapiro, Leonard, and Reddaway, Peter (eds) (1967), *Lenin: The Man, The Theorist, The Leader, A Reappraisal* (London: Pall Mall).

Sarkesian, Sam C. (ed.) (1975), *Revolutionary Guerrilla Warfare* (Chicago: Precedent).

Schelling, Thomas C. (1966), *Arms and Influence* (New Haven, Conn.: Yale University Press).

Schmidt, Dana Adams (1974), *Armageddon in the Middle East* (New York: John Day).

Schweisfurth, Theodor (1979), *Sozialistisches Volkerrecht?* (Berlin: Springer-Verlag).

Sejna, Jan (1982), *We Will Bury You* (London: Sidgwick & Jackson).

Seton-Watson, Hugh (1960), *Neither War Nor Peace* (New York: Praeger).

Shackleton, The Rt Hon. Lord *Review of the Operation of the Prevention of Terrorism (Temporary Provisions) Acts 1974 and 1976*, Cmnd 7324 (London: HMSO).

Shaw, Jennifer, Gueritz, Rear Admiral E. F., and Younger, Major-General A. E. (eds) (1979), *Ten Years of Terrorism, Collected Views* (London: Royal United Services Institute for Defence Studies).

Shirer, William L. (1960), *The Rise and Fall of the Third Reich* (New York: Simon & Schuster).

Shubber, Sami (1973), 'Aircraft hijacking under the Hague Convention 1970 - a new regime?', *International and Comparative Law Quarterly*, vol. 22, pt 4, October, pp. 687-726.

Sidelnikov, Col. I. (1973), 'Peaceful coexistence and the security of People', *Kraznaya Zvezda*, 14 August.

Silj, A. (1977), *Mai piu senza fucile: Alle Origini delle BR e dei NAP* (Florence: Vallecchi).

Skolnick, Jerome H. (1969), *The Politics of Protest* (New York: Ballantine Books).

Smith, Colin (1976), *Carlos: Portrait of a Terrorist* (New York: Holt, Rinehart & Winston).

Soccorso Rosso (1976), *Brigate Rosse* (Milan: Feltrinelli).

Solodvnikov, V. G. (1968), 'The Soviet Union and Africa', *Africa in Soviet Studies*, vol. 1, pp. 9-21.

Soloviev, Alexandre V. (ed.) (1965), *A Century of Political Life in Russia (1800-1896)*, Russian Reprint Series (The Hague: Europe Printing).

Solzhenitsyn, Aleksandr I. (1973-4), *The Gulag Archipelago 1918-1956*, trans. Thomas P. Whitney (New York: Harper & Row).

Solzhenitsyn, Aleksandr I. (1980), *The Mortal Danger* (New York: Harper & Row).

Sonyei, Dr Salahi R. (1978), *Displacement of the Armenians: Documents* (Ankara: Belgeler, Turk Tarih Kurumu Belleteninde Yayinlanmistrir). A compilation of documents from F.O.371/9158,E.5523.

Souvarine, Boris (1920), *The Third International* (London: British Socialist Party).

Souvarine, Boris (1935), *Staline* (Paris: Editions Plon).

Soviet Association of International Law (ed.) (1970), *Soviet Yearbook of International Law, 1969* (Moscow: Nanka).

Soviet Association of International Law (ed.) (1979), *Soviet Yearbook of International Law, 1977* (Moscow: Nanka).

Speier, Hans (1966), *Revolutionary War* (Santa Monica, Calif.: Rand, September), P-3445.

Spiridovich, General A. (1930), *Histoire du terrorisme russe 1886-1917*, trans. Vladimir Lazarevski (Paris: Payot).

Staar, Richard F. (ed.) (1976) *Yearbook on International Communist Affairs 1976* (Stanford, Calif.: Hoover Institution).

Stalin, Joseph V. (1945), *Problems of Leninism* trans. from 11th Russian edn (Moscow: Foreign Languages Publishing House).

Stalin, Joseph V. (1973), *The Essential Stalin: Major Theoretical Writings, 1905-52*, ed. Bruce Franklin (London: Croom Helm).

Starke, J. (1967), *An Introduction to International Law*, 6th edn (London: Butterworth).

Sterling, Claire (1978), 'The terrorist network', *Atlantic Monthly*, November.

Sterling, Claire (1981), *The Terror Network* (New York: Holt, Rinehart & Winston).

Stevenson, William (1976), *Ninety Minutes at Entebbe* (New York: Bantam).

Stone, J. (1958), *Aggression and World Order: A Critique of United Nations Theories of Aggression*, Library of World Affairs No. 39 (London: Stevens).

Stone, J. (1959), *Legal Controls of International Conflict: A Treatise on the Dynamics of Disputes and War Law* (London: Stevens).

Stone, Julius (1977), 'Hopes and loopholes in the 1974 definition of aggression', *American Journal of International Law*, vol. 71, no. 2, April, pp. 224-46.

Terkhov, V. (1974), 'International terrorism and the struggle against it', *Novoye Vremya*, 15 March.

Thomas, Hugh (1979), *The Spanish Civil War*, 3rd edn (Harmondsworth: Penguin).

Thompson, W. Scott (1976), 'Political violence and the "correlation of forces" ', *Orbis*, vol. 19, no. 4, Winter, pp. 1270-88.

Tinnin, David (1976), *Hit Team* (London: Weidenfeld & Nicolson).

Tkachenko, V. (1972), 'Latin America: problems of the liberation struggle', *International Affairs* (Moscow), no. 5, May.

Tokes, Rudolf L. (ed.) (1975), *Dissent in the USSR* (Baltimore, Md: Johns Hopkins University Press).

Tolstoy, Nikolai (1981), *Stalin's Secret War* (London: Jonathan Cape).

Trotsky, Leon (1961), *Terrorism and Communism* (Ann Arbor, Mich.: Ann Arbor Paperback; 1st edn 1920).

Trotsky, Leon (1974), *Against Individual Terror* (New York: Pathfinder Press, April).

Truman, Harry S. (1956), *Memoires*, 2 vols (Garden City, NY: Doubleday).

Tyunkov, V. (1977), 'USSR-PLO: firm support', *New Times,* no. 37, September.

Ulam, Adam B. (1965), *Lenin and The Bolsheviks* (London: Fontana/Collins).

Valenta, Jiri (1982), 'Soviet use of surprise and deception', *Survival,* vol. 24, no. 2, March/April, pp. 50-61.

Vigor, P. H. (1975), *The Soviet View of War Peace and Neutrality* (London: Routledge & Kegan Paul).

Vincent, R. J. (1975), *Military Power and Political Influence: The Soviet Union and Western Europe,* Adelphi Paper No. 119 (London: Institute for International and Strategic Studies).

Vinci, Piero (1979), 'Some considerations on contemporary terrorism', *Terrorism: An International Journal,* vol. 2, nos 3 and 4, pp. 149-57.

Visscher, Charles de (1960), *Theories et Realities en Droit International Public,* 3rd edn (Paris: Editions A. Pedone).

Walzer, Michael (1980), *Just and Unjust Wars* (Harmondsworth: Penguin).

Wilkinson, Paul (1974), *Political Terrorism* (London: Macmillan).

Wilkinson, Paul (1976), 'Terrorism versus liberal democracy - the problems of response', *Conflict Studies,* no. 67, London Institute for the Study of Conflict, January.

Wilkinson, Paul (1977), *Terrorism and the Liberal State* (London: Macmillan; New York: University Press, 1979).

Wilkinson, Paul (1979), 'Terrorism, international dimensions', *Conflict Studies,* no. 113, London Institute for the Study of Conflict.

Williams, Maureen, and Chatterjee, S. J. (1976), 'Suggesting remedies for international terrorism: use of available means', *International Affairs,* vol. 4, November, pp. 1069-93.

Wolfe, Thomas W. (1971), *Some Foreign Policy Aspects of the CPSU 24th Party Congress* (Santa Monica, Calif.: Rand, May), P-4644.

Wolfe, Thomas W. (1973), *The Global Strategic Perspective from Moscow* (Santa Monica, Calif.: Rand, March), P-4978.

Wolin, Simon, and Slusser, Robert M. (eds) (1957), *The Soviet Secret Police* (London: Methuen).

Wykert, John (1979), 'A meeting on terrorism', *Psychiatric News,* vol. 14, no. 8 (20 April), pp. 1-13.

Yodfat, A. (1969), 'Moscow reconsiders Fatah', *New Middle East* (London), no. 13, December.

Yodfat, Aryeh (1973), *Arab Politics in the Soviet Mirror* (Jerusalem: Israel Universities Press).

Zakharov, Marshal M.V. (1970), 'Leninizm i sovetskaya voyennaya nauka', *Krasnaya zvezda*, 5 April.

Zamyatin, Leonid (1979), 'New contribution to the cause of detente', *Liternaturnaya gazeta*, 7 November.

Zawodny, J. K. (1979a), 'Internal organizational problems and the sources of tensions of terrorist movements as catalysts of violence', *Terrorism: An International Journal*, vol. 1, nos 3 and 4, pp. 277-85.

Zawodny, J. K. (1979b), 'Infrastructures of terrorist organizations', paper delivered at the Conference on Psychopathology and Political Violence: Terrorism and Assassination, 16-17 November.

Index